CREATIVE SCHOOLS

'Make me care. Sir Ken and Lou turn these three words into a mantra for the future of education. We don't do education to students, we do it with them. I hope every teacher and every parent reads this'
Seth Godin, author of *Stop Stealing Dreams*

'Ken Robinson's *Creative Schools* offers a brilliant and compelling vision for what education must become. His powerful call to action cites wonderful examples where the education of the future is happening today. Don't miss this important book!' Tony Wagner, author of *Creating Innovators* and *The Global Achievement Gap*

'Sir Ken Robinson does it again with this compelling book. His explanations and examples are spot on'
Elliot Washor, author of *Leaving to Learn*

"This is the book we have been waiting for from Sir Ken Robinson – laying out what is fundamentally wrong with our education systems, and correspondingly showing what and how it should and could be different. He makes creativity, and much more, come alive. Don't start reading this book unless you have three hours before you, as you will have difficulty putting it down' Michael Fullan, author of *The Principal: Three Keys to Maximizing Impact*

'Forget the chatter about disruptive technological and economic forces in education. Ken Robinson and Lou Aronica vividly describe the disruptions that are needed if we are to have quality education in our time' Howard Gardner, author of *Five Minds for the Future*

'A comprehensive and compelling statement of why creativity matters for everyone, what it looks like in action, and how to get there. Inspiring and so readable you will feel Sir Ken is talking directly to you'
Andy Hargreaves, author of *Professional Capital*

'Ken Robinson is the world's most potent advocate of global education transformation; his clarity, passion and insight have inspired millions, including me. This book is not only a catalyst, or call to action; it is a manifesto; a practical exploration and celebration of what is possible. Now it's up to us; we must read, react and accelerate the revolution'
Richard Gerver, author of *Creating Tomorrow's Schools Today*

'One of those rare books that not only inspires and brings a new sense of possibility to the goal of transforming education, but also lays out an actionable strategy . . . This is a global game-changer and I'm in'
Brené Brown, Ph.D., author of *Daring Greatly*

ABOUT THE AUTHOR

Sir Ken Robinson, PhD, is an internationally recognized leader in the development of creativity, innovation and human potential. He advises governments, corporations, education systems and some of the world's leading cultural organizations. The videos of his famous talks to the prestigious TED Conference have been watched by an estimated 300 million people in over 150 countries.

Lou Aronica is the author of two novels and co-author of several works of non-fiction, including *The Culture Code* (with Clotaire Rapaille) and *The Element*.

KEN ROBINSON

Creative Schools

with Lou Aronica

PENGUIN BOOKS

PENGUIN BOOKS

UK | USA | Canada | Ireland | Australia
India | New Zealand | South Africa

Penguin Books is part of the Penguin Random House group of companies
whose addresses can be found at global.penguinrandomhouse.com.

First published in the United States of America by Viking Penguin,
a member of Penguin Group (USA) LLC 2015
First published in Great Britain by Allen Lane 2015
Published in Penguin Books 2016
004

Printed in Great Britain by Clays Ltd, St Ives plc

A CIP catalogue record for this book is available from the British Library

ISBN: 978–0–141–97857–4

www.greenpenguin.co.uk

Penguin Random House is committed to a
sustainable future for our business, our readers
and our planet. This book is made from Forest
Stewardship Council® certified paper.

*To Bretton Hall College, Wakefield (1949–2001),
and all who sailed in her.*

Acknowledgments

I've spent my life working in education. Along the way, I've been inspired by many extraordinary teachers, scholars, and practitioners in all sorts of fields. There are, as they say, far too many to thank individually. The scale of my debt should become obvious as you read these pages, and especially to all of those in schools and elsewhere whose work we reference and describe. Nonetheless, I do need to thank some specific people who had a direct hand in producing this book.

First, I want to thank Lou Aronica, my cowriter and collaborator. He conducted and drafted many of the interviews and case studies that we feature here and, from start to finish, has been an expert and wise partner in the whole process. I'm immensely grateful. Thank you, Lou.

John Robinson did much of the background research and fact-checking. He contributed enormously in many other ways to the overall process of enquiry and to making this for me an enjoyable, as well as an important, project.

Our literary agent, Peter Miller, was as professional as ever in ensuring the best route to publication. Kathryn Court and Tara Singh Carlson at Penguin have been expert partners in bringing the book into the world in its present form.

Jodi Rose was, as she always is, a maestro in making sure that all the moving parts of a complex schedule were properly prioritized and in always helping me see when things I thought really mattered really didn't.

My daughter, Kate Robinson, was a constant source of constructive support, sharing, as she does, a passion for these issues. My son, James, pressed me, as he always does, to be clearer and sharper in saying what I mean and meaning what I say.

Above all, I'm grateful, in more ways than I can say, to Terry, my partner in work and life, who sustains me always with her conviction that what we do matters. Her unerring sense of the right path to take and the right values to uphold challenges me every day. A constant guide and mentor, it's hard to imagine what I would achieve without her.

Introduction
One Minute to Midnight

ARE YOU CONCERNED about education? I am. One of my deepest concerns is that while education systems around the world are being reformed, many of these reforms are being driven by political and commercial interests that misunderstand how real people learn and how great schools actually work. As a result, they are damaging the prospects of countless young people. Sooner or later, for better or for worse, they will affect you or someone you know. It's important to understand what these reforms are about. If you agree that they're going in the wrong direction, I hope you will become part of the movement to a more holistic approach that nurtures the diverse talents of all our children.

In this book, I want to set out how the standards culture is harming students and schools and to present a different way of thinking about education. I want to show too that whoever and wherever you are, you do have the power to make the system change. Changes are happening. All around the world, there are many great schools, wonderful teachers, and inspiring leaders who are working creatively to provide students with the kinds of personalized, compassionate, and community-oriented education they need. There are entire school districts and even national systems that are moving in the same direction. People at all levels of these systems are pressing for the changes I'm arguing for here.

In 2006, I gave a talk at the TED conference in California

called "Do Schools Kill Creativity?" The essence of that talk was that we're all born with immense natural talents, but by the time we've been through education far too many of us have lost touch with them. As I put it then, many highly talented, brilliant people think they're not because the thing they were good at in school wasn't valued or was actually stigmatized. The consequences are disastrous for individuals and for the health of our communities.

It has proven to be the most watched talk in the history of TED. It has been viewed online more than thirty million times and has been seen by an estimated three hundred million people worldwide. I know that's not as many views as Miley Cyrus gets. But I don't twerk.

Since that talk was posted online, I've heard from students all around the world who say they've shown it to their teachers or parents, from parents who say they've shown it to their children, from teachers who've shown it to their principals, and from superintendents who've shown it to everybody. I take this as evidence that I'm not alone in thinking this way. And these are not recent concerns either.

I was speaking last year at a U.S. college in the Midwest. Over lunch, one of the faculty said to me, "You've been at this a long time now, haven't you?" I said, "At what?" He said, "Trying to change education. How long is it now? Eight years?" I said, "What do you mean, eight years?" He said, "You know, since that TED talk." I said, "Yes, but I was alive before that. . . ."

I've now worked in education for more than forty years as a teacher, researcher, trainer, examiner, and adviser. I've worked with all sorts of people, institutions, and systems in education and with businesses, governments, and cultural organizations. I've directed practical initiatives with schools, districts, and governments; taught in universities; and helped to set up new institutions.

In all of this, I've been pushing for more balanced and individualized and creative approaches to education.

In the last ten years especially, I hear people everywhere saying how exasperated they are by the deadening effects of testing and standardization on them, their children, or their friends. Often they feel helpless and say there's nothing they can do to change education. Some people tell me they enjoy my talks online but are frustrated that I don't say what they can do to change the system. I have three responses. The first is, "It was an eighteen-minute talk; give me a break." The second is, "If you're really interested in what I think, I've published various other books, reports, and strategies on all of this, which you may find helpful."[1] The third response is this book.

I'm often asked the same questions: What's going wrong in education and why? If you could reinvent education, what would it look like? Would you have schools? Would there be different types? What would go on in them? Would everyone have to go, and how old would they have to be? Would there be tests? And if you say I can make a difference in education, where do I begin?

The most fundamental question is, *what is education for?* People differ sharply on this question. Like "democracy" and "justice," "education" is an example of what the philosopher Walter Bryce Gallie called an "essentially contested concept." It means different things to different people according to their cultural values and how they view related issues like ethnicity, gender, poverty, and social class. That doesn't mean we can't discuss it or do anything about it. We just need to be clear on terms.[2] So, before we go on, let me say a few words about the terms "learning," "education," "training," and "school," which are sometimes confused.

Learning is the process of acquiring new knowledge and skills. Human beings are highly curious learning organisms. From the moment they're born, young children have a voracious appetite for learning. For too many, that appetite starts to dull as they go through school. Keeping it alive is the key to transforming education.

Education means organized programs of learning. The assumption of formal education is that young people need to know, understand, and be able to do things that they wouldn't if left to their own devices. What those things are and how education should be organized to help students learn them are core issues here.

Training is a type of education that's focused on learning specific skills. I remember earnest debates as a student about the difficulty of distinguishing between education and training. The difference was clear enough when we talked about sex education. Most parents would be happy to know their teenagers had sex education at school; they'd probably be less happy if they'd had sex training.

By *schools*, I don't mean only the conventional facilities that we are used to for children and teenagers. I mean any community of people that comes together to learn with each other. School, as I use the term here, includes homeschooling, un-schooling, and informal gatherings both in person and online from kindergarten to college and beyond. Some features of conventional schools have little to do with learning and can actively get in the way of it. The revolution we need involves rethinking how schools work and what counts as a school. It's also about trusting in a different story about education.

We all love stories, even if they're not true. As we grow up, one of the ways we learn about the world is through the stories we hear. Some are about particular events and personalities within our personal circles of family and friends. Some are part of the larger cultures we belong to—the myths, fables, and fairy tales about our own ways of life that have captivated people for generations. In stories that are told often, the line between fact and myth can become so blurred that we easily mistake one for the other. This is true of a story that many people believe about education, even though it's not real and never really was. It goes like this:

Young children go to elementary school mainly to learn the basic skills of reading, writing, and mathematics. These skills are essential so they can do well academically in high school. If they go on to higher education and graduate with a good degree, they'll find a well-paid job and the country will prosper too.

In this story, real intelligence is what you use in academic studies: children are born with different amounts of this intelligence, and so naturally some do well at school and some don't. The ones who are really intelligent go on to good universities with other academically bright students. Those who graduate with a good university degree are guaranteed a well-paid professional job with their own office. Students who are less intelligent naturally do less well at school. Some may fail or drop out. Some who finish high school may not go any further in education and look for a lower-income job instead. Some will go on to college but take less academic, vocational courses and get a decent service or manual job, with their own toolkit.

When it's put so baldly, this story may seem too much of a caricature. But when you look at what goes on in many schools, when you listen to what many parents expect of and for their children, when you consider what so many policymakers around the world are actually doing, it seems that they really believe that the current systems of education are basically sound; they're just not working as well as they should because standards have fallen. Consequently, most efforts are focused on raising standards through more competition and accountability. You may believe this story too and wonder what's wrong with it.

This story is a dangerous myth. It is one of the main reasons why so many reform efforts do not work. On the contrary, they often compound the very problems they claim to be solving. They include the alarming rates of nongraduation from schools and colleges, the levels of stress and depression—even suicide—among students and their teachers, the falling value of a university degree, the rocketing costs of getting one, and the rising levels of unemployment among graduates and nongraduates alike.

Politicians often scratch their heads over these problems. Sometimes, they punish schools for not making the grade. Sometimes, they fund remedial programs to get them back on track. But the problems persist and in many ways they're getting worse. The reason is that many of these problems are being caused by the system itself.

All systems behave in ways that are particular to them. When I was in my twenties in Liverpool, I made a visit to an abattoir. (I don't remember why now. I was probably on a date.) Abattoirs are designed to kill animals. And they work. Very few escape and form survivors clubs. As we came to the end, we passed a door that was marked "veterinarian." I imagined this person was fairly depressed at the end of an average day, and I asked the guide why the abattoir had a veterinarian. Wasn't it a bit late for that? He said that the veterinarian came in periodically to conduct random autopsies. I thought, he must've seen a pattern by now.

If you design a system to do something specific, don't be surprised if it does it. If you run an education system based on standardization and conformity that suppresses individuality, imagination, and creativity, don't be surprised if that's what it does.

There's a difference between symptoms and causes. There are many symptoms of the current malaise in education, and they won't be relieved unless we understand the deeper problems that underlie them. One is the industrial character of public education. The issue in a nutshell is this: most of the developed countries did not have mass systems of public education much before the middle of the nineteenth century. These systems were developed in large part to meet the labor needs of the Industrial Revolution and they are organized on the principles of mass production. The standards movement is allegedly focused on making these systems more efficient and accountable. The problem is that these systems are inherently unsuited to the wholly different circumstances of the twenty-first century.

In the last forty years, the population of the world has doubled from less than three billion to more than seven billion. We are the largest population of human beings ever to be on Earth at the same time, and the numbers are rising precipitously. At the same time, digital technologies are transforming how we all work, play, think, feel, and relate to each other. That revolution has barely begun. The old systems of education were not designed with this world in mind. Improving them by raising conventional standards will not meet the challenges we now face.

Don't mistake me; I'm not suggesting that all schools are terrible or that the whole system is a mess. Of course not. Public education has benefited millions of people in all sorts of ways, including me. I could not have had the life I've had but for the free public education I received in England. Growing up in a large working-class family in 1950s Liverpool, my life could have gone in a completely different direction. Education opened my mind to the world around me and gave me the foundations on which I've created my life.

For countless others, public education has been the path to personal fulfillment or the route out of poverty and disadvantage. Numerous people have succeeded in the system and done well by it. It would be ridiculous to suggest otherwise. But far too many have not benefited as they should from the long years of public education. The success of those who do well in the system comes at a high price for the many who do not. As the standards movement gathers pace, even more students are paying the price of failure. Too often, those who are succeeding are doing so in spite of the dominant culture of education, not because of it.

So what can you do? Whether you're a student, an educator, a parent, an administrator, or a policymaker—if you're involved in education in any way—you can be part of the change. To do that, you need three forms of understanding: a *critique* of the way things are, a *vision* of how they should be, and a *theory of change* for how to move from one to the other. These are what I offer in this book, based on my own experience and that of many other people too. Three types of material are woven through the following chapters: analysis, principles, and examples.

If you want to change education, it's important to recognize what sort of system it is. It is neither monolithic nor unchanging, which is why you can do something about it. It has many faces, many intersecting interests, and many potential points of innovation. Knowing this helps to explain why and how you can change it.

The revolution I'm advocating is based on different principles from those of the standards movement. It is based on a belief in the value of the individual, the right to self-determination, our potential to evolve and live a fulfilled life, and the importance of civic responsibility and respect for others. As we go on, I'll elaborate on what I see as the four basic purposes of education: personal, cultural, social, and economic. As I see it, the aims of education are *to enable students to understand the world around them and the talents within them so that they can become fulfilled individuals and active, compassionate citizens.*

This book is full of examples from many sorts of schools. It draws on the work of thousands of people and organizations working to transform education. It is also supported by the most current research available that is being put into effective practice. My aim here is to offer a coherent overview of the changes that are urgently needed in and to schools. It includes the transforming context of education, the dynamics of changing schools, and core issues of learning, teaching, curriculum, assessment, and policy. The inevitable price of a big picture is reduced detail in parts of it. For that reason, I refer you often to the work of others, which dwells more deeply than I can here on some of the issues I need to cover more quickly.

I'm fully aware of the intense political pressures bearing down on education. The policies through which these pressures exert themselves must be challenged and changed. Part of my appeal (as it were) is to policymakers themselves to embrace the need for radical change. But revolutions don't wait for legislation. They emerge from what people do at the ground level. Education doesn't happen in the committee rooms of the legislatures or in the rhetoric of politicians. It's what goes on between learners and teachers in actual schools. If you're a teacher, for your students *you are* the system. If you're a school principal, for your community *you are* the system. If you're a policymaker, for the schools you control *you are* the system.

If you're involved in education in any way you have three options: you can make changes within the system, you can press for changes to the system, or you can take initiatives outside the system. A lot of the examples in this book are of innovations within the system as it is. Systems as a whole are capable of changing too, and in many ways they already are. The more innovation there is within them, the more likely they are to evolve as a whole.

For most of my life, I lived and worked in England. In 2001, my family and I moved to the United States. Since then, I've traveled extensively throughout the country working with teachers, school districts, professional associations, and policymakers at all levels of education. For these reasons, this book looks especially at what is happening in the United States and in the U.K. But the issues affecting education are global, and there are examples throughout the book from other parts of the world.

The focus of the book is mainly on education from early childhood to the end of high school. The issues we deal with have major implications for secondary education too, and many of those institutions are changing radically with the world around them. I refer generally to those changes, but looking at them properly would take a book of its own.

In a recent interview, I was asked about my theories. I replied that they are not simply theories. I do offer various theoretical perspectives on the approach I'm suggesting, but what I'm arguing for is not hypothetical. It's based on long experience and study of what works in education, what motivates students and teachers to achieve their best and what does not. In doing this, I stand in a long tradition. The approach I'm recommending has deep roots in the history of teaching and learning since ancient times. It is not a fashion or trend. It is based on principles that have always inspired transformative education, principles that industrial education, for all else it has achieved, has systematically pushed to the margins.

The challenges we face on Earth are not theoretical either; they are all too real and they are mostly being created by people. In 2009, the BBC's *Horizon* series aired an episode about how many people can live on Earth. It was called *How Many People Can Live on Planet Earth?* (The BBC has a gift for titles.) There are now 7.2 billion people on Earth. That's nearly twice as many as in 1970, and we're heading for nine billion by the middle of the century and twelve billion by the end of it. We all have the same basic needs for clean air, water, food, and fuel for the lives we lead. So how many people can the Earth sustain?

The episode consulted some of the world's leading experts on population, water, food production, and energy. They concluded that if everyone on Earth consumed at the same rate as the average person in India, the Earth could sustain a maximum population of fifteen billion. On that basis, we are halfway there. The trouble is that we don't all consume at that rate. If everyone consumed at the same rate as the average person in North America, we're told, the planet could sustain a maximum population of 1.5 billion. We are nearly five times past that already.

So, if everyone wanted to consume as we do in North America, and it seems they do, by the middle of the century we would need five more planets to make that feasible. The need for radical innovation in how we think, live, and relate to each other could hardly be more pressing. In the meantime, we are as divided as ever by cultural differences and by economic competition for the same resources.

It's often said that we have to save the planet. I'm not so sure. The Earth has been around for almost five billion years, and it has another five billion years to run before it crashes into the sun. As far as we know, modern human beings like us emerged less than two hundred thousand years ago. If you imagine the whole history of the Earth as one year, we showed up at less than one minute to midnight on December 31. The danger is not to the planet, but to the conditions of our own survival on it. The Earth may well conclude that it tried humanity and is not impressed. Bacteria are much less trouble, which may be why they've survived for billions of years.

It was probably this sort of thing that the science fiction writer and futurist H. G. Wells had in mind when he said that civilization is a race between education and catastrophe. Education is indeed our best hope. Not the old style of industrial education, which was designed to meet the needs of the nineteenth and early twentieth centuries, but a new style of education suited

to the challenges we now face and the real talents that lie deep
within us all.

As we face a very uncertain future, the answer is not to do
better what we've done before. We have to do something else. The
challenge is not to fix this system but to change it; not to *re*form
it but to *trans*form it. The great irony in the current malaise in
education is that we actually know what works. We just don't do
it on a wide enough scale. We are in position as never before to
use our creative and technological resources to change that. We
now have limitless opportunities to engage young people's imaginations and to provide forms of teaching and learning that are
highly customized to them.

Although education is now a global issue, it is inevitably a
grassroots process. Understanding that is the key to transformation. The world is undergoing revolutionary changes; we need a
revolution in education too. Like most revolutions, this one has
been brewing for a long time, and in many places it is already
well under way. It is not coming from the top down; it is coming,
as it must do, from the ground up.

Contents

Civilization is a race between education and catastrophe.
— H. G. Wells

CHAPTER ONE

Back to Basics

D R. LAURIE BARRON would have forgiven her students and colleagues if they'd fitted her office with a revolving door before her first day as principal of Smokey Road Middle School in Newnan, Georgia. After all, the school had been open for only five years, and it had already seen four other principals. "It wasn't that we had poor or ineffective leaders," she told me. "In fact, most of those leaders who preceded me were very successful, older principals. Three of them became superintendents. It was the lack of stable leadership. They weren't there long enough to make anything happen."

This was especially problematic in Smokey Road, where the numbers were not in the school's favor. Located about thirty-five miles from Atlanta, nearly 20 percent of Newnan's population are living below the poverty line, and more than 60 percent of Smokey Road's students qualify as economically disadvantaged. When Laurie arrived at Smokey Road in 2004, the school consistently had the lowest academic achievement of the five middle schools in its district. It also had the highest number of absences, the highest number of discipline referrals, the highest number of charges filed with the juvenile justice system, and the highest number of students placed in alternative education systems because of discipline problems. Smokey Road needed help at a variety of levels, but Laurie decided that what it needed first was a sense of stability and safety.

"I spent that first year jumping over tables breaking up fights. People would ask me what kind of data I had, and I would tell them that I jump over tables; I don't know anything about data. I'm very organized and data driven, but when I look back over my notebooks for my nine years there, I realize I don't have any notebooks from that first year. The only thing I did that first year was to try to establish safety. None of the students felt comfortable, because there were all kinds of confrontations going on."

Laurie spent a great deal of time in her initial year getting kids out of each other's faces and, more often than she wanted, sending them home on suspension. It was necessary. Laurie realized that learning was nearly impossible when students were either picking fights or worried about getting into a fight. By the end of that first year, she'd put enough ground rules in place for the students to begin to understand what kind of behavior was expected of them. Most important of all, she came back for a second year. This put a halt to the revolving door and allowed the school to get to work on a productive long-term plan—a plan that had to break the habits that had become ingrained in the school's culture.

"Our school wasn't perceived as a good school, but this was just accepted. No one was disappointed in how we were performing. It was almost like, 'Hey, you're doing a good job with what you've got.' It was fine to be what we were. That second year was when we really started to think about what we wanted to be about. We needed to get the kids to the point where they wanted to be here. We spent the whole year developing our mission and vision. That's when we realized that we needed to get to know these kids. It was a very long process with involvement from teachers, students, business partners, and community members. We organized a parent-teacher organization. I believe a lot of the teachers believed in the kids, but holistically as a school, I don't think *we* believed in the kids, and our community didn't believe in the kids. I think some of the teachers did, because we had some quality teachers there who are still there today, but we didn't have a big-picture mission."

This vision evolved into a four-step plan. The first step was making sure that the kids came to school in the first place. Smokey Road had a very poor attendance record, and Laurie realized that the school had not created a culture where kids felt that it mattered that they were there—and that *she* was part of the problem. "I was suspending them all the time for fighting," she said, "so I certainly wasn't showing them that I wanted them to be there."

Next, she and her team needed to make the students feel safe while they were at the school. The confrontations at Smokey Road rarely got to the point where anyone was getting seriously hurt, but the regular outbreaks had to stop if the kids were going to feel secure and undistracted.

After this, the next step was to help students feel valued as individuals. The true turnaround came when Laurie and her staff realized that they needed to deal with every student based on the needs and interests of each individual. (More on this in a moment.)

The fourth step was teaching the appropriate curriculum that the students needed for future success. It's notable that Laurie saw this as the last of the four key steps. Curriculum was important, but only once the other objectives were in place. The same was true with evaluating her teachers.

"We really didn't focus on teaching, because we had been teaching all along. I didn't feel that the problem was that teachers didn't know how to teach. It was that there were so many hindrances to teaching curriculum. I felt that if we could give them the kids for seventy-five minutes, they could do something with them. Once we had those other things in place, then we could look at the teachers. Before then, we couldn't tell if the teacher struggled or not, because the problem could have been safety and classroom management or building relationships with kids. We were in every classroom every week. I had two assistant principals, and the three of us would visit every teacher every week. We couldn't do that when we had seventy kids in our office every day for disciplinary reasons."

Only when Laurie started to think about what mattered to her kids did things start to change at Smokey Road. "Whatever is important to the student is the most important thing. Nothing is more important than something else: football, band, math, English. We weren't going to tell the students that football wasn't important, that math was what was important. Our approach was that if football was most important to you, then we were going to do whatever it takes to keep you in football. When we started taking that approach, when kids started seeing that we valued what they valued, they started giving back to us what we valued. Once we started building relationships with the kids, they'd feel guilty about letting us down. They might not like math, but they didn't want to let that math teacher down. Then the teachers could finally teach, instead of writing discipline referrals.

"I've got some teachers who couldn't care less about football, but they'll go to the football game and cheer on Bobby and then use Bobby in a science equation the next day. Bobby will do all the science in the world for that teacher."

This kind of approach required Laurie to forgo the models she was getting from the state and from the federal government, and to let go of any elements of "we've always done it that way" thinking that might have remained. And it worked brilliantly with so many of the students. One of her students was a good athlete, but he failed sixth grade, largely because he'd received thirty-three discipline referrals. When Laurie finally got him to see that she agreed that athletics were the most important thing in his life, the discipline problems abated. "He had two referrals total in seventh and eighth grades. And he passed every standardized test. He was black, special education, free and reduced-cost lunch—he was a statistic waiting to happen. We told him that football could be more important than anything else he did, but we would have to help him get through that."

She gave me another example. "We have a girl in chorus: white female, special education, economically disadvantaged. Her father died when she was in fourth grade. She shut down, didn't want to do anything. She was failing sixth grade. My chorus teacher saw something in her and gave her a solo. She sang the solo in November and made all A's the rest of the year. She would have never made it, but the teacher said that all she wanted to do was sing. You've got to listen to what's important to the child.

"Our teachers don't get in front of the class and say, 'You all have to pass the math test.' They go to each kid: 'Hey, you want to be in band; you want to play first chair? Doing well in math is going to help you.' You can get anyone to do you a favor. You can't get groups to follow a mandate." The change in Smokey Road was obvious to everyone, and the stats improved dramatically as well. Test scores were up in every subgroup—special education student test scores improved 60 percent in math and reading—and there was a dramatic increase in attendance and a significant drop in discipline referrals.

The turnaround at Smokey Road was so profound that the school was named a Georgia Title I Distinguished School and a 2011 MetLife Foundation–NASSP Breakthrough School for being high achieving while serving a large number of students living in poverty. Laurie Barron herself was named 2013 MetLife/NASSP National Middle Level Principal of the Year.[1]

What Laurie Barron saw at Smokey Road was a school in desperate need of reform—not the kind of reform that comes from state mandates or federal standards, but the kind that comes from the ground up when you truly understand your students and your educators. Laurie embodies the kind of reform so necessary in our schools. But, as we're about to see, "reform" has different definitions for different people.

The Standards Movement

Reform isn't new in education. There have always been debates about what education is for and what should be taught and how. But now it's different. The modern standards movement is global. Pasi Sahlberg, a leading commentator on international trends in education, deftly refers to it as the Global Education Reform Movement, or GERM. It certainly does seem to be contagious, to judge by how many countries are catching the bug. National education policies used to be mainly domestic affairs. These days, governments scrutinize each other's education systems as earnestly as their defense policies.

The political stakes are high. In 1992, Bill Clinton said he wanted to be known as the education president. So too did George W. Bush, who made education reform a top priority of his first presidential term. In January 2002, on the eve of Martin Luther King Jr. weekend, Bush said he believed education was the civil rights issue of the time, going on to say, "We have overcome the institutionalized bigotry that Dr. King fought. . . . Now our challenge is to make sure that every child has a fair chance to succeed in life."[2] President Obama made reforming education one of the highest priorities of his administration. China is promoting massive reforms in education as a centerpiece of national transformation.[3] Dilma Rousseff, the first female president of Brazil, put education at the heart of her government's strategy for renewal.[4] Wherever you look, education is high on the agenda of governments around the globe.

Since 2000, the standards movement has been turbocharged by the league tables of the Program for International Student Assessment (PISA). These tables are based on student performance in standardized tests in mathematics, reading, and science, which are administered by the Paris-based Organisation for Economic Co-operation and Development (OECD). PISA runs the tests every three years with groups of fifteen-year-olds in countries around the world. The number of countries taking part has increased from thirty-two in 2000 to sixty-five in 2012, and the number of students being tested has almost doubled from 265,000 in 2000 to 510,000.[5]

The political impact of PISA has grown too. In 2001, the results attracted relatively mild attention in the European press. In 2013, they made headlines around the world and sent tremors through governments everywhere.[6] Ministers of education now compare their respective rankings like bodybuilders flexing their biceps. Like the press, they seem to treat the rankings as an absolute measure of their success.

When the Chinese district of Shanghai took part in PISA for the first time in 2009, it took the top spot in all three categories. That result shook Western states to the core. In 2012, Shanghai was at the top again, followed by Singapore, Hong Kong, and Chinese Taipei. The Western press speculated feverishly about the power of "the Asian model" of education and delivered a louder call to politicians in their own countries to do more to raise standards and keep pace with global competition.

U.S. Secretary of Education Arne Duncan commented, "The big picture of U.S. performance on the 2012 PISA is straightforward and stark: It is a picture of educational stagnation." These results, he said, "must serve as a wake-up call against educational complacency and low expectations. The problem is not that our fifteen-year-olds are performing worse today than before. . . . [It is that] our students are basically losing ground. We're running in place, as other high-performing countries start to lap us."[7] Appropriately enough, the major education initiative by the Obama administration is called Race to the Top, a national program of financial incentives for school improvement that is driven by standards and testing.[8]

Why is education such a hot political issue? The first reason is *economic*. Education has huge implications for economic prosperity. In the last twenty-five years, business has been transformed by the rapid developments in digital technology and massive population growth. In the process, economic competition has intensified in trade, manufacturing, and services. Governments know that a well-educated workforce is crucial to national economic prosperity, and their policies are peppered with rhetoric about innovation, entrepreneurship, and "twenty-first-century skills." It's why they spend so much money on education and why it's one of the world's biggest businesses. In the United States alone, education and training cost $632 billion in 2013.[9] Worldwide, the figure was more than $4 trillion.[10]

The second reason is *cultural*. Education is one of the main ways that communities pass on their values and traditions from one generation to the next. For some, education is a way of preserving a culture against outside influences; for others, it is a way of promoting cultural tolerance. It is partly because of its cultural significance that there is such political heat around the content of education.

The third reason is *social*. One of the declared aims of public education is to provide all students, whatever their backgrounds and circumstances, with opportunities to prosper and succeed and to become active and engaged citizens. In practice, governments also want education to promote whatever attitudes and behaviors they think necessary for social stability. Those vary, of course, from one political system to another.

The fourth reason is *personal.* Most statements of public policy for education contain ritual passages about the need for all students to realize their potential and to live fulfilled and productive lives.

So how are governments going about achieving these goals?

Taking Control

Governments everywhere are now yanking firmly on the reins of public education, telling schools what to teach, imposing systems of testing to hold them accountable, and levying penalties if they don't make the grade. In some countries, governments have always had a strong role in education. In others, politicians have traditionally kept their distance from schools. In the United States, for example, education is mainly organized at the state level and, until recently, the role of the federal government was relatively weak. All that changed in 2001 when Congress passed the No Child Left Behind Act (NCLB). In the years since, federal and state governments combined have spent more than eight hundred billion dollars on thousands of programs and new systems of testing.[11]

Although there are some important differences between countries, the reform strategies in many of them do have various features in common. The typical reform story goes like this:

A high-performing education system is critical to national economic prosperity and to staying ahead of our competitors. Standards of academic achievement must be as high as possible, and schools must give priority to subjects and methods of teaching that promote these standards. Given the growth of the knowledge economy, it's essential that as many people as possible go on to higher education, especially four-year colleges and universities.

Because these matters are too important to be left to the discretion of schools, government needs to take control of education by setting the standards, specifying the content of the curriculum, testing students systematically to check that standards are being met, and making education more efficient through increased accountability and competition.

Like the general story of education I gave earlier, this reform story looks highly plausible. It is also deeply flawed, as we'll see. But let's look first at how this story is being played out in practice.

Raising Standards

Raising standards in education certainly seems like a good idea. There's no point lowering them. But standards of what? Why do we choose them, and how do we implement them? A common mantra is that schools have to get "back to basics." It's a phrase with an appealing, folksy ring that suggests a commonsense, down-to-earth approach. It's like eating your vegetables and getting enough sleep. What are these basics the schools should be getting back to? The reform movement has four priorities: the three R's, raising academic standards, STEM disciplines, and going to college.

In some countries, including the U.K. and the United States, a long-term concern has been that standards are too low in *literacy* and *mathematics*. The reformers are not wrong about this. There are problems, and they are not new. In 1983, the U.S. Department of Education published "A Nation at Risk."[12] The report warned that the United States was drowning under a "rising tide of mediocrity" that threatened the future of the country's economy and social well-being. The reformers give high priority to teaching correct grammar, spelling, and punctuation, along with basic mathematics.

The standards movement is concerned with raising *academic standards* in particular. Again, that may seem reasonable. But academic work is only part of education. It mainly involves certain sorts of analytical reasoning, especially with words and numbers, and a focus on what is usually called "propositional knowledge." For various reasons, as we'll see, education is dominated by this idea.

Ironically, the standards movement is also supposed to be about preparing students for the world of work and tackling overseas competition, hence the emphasis on the STEM disciplines: science, technology, engineering, and math. You may see a curious contradiction here. On one hand, politicians are pushing for more academic work in schools; on the other, they say they're all about economic relevance. Yet academics are often thought to be remote from the real world, living in ivory towers, immersed in pure theory. How academic work in the modern world came to be seen as the economic salvation of nations is an interesting issue to which we will return.

Finally, many countries are increasing the numbers of students who go to college. In Europe and the United States in the fifties and sixties, about one in twenty people went to college. Between 1970 and 2000, there was a global increase of almost 300 percent.[13] In the developed economies at least, about one in three high school graduates now heads for college. Getting to college is now widely seen as the ultimate purpose of high school.[14]

So what are the reformers doing to promote this agenda? There are three main strategies: standardization, competition, and corporatization.

STANDARDIZATION

Formal education is made up of three main elements: curriculum, teaching, and assessment. The basic strategy is to standardize them as much as possible. Many countries now have firm guidelines for what schools should teach, usually year by year, in some sort of national curriculum. This is true in England, France, Germany, China, and many other countries. Some countries have looser frameworks, including Finland, Scotland, and, so far, the United States and Singapore.

Most national curricula are based on the idea of discrete subjects. In most systems there is a hierarchy to these subjects. At the top are literacy, mathematics, and now the STEM disciplines. Next come the humanities, including history, geography, and social studies. Because the standards movement emphasizes academic study, it places less value on practical disciplines like art, drama, dance, music, design, and physical education and on "soft subjects" like communications and media studies, which are all thought to be nonacademic. Within the arts, visual arts and music are usually given higher priority than drama and dance. Often these last two are not taught at all. Vocational programs like shop and home economics have also disappeared from many schools. In some countries, provision for all of these "nonessential" disciplines has been devastated.

In terms of *teaching*, the standards movement favors direct instruction of factual information and skills and whole-class teaching rather than group activities. It is skeptical about creativity, personal expression, and nonverbal, nonmathematical modes of work and of learning by discovery and imaginative play, even in preschool.

When it comes to *assessment*, the standards movement emphasizes formal, written examinations and extensive use of multiple-choice tests so that students' answers can be easily codified and processed. It is skeptical too of course work, portfolios, open-book tests, teacher evaluation, peer assessment, and other approaches that are not so easily quantifiable. This is partly why students spend so much time sitting at desks, working on their own.

COMPETITION

One of the aims of testing is to increase competition between students, teachers, and schools, on the assumption that it will drive up standards. In this new environment, students compete with each other, teachers are judged mainly on their students' test results, and schools and districts go head-to-head to win resources. Standards-based tests influence funding allocations, staff promotions, and whether or not schools stay open or are placed under different leadership. This is why they are called "high-stakes" assessments. As we've seen, the competition is now increasingly international in character.

CORPORATIZATION

For more than a hundred years, mass education in the industrialized countries was paid for by taxation and was seen as an investment in the public good. Some governments are now encouraging investment in education by private corporations and entrepreneurs. Their involvement ranges from selling products and services to schools to running their own schools for commercial profit. Governments are promoting different categories of public school—such as academies, charters, and free schools—in which some strictures of the standards movement are deliberately relaxed. There are several motives here. One is to intensify competition; a second is to promote diversity of provision; a third is to ease the burden on the public purse; and a fourth is profit. As I said, education is one of the world's biggest businesses.[15]

How's It Going?

If the standards movement were working as intended, there would be nothing more to say. But it isn't. Take the three R's. In spite of the billions of dollars spent, the standards movement has been at best a partial success. Countries like the United States and England have sacrificed much in a desperate drive to raise standards in literacy and numeracy. Yet test scores in the targeted disciplines have hardly improved.

In 2012, 17 percent of high school graduates in the United States were unable to read or write fluently and had basic problems with spelling, grammar, and punctuation (below level 2 on the PISA scales).[16] More than 50 percent of adults were below level 3 of literacy.[17] "Although a few scores on the National Assessment of Educational Progress (NAEP) have slowly inched upward," said Paul R. Lehman, a past president of the National Association for Music Education, in 2012, "many have remained essentially unchanged in recent years, and in March 2013, Arne Duncan warned Congress that more than 80 percent of the nation's schools will likely be labeled as failing in 2014 under NCLB."[18]

The problems are not only in "basic skills." American students struggle with elementary cultural knowledge. In 2006, *National Geographic* ran a survey of cultural knowledge in America. Twenty-one percent of young adults aged eighteen to twenty-four could not identify the Pacific Ocean on the map. Even more alarmingly (for me, anyway), 65 percent could not identify the U.K. on a map, which is a disgrace by anyone's standards.[19] The situation isn't much better in the U.K. itself, wherever it is.[20]

The standards movement is not meeting the *economic* challenges we face. One of the declared priorities is to prepare young people for work. And yet, youth unemployment around the world is at record levels. There are about six hundred million people on Earth between the ages of fifteen and twenty-four. About seventy-three million of them are long-term unemployed.[21] That's the largest number ever recorded—nearly 13 percent of the total population in that age group. From 2008 to 2013, youth unemployment in Europe increased dramatically, reaching almost 24 percent.[22]

The blight of unemployment is even affecting young people

who've done everything that was expected of them and graduated from college. Between 1950 and 1980, a college degree was pretty much a guarantee of a good job. If you had a degree, employers formed a line to interview you. They don't now.[23] The essential problem is not the quality of degrees, but the quantity. Academic qualifications are a form of currency, and like all currencies their value varies with market conditions. A college degree used to be so valuable because relatively few people had one. In a world bristling with graduates, a college degree is no longer the distinction it once was.

The recession of 2008 left many college graduates struggling to find jobs that used their degrees in any meaningful way. Recent graduates naturally need some time to get a start in their chosen fields. Even so, the numbers who are unemployed or "underemployed"—working in a job that typically does not require a bachelor's degree—have risen since the 2008 recession. In addition, the quality of jobs held by the underemployed has declined. Many recent graduates now have to accept low-wage jobs or part-time work to pay the bills.[24]

The prospects for college graduates have been deteriorating in many parts of the world. In 1999, China began a massive expansion of universities and colleges. Since then, graduate unemployment has become more and more serious. In 1999, there were 840,000 undergraduates in China. The class of 2013 included almost seven million graduates. China's Ministry of Education has observed ruefully that "even if 80 percent of undergraduates gain some form of first employment, the number without jobs will still be large."[25]

For some careers, having a degree is still important. And, on balance, graduates can still expect to earn a lot more over their lifetimes than nongraduates. But having a degree is no longer a guarantee of work in any field, and in some it's an expensive irrelevance.

Of course, some people go to college because they really do want to pursue their academic studies. But to judge by the low graduation rates (more than 40 percent of U.S. college students do not complete a college degree),[26] a sizable number, especially in the West, trudge off to higher education because it's what you do after high school. Many have no particular sense of purpose when they get there, and a significant number leave early without graduating. Others graduate with no clear idea of what to do next. Many are saddled with debt. In 2014, the average student graduating from college in the United States after four to six years was carrying a loan debt of between twenty and a hundred thousand dollars.[27] In the United States, the burden of student debt has grown each year since 2004, from just over $300 billion to $1.3 trillion in 2013—higher than all forms of credit card debt combined.[28]

There is an ever-widening skills gap between what schools are teaching and what the economy actually needs.[29] The irony is that in many countries there's plenty of work to be done but, despite the massive investments in education, too many people don't have the skills that are needed to do it. Although all the rhetoric of the standards movement is about employability, the emphasis has not been on courses that prepare people directly for the work but on raising standards in academic programs.

Yong Zhao is presidential chair and director of the Institute for Global and Online Education in the College of Education at the University of Oregon. He calculates that in the twenty-eight years from 1977 and 2005 more than a million jobs annually disappeared from existing firms in the United States. During that same time, new firms created more than three million jobs a year. Many of these new jobs needed significantly different skill sets from the old, lost jobs—and there was very little advance warning over what those skill sets might be. The work went to employees who had refined those talents already and to people with the creative and entrepreneurial ability to make career and training adjustments.[30]

Our communities depend on an enormous diversity of talents, roles, and occupations. The work of electricians, builders, plumbers, chefs, paramedics, carpenters, mechanics, engineers, security staff, and all the rest (who may or may not have college degrees) is absolutely vital to the quality of each of our lives. Very many people in these occupations enjoy them enormously and gain great fulfillment from them. One effect of the emphasis on academic work in schools is that the education system is not focused on these roles and typically considers them second-rate options for people who don't make the academic cut.

As the story goes, the smart kids go to college. The others may leave school early and look for a job or apply for a vocational course to learn a trade of some sort. Either way, they have taken a step down the status ladder in education. This academic/vocational caste system is one of the most corrosive problems in education.

Let me step back here for a second for a quick story to illustrate what we're missing by creating this divide. As with most schools in the United States, the shop program at Analy High School in Sebastopol, California, had become largely irrelevant. The main shop room had become little more than a glorified storage room. The school's priorities were firmly focused on college readiness and success at standardized tests, and vocational programs had taken a backseat.

But Sebastopol is also the home of *Make* magazine, one of the leading voices of the maker movement. *Make* proposed that a group of students from Analy come to their offices to explore the possibilities involved in creating things with 3-D printers, computer-aided design, and more. The program was so popular that *Make* could no longer accommodate it in their offices, so they agreed to donate equipment to Analy if the school would ramp up their vocational program.

Casey Shea, a teacher at Analy, ran with the idea. The shop room was cleaned up, new equipment was moved in, and others in the community donated materials, more equipment, cash, and expertise. The program became hugely popular very quickly—and not just among the "shop kids."

"There's a big range, from people struggling in Algebra 1 to people in AP Calculus," Casey told me. "At least half, if not more, of the kids are on what would traditionally be called the 'academic track.' I think it's because we have the cool factor of 3-D printers, electronics, and robotics."

The program is also doing so much more than showing kids how to use a vinyl cutter. "What's really exciting is the entrepreneurship angle. That has more promise in it than just college attendance, because these kids are getting the sense that their ideas can be transformed into marketable commodities. In my mind, it opens up a whole new way of walking through the world than, 'OK, I'm going to work in the video store.' They designed really cool ornaments for the holidays and we sold more than a thousand dollars' worth of stuff. We just put together a coaster set for a local microbrewery. We've got a tremendous community of artistic people and small businesses that I'm sure would be willing to do what the brewery did. The kids would have to go to the business and make the pitch and figure out what the cost would be by doing an analysis of material and time and all the other costs. I'm talking with a finance teacher we have to set this up as a business class on student enterprise, with real outcomes."

Healthy economies depend on people having good ideas for new businesses and the ability to grow them and create employment. In 2008, IBM published a survey of what characteristics organization leaders need most in their staff. They spoke with fifteen hundred leaders in eighty countries. The two priorities were *adaptability to change* and *creativity in generating new ideas*. They found these qualities lacking in many otherwise highly qualified graduates.[31] Few if any of the abilities that entrepreneurs need are facilitated by the strategies that reformers value so much. On the contrary, standardized education can crush creativity and innovation, the very qualities on which today's economies depend.

Unsurprisingly, as Yong Zhao points out, there is an inverse relationship between countries that do well on standardized tests and those that demonstrate entrepreneurial flair.[32]

I have mentioned that the top-performing school system according to the latest PISA tables is Shanghai. Shanghai is less impressed by its own performance than everyone else seems to be. Yi Houqin, a high-ranking official in the Shanghai Education Commission, recently said that he was pleased but not surprised at how well their students had done. After all, the system is focused on drilling them in rote learning to succeed in just these sorts of tests. That is not the point. He said that the commission was considering stepping away from PISA testing at some point. "Shanghai does not need so-called '#1 schools.'" he said. "What it needs are schools that follow sound educational principles, respect principles of students' physical and psychological development, and lay a solid foundation for students' lifelong development."[33]

In 1982, Wayne Gretzky was the top-scoring ice hockey player in the world. His secret, he said, was simple. Other players tend to race to where the puck is. Gretzky said that he went where the puck was going to be. It's hard to resist the thought that in the mad rush to standardization, many countries are now dashing to where they think the puck is rather than where it's really going to be.

Unemployment is not only an economic issue; it's a scourge

that that can destroy lives and whole communities. In many countries, there is a growing problem of "social exclusion." In the developed economies, there is a widening gap between the wealthy, the middle classes, and those who live in poverty. According to a 2012 study by the U.S. Census Bureau, the "poverty gap" in the United States was $178 billion.[34] Poverty and social deprivation can have toxic effects on young people's educational achievements. Some fight determinedly against their circumstances and triumph over them. Others do not. Education is not the only source of the income gap, but the forms of education that the standards movement is promoting are exacerbating it. The drab nature of standardized education does little to inspire and empower those caught in poverty.

Externalities

The standards movement is not achieving the objectives it has set for itself. Meanwhile, it is having catastrophic consequences on student engagement and teacher morale.

In 1970, the United States had the highest rates of high school graduation in the world; now it has one of the lowest. According to the OECD, the overall U.S. graduation rate is now around 75 percent, which ranks the United States twenty-third out of twenty-eight countries surveyed. In some states and districts the graduation rate is much lower.[35] Overall, about seven thousand young people drop out of the nation's high schools every day, close to one and a half million a year. Some of these so-called dropouts go on to other forms of education, in community colleges, for example, or they study for the GED test. But there are still huge numbers of young people deciding that conventional education is just not for them. There are similarly bleak statistics in other countries. The social and economic costs are enormous.

In general, high school graduates are more likely to find employment, to earn at higher levels, and to pay more taxes than nongraduates. They're more likely to go on to college or other learning programs. They're more likely to engage in their communities and less likely to depend on social welfare programs. According to one estimate, if the numbers of young people leaving school early could be cut in half, the net gain to the U.S. economy from savings in social programs and gains in additional tax revenues could be around ninety billion dollars a year—that's almost a trillion dollars in just over ten years.[36] That's a big number. But think too of the benefits to all of us of hundreds of thousands of young people moving on every year to lives that are more productive and fulfilling.

One of the key agenda items for NCLB was closing the "achievement gap" between socioeconomic groups. There's little evidence that this has happened. "It has been twelve years since No Child Left Behind became the law of the land," wrote Daniel Domenech, executive director of the School Superintendents Association, in 2013.[37] "The standards and accountability movement swept the nation, followed by an education reform agenda often driven by noneducators. Still today half of African-American and Latino students fail to graduate from our high schools. They drop out in disproportionate numbers from our schools. The numbers for attending and graduating from college are dismal."

Meanwhile, the teacher attrition rate is alarmingly high. In the United States, more than a quarter of a million teachers leave the profession every year, and it is estimated that more than 40 percent of new teachers leave the profession within the first five years. This scenario is especially bleak in high-poverty schools, where turnover is approximately 20 percent every year.[38]

Much of the cause of the teacher attrition rate is the condition under which many teachers work. "The data suggest that school staffing problems are rooted in the way schools are organized and the way the teaching occupation is treated and that lasting improvements in the quality and quantity of the teaching workforce will require improvements in the quality of the teaching job."[39]

THE SCHOOL-TO-PRISON PIPELINE

For some, not completing high school can have disastrous consequences. The United States has the highest rate of incarceration of any country in the world. Roughly one in thirty-five adults is in the correctional system, either in jail, on probation, or on parole. It's not true, of course, that pulling out of high school inevitably leads young people into trouble. Many so-called high school dropouts have gone on to have extraordinary, successful lives. What is true is that a very high proportion of people who are long-term unemployed, homeless, on welfare, or in the correctional system did not graduate from high school. In the United States, more than two-thirds of all male prisoners in state and federal facilities do not have a high school diploma.

It costs on average eleven thousand dollars a year in the United States to educate a student in high school. It costs more than twenty thousand dollars a year to keep him or her in jail.[40] The annual cost is almost seventy billion dollars. This number equates to a 127 percent funding increase from 1998 to 2007. By comparison, there was only a 21 percent increase in funding in higher education over the same period.[41] Go figure, as they say.

I say "so-called dropouts" because the term implies that these young people have failed the system. It's often more accurate to say that the system has failed them. Every individual who leaves school early has personal reasons for doing so. They may have family difficulties, be under peer pressure, or just find the whole story unconvincing. Whatever the reason for it, dropping out is a symptom of a deeper problem in the system as a whole, not the problem itself. If you were running a business and every year you lost more than a third of your customers, you might start to wonder if the real problem was them or your business.

DISENGAGEMENT

The nongraduation figures are stark enough. But they don't take into account the millions of other students who stay in education but are bored and disaffected by the whole process. One North American study puts the figure in high schools at 63 percent.[42] These are students who stay with the program reluctantly but have little interest in what they're doing and largely wait for the day to be over and for the time to come when they can graduate and get on with the rest of their lives.

ANXIETY AND PRESSURE

What price is really being paid by students and teachers in this massive international effort to move up the PISA ranks? South Korea, for example, has ranked in the top five of every PISA program. South Korea spends about $8,200 on each student. This represents almost 8 percent of the country's GDP, the second highest among OECD countries.[43] South Korean parents spend thousands of dollars on after-school tuition. But the real costs of South Korea's high performance on international tests is very much higher; the country now has the highest suicide rate of all industrialized OECD countries.[44]

In the last forty-five years, suicide rates have increased by 60 percent worldwide. Suicide is now among the three leading causes of death among those age fifteen to forty-four. These figures do not include suicide *attempts*, which can be as many as twenty times more frequent than completed suicide. It used to be that the highest suicide rates were among elderly men. Suicide rates among young people have been increasing to such an extent that they are now the group at highest risk in a third of both developed and developing countries.[45]

Back to Basics

The standards movement came about because of legitimate concerns about standards in schools. There are many factors that affect students' achievement in schools. They may include student motivation, poverty, social disadvantage, home and family circumstances, poor facilities and funding in schools, the pressures of testing and assessment, and myriad others. These factors cannot be ignored, and any attempt to raise achievement in schools has to take them fully into account. But they are never the whole story. There are well-endowed schools in affluent areas where students are disaffected and underachieving too. Circumstances are not destiny. To show this, we give examples throughout this book of difficult schools in "deprived areas" where achievement has been transformed by creative approaches to teaching and learning.

In some cases, low standards were undoubtedly because of shortcomings in the schools themselves and in the quality and methods of teaching. They may include the misapplication of some of the core ideas of "progressive" education and of misconceived polarities with "traditional" education, which I'll come back to. Whatever the reasons, research and practical experience show time and again that the critical factors in raising student achievement on all fronts are the motivation and expectations of students themselves. The best ways to raise them are to improve the quality of teaching, have a rich and balanced curriculum, and have supportive, informative systems of assessment. The political response has been the opposite: to narrow the curriculum and wherever possible to standardize content, teaching, and assessment. It has proved to be the wrong response.

The evidence is everywhere that the standards movement is largely failing by its own terms and creating more problems than it is solving. In the meantime, some of the countries that are succeeding best in the limited terms of the PISA league tables are now turning away from that agenda to cultivate skills and attitudes in students that the standards movement has been systematically stifling. The need for this shift is urgent.

The fact is that our children and our communities need a different sort of education, based on different principles from those that are driving the standards movement. To understand what this sort of education looks and feels like, we really do need to get back to basics. They are not a particular set of subjects or teaching methods or assessment strategies. They are the underlying purposes that education is meant to serve in the first place.

To meet them, we need a radical change in how we think about and do school—a shift from the old industrial model to one based on entirely different principles and practices. People do not come in standard sizes or shapes, nor do their abilities and personalities. Understanding this basic truth is the key to seeing how the system is failing—and also how it can be transformed. To do that we have to change the story: we need a better metaphor.

CHAPTER TWO

Changing Metaphors

STEVE REES was an architect in Kansas City with grown children. One day he was invited to a career lunch at DeLaSalle Education Center, a charter high school dedicated to addressing the needs of the city's at-risk students. Steve knew going into the lunch that many DeLaSalle students had been kicked out of other schools and that a fair number of them had troubled pasts. What he discovered at the lunch was that these students had a far greater desire to do something with their lives than he would ever have guessed.

"There was a large number of kids who had not been able to find a course that worked for them," he told me. "There were kids that had learning and emotional issues and social issues, but there was a lot of potential there." Steve decided to take an active role in the school. He set up a program for some of DeLaSalle's seniors that allowed them to take junior college classes. He also set up a mentoring program where he paired DeLaSalle students with adults in the Kansas City business community. These adults volunteered to take a student to lunch, spend time with the student in the volunteer's workplace, and then have a follow-up lunch. The kids gained a glimpse into their potential futures, and the mentors forged emotional ties that many of them didn't expect and that they found hugely rewarding.

The program made an impact, but Steve felt that it was just a start. Around this time, he sold his architectural practice and left the country for two years. He never stopped thinking about DeLaSalle, though, or the effect the kids had on him. "They had quite a bit of grit, even if it was misdirected."

When he came back to the area, he returned to DeLaSalle and asked the school's administrators if he could teach a class in creativity and entrepreneurial studies. The school quickly agreed. "We did things like build a bridge out of toothpicks and think about how you would write a book or how you would do any number of things. It was just to get them to start thinking about process. What would it mean to run a barbershop? If you wanted to make $80,000 a year, how do you do that running a barbershop? The kids would read *The New York Times* business section to each other."

This was a very positive step, with a strong level of student engagement. But the real breakthrough was just around the corner. Steve is a self-described "car guy," and one of the things he would do with his students was design vehicles at the conceptual stage. "We would design the body, not the real workings. The kids would do their own small models, and we would pick one and do a full-size model out of Styrofoam. The kids started saying, 'Why can't we build a real car?' They weren't afraid to ask ridiculous questions. I kept saying that we couldn't do that, but after about a hundred times, I thought, 'These kids are thinking outside the box and I need to find a way to make that happen.'"

Steve tracked down an old Indy racing car that had crashed, and he had it delivered to his students. They moved from imagining with toothpicks and Styrofoam to doing something much more tangible: restoring the car. Because it had been used for racing in a former life, the car was extremely lightweight. Steve realized he could teach his students environmental responsibility and new technology at the same time by helping them to turn the racer into an electric vehicle.

At this point, the program was more than DeLaSalle could handle, so Steve turned it into a nonprofit organization and named it Minddrive. He received some sponsorship money from Bridgestone, who also took that first car to their testing facility and found that it was operating at the equivalent of 445 miles per gallon. "Suddenly the kids felt that they'd done something significant. They felt empowered. And in the process, they learned something about mechanics, technology, and building a team."

As I write this, Minddrive's students have built four cars—a recycled 1999 Lola Champ Car, a recycled 2000 Reynard Champ Car, a 1977 Lotus Esprit, and a 1967 fully converted, electric Karmann Ghia. In 2012, they drove their Lotus from San Diego to Jacksonville, making forty charging stops along the way and doing presentations at every stop to audiences including school groups, trade schools, civic groups, and the Sierra Club.

In 2013, they drove another car, their Karmann Ghia, from Akron to Washington, D.C., this one equipped with a device that turned mentions on social networks into "social fuel." A wide range of social media picked up the campaign, news programs in several foreign countries carried their story, and public figures like Richard Branson and Nancy Pelosi even wrote posts about it.

There are students from seven other area schools involved in Minddrive now. "All of these kids are interested in cars because it represents freedom," Steve said, "and they're all interested in the Internet because it's an inexpensive way for them to communicate. We started out getting students from the counselors at the schools. Then we started getting word of mouth, and we now have issues over how to select kids for the program. We went to DeLaSalle this last year and just put up a poster saying we were going to have a meeting at the gym at ten thirty. Out of the 180 kids at the school, 53 showed up. These are kids that are willing to give up their Saturdays to get involved in this.

"In our program they gain confidence in being able to do something, and they find it somewhat amazing. We always try to do something extraordinary as an endgame, like going cross country in an electric car. When they get it done, those kids feel like they can do anything, and it's influencing other kids in the school. They're seeing these Minddrive kids as success stories in the hall. Our kids feel special. They wear their T-shirts to school."

While the accomplishments of the Minddrive students are fascinating enough in themselves, what makes the accomplishments more instructive is that they are coming from kids who for years had been written off as low achievers. "These were at-risk kids from the lower 20 percent of education. We're getting our students kind of late in the game, and if they come into our class as juniors and can't even read a ruler, that kind of tells a story right there. We're having an influence even on students that have very little academic capability. We find that they're able to have a different vision of their future; they're able to find a passion, and make some pretty amazing changes in their lives. We have a girl who went from having F's and everyone telling her she had no chance to being on the honor roll and going to college.

"The true value is borne out in their core school. Just about across the board the kids' grades have gone up. This year, we had twelve students who were seniors. They all graduated, and 80 percent of them are going to college. We don't really care if they go to college or not. Life sustainability is really our goal. We want kids to have a family, a home, and a car."

Alternative Education

A few years ago, I was invited to a meeting in Los Angeles of alternative education programs. These are programs that are designed to reengage young people who are either failing in school or have pulled out of it altogether. The meeting included all sorts of programs based in technology, the arts, engineering, community initiatives, and business and vocational projects. For all their differences, these programs have some common features. They work with students who are doing least well in conventional education: the low achievers, the alienated, the ones with low self-esteem and little optimism for their own futures. These programs offer these disaffected young people a different sort of learning experience.

Often they work on practical projects or in the community helping others, or on artistic productions and performances. They work collaboratively in groups. Along with their regular teachers, they work with people from other fields as mentors and role models: engineers, scientists, technologists, artists, musicians, business leaders, and so on. Often these alternative education programs have spectacular results.

Students who've been slumbering through school wake up. Those who thought they weren't smart find that they are. Those who feared they couldn't achieve anything discover they can. In the process, they build a stronger sense of purpose and self-respect. Usually, their achievements in conventional schoolwork improve enormously too. Kids who thought they had no chance of going to college find that they do. Those who don't want to go to college find there are other routes in life that are just as rewarding.

What struck me is that these programs are called "alternative education." If all education had these results, there'd be no need for an alternative. Of course, the success of alternative education projects like Minddrive is not automatic or guaranteed. It takes care, passion, and expertise on the part of the adults, and trust, willingness, and commitment from the students. Each program, each relationship has to be as carefully handcrafted as the cars the Minddrive students make. But these programs show vividly that these students are not incapable of learning and are not inevitably destined to fail. They were alienated and marginalized by the system itself. So are many others, including many who stay in the system. The essential reason is that mass education operates on different principles from those exemplified by Minddrive. So what are these principles and how did public education get to be this way in the first place?

Industrial Education

In the developed world, we take for granted that children start school around the age of five and go through about twelve years of compulsory schooling. Going to school seems like the natural order of things, like driving on the right (or left) side of the road. But mass systems of public education are a relatively recent innovation. They mostly came into being in the middle of the nineteenth century as part of the Industrial Revolution, which began to gather force in Europe about a hundred years earlier.

In earlier times, the vast majority of people lived in the countryside and worked on the land. Cities were mainly small centers of trade and commerce. In sixteenth-century Europe, about 5 percent of the total population lived in cities.[1] The rural majority lived and worked under the feudal rules of the old aristocracies. Their lives were shaped by the rhythms of the seasons and the rituals of their beliefs. They were mostly illiterate and had little education beyond learning whatever craft or trade they practiced to earn a living. Schooling was for the wealthy and those who joined the church.

The Industrial Revolution changed everything. From the middle of the eighteenth century, a succession of technological innovations transformed traditional methods of making goods and materials, especially wool and cotton. They also led to entirely new sorts of products, made from iron and steel. Machine tools and steam engines forged revolutionary forms of transport that carried people and products farther and more quickly than ever before—on railways, over iron bridges, and around the globe on mechanical ships. Industrialism generated a massive demand for energy from coal and gas, and with that demand, whole new industries arose in mining and refining raw materials. Tidal waves of people surged from the countryside to the cities to work in factories, shipyards, and mills. Others dug underground for the coal and ores on which the factories depended.

As the Industrial Revolution barreled forward in the nineteenth century, a new sort of society began to form. At its base was a new urban working class of men, women, and children who sold their physical labor to turn the vast machinery of industrialism. The working classes often lived and worked in pitiless conditions of dire poverty, ill health, and the constant risk of physical injury and accidental death. They were the faceless infantry of industrialism.

Between the working classes and the old nobility there emerged a new "middle class" of people who prospered in the new economies. They included the owners and masters of industry; lawyers, doctors, and accountants; and entrepreneurs and the investors and financiers on whom they often depended. Some in the middle classes had risen from poverty through their own flair and determination. Overall, these middle classes had high aspirations for themselves and their families, and they had the money and the means to fulfill them. For different reasons, both the working and the middle classes began to press politically for a greater say in how they were governed. As they did, the feudal grip of the old aristocracies began to slacken, and a new political order began to take shape.

As it did, numerous institutions sprang up across Europe and

North America to promote commerce, trade, technology, and the flow of ideas between the arts and the sciences. At the same time, new philanthropic institutions tried to alleviate the often appalling conditions of the working classes with charitable programs in health, education, and social welfare.

It was in all these tumultuous circumstances that the demand grew for organized systems of mass education. Income from taxation and the growing spending power of the middle classes made it possible to pay for them. These systems were shaped by many forces.

Industrial Purposes

Industrialism needed armies of *manual* workers for the repetitive and exhausting labor in the mines, factories, railways, and shipyards. It needed more-skilled *technical* workers in engineering and all the associated trades and crafts of mining, manufacturing, and construction. It needed cohorts of *clerical and administrative* workers to manage the new bureaucracies of trade and manufacturing. It needed a smaller *professional* class of lawyers, doctors, scientists, and academics to provide expert services to those who could afford them. Some industrial countries—especially Britain—had extensive colonial interests for which they needed an even smaller *ruling* class of diplomats, ambassadors, and civil servants to run the business of empire at home and overseas.

From the outset, mass education had strong social purposes too. In the United States, it was intended to produce an educated citizenry for the well-being of democracy. As Thomas Jefferson put it, "If a nation expects to be ignorant and free, in a state of civilization, it expects what never was and never will be."[2] Some saw mass education as a mode of social control. For many, education was a means of promoting social opportunity and equity. For some, going to the right school and mixing with the right people was an essential process of social grooming for the children of the middle and upper classes. And it still is.

All of these interests are evident in the *structure* and *organizational principles* of mass education.

Industrial Structures

Industrialism needed a lot more manual workers than it did college graduates. So mass education was built like a pyramid, with a broad base of compulsory elementary education for all, a smaller sector of secondary education, and a narrow apex of higher education.

In elementary schools, the emphasis was on literacy and numeracy. In most countries, there were different types of secondary school: those with a mainly academic curriculum and those with a more practical bias. In Germany, for example, the *hauptschule* is for children who are expected to work in trades, whereas the *realschule* is for white-collar jobs such as banking, and the *gymnasium* is for students planning to go to college. In 1944, the British government set up three types of secondary schooling: selective grammar schools, to prepare a minority of students for administrative and professional occupations and college; technical schools, for those likely to take up a trade; and secondary moderns, to prepare the rest for blue-collar jobs.

For much of the industrial era, the majority of young people left school before the age of fourteen, mainly for manual and service work. That was true of my parents and grandparents. Some went on to clerical or technical training, or trade apprenticeships. A few went to college and qualified for the professions. I was the first in my own family to do that, in 1968. Those who went to the right universities from the right families might take their place in government and colonial administration. I didn't do that.

Industrial Principles

The purpose of industrial manufacturing is to produce identical versions of the same products. Items that don't *conform* are thrown away or reprocessed. Systems of mass education were designed to mold students to certain requirements. Because of that, not everyone makes it through the system, and some are rejected by it.

Industrial processes demand *compliance* with specific rules and standards. This principle is still applied to education. The standards movement is based on compliance in curriculum, teaching, and assessment.

Industrial processes are *linear*. Raw materials are turned into products through sequential stages, each with some form of testing as a gateway to the next. Mass education was designed as a series of stages, from elementary school to high school to higher education. Students are typically organized into separate year groups and progress through the system in batches that are defined by date of birth. There are variations in national systems, but in most of them periodic tests determine who goes down which route and when.[3]

Industrial production is related to *market demand*. If it rises or falls, manufacturers adjust production to meet it. Because industrial economies needed comparatively few administrative and professional workers, the number of students admitted to universities was tightly controlled. In our times, the demand for intellectual labor has grown, and the doors to universities have been flung open to increase the flow of graduates into the economy. The emphasis on STEM disciplines is another example of market principles being applied to education.

As in typical factories, high schools and higher education in particular are organized around the *division of labor*. In high schools, the day is usually segmented into regular chunks of time.

When the bell rings, everyone changes task (and often rooms) and starts doing something else instead. Teachers specialize in particular subjects and move through the day from class to class in separate segments.

While these principles may work well in manufacturing products, they can cause all kinds of problems in educating people.

Human Problems

The problem with *conformity* in education is that people are not standardized to begin with. Let me be clear: in challenging the idea of conformity in schools, I'm not advocating antisocial behavior. All communities depend on agreed conventions of conduct. If people consistently flout them, the community itself may founder. By conformity, I mean the institutional tendency in education to judge students by a single standard of ability and to treat those who don't meet it as "less able" or "disabled"—as deviations from the norm. In this sense, the alternative to conformity is not condoning disruption; it is celebrating diversity. Students' individual talents take many forms and they should be fostered in similarly diverse ways.

Every individual is unique. We all differ physically and in our talents, personalities, and interests. A narrow view of conformity inevitably creates enormous numbers of nonconformists who may be rejected by the system or be earmarked for remedial treatment. Those who meet the system specifications are likely to do well; those who don't are not.

This is one of the core issues in promoting a culture of strict *compliance* in education. I'm not talking here about standards of behavior and social conduct, but about whether and how students are encouraged to ask questions, to look for alternative and unusual answers, and to exercise their powers of creativity and imagination. Strict compliance is essential in manufacturing products, but people are different. It's not just that we come in all shapes and sizes. In the right circumstances, we are also highly imaginative and creative. In a culture of compliance, these capacities are actively discouraged, even resented.

The principle of *linearity* works well for manufacturing; it doesn't for people. Educating children by age group assumes that the most important thing they have in common is their date of manufacture. In practice, different students learn at different rates in different disciplines. A child with natural ability in one area may struggle in another. One may be equal to older children in some activities and behind younger ones in others. We don't apply this batching principle outside of schools. We don't keep all the ten-year-olds away from the nine-year-olds, in separate facilities. This form of segregation mainly happens in schools.

The principle of *supply and demand* does not work with people's lives either, because life itself is not linear. If you ask middle-aged and older people if they are doing exactly what they had in mind when they were in high school, very few say they are. The lives we create are the result of all sorts of currents and crosscurrents, most of which we can't anticipate in advance.[4]

Paying the Real Price

Industrial processes commonly overlook the value of raw materials that are not relevant to what is being made. The same is true in education. The preoccupation with particular subjects and types of ability means that students' other talents and interests are almost systematically marginalized. Inevitably, many people don't discover what they're really capable of at schools, and their lives may be impoverished as a result.

Most industrial processes generate huge amounts of waste and low-value by-products. So does education. As we've seen, they include dropping out, disengagement, low self-esteem, and limited employment opportunities for those who don't succeed, or whose talents are not valued, in the system.

Industrial processes can create catastrophic problems in the environment. Often, it's left to others to clean up the mess. Economists describe these as "externalities." Chemicals and toxic waste products run off into rivers and oceans, polluting the environment and damaging delicate ecosystems. Smoke from factories and engines chokes the atmosphere and creates multiple health problems for the people who breathe it. Cleaning up the mess can carry a multibillion-dollar price tag. But it's not the producers who usually pay the price; it's the taxpayers. The producers don't see the waste as their problem. It's the same with education.

The students who feel alienated by current systems of standardization and testing may walk out the door, and it's left to them and others to pay the price in unemployment benefits and other social programs. These problems are not accidental by-products of standardized education; they are a structural feature of these systems. They were designed to process people according to particular conceptions of talent and economic need and were bound to produce winners and losers in just those terms. And they do. Many of these "externalities" could be avoided if education genuinely gave all students the same opportunities to explore their real capabilities and create their best lives.

So, if these industrial principles don't work well for education, what does? What sort of system is education, and how can it be changed? A good way to think about this transformation is to change metaphors. If you think of education as a mechanistic process that's just not working as well as it used to, it's easy to make false assumptions about how it can be fixed; that if it can just be tweaked and standardized in the right way it will work efficiently in perpetuity. The fact is that it won't, because it's not that sort of process at all, however much some politicians would like it to be.

Mechanisms and Organisms

If you've read my book *The Element*, you may remember the story of Richard Gerver, who became head teacher at Grange Primary School in central England, and how he helped to create Grangeton, a working "town" within the school where every "job" was done by students. Through their work in the town, these students learned the core disciplines—and much more—at a high level, while also experiencing extraordinary degrees of engagement.[5]

When Richard got to Grange, the school had been underperforming for years and student enrollment was falling. The school had a poor reputation and was generally in a precarious state. This is when many people start talking about going back to basics. The thought came to Richard's mind as well, but not in the same way.

"The 'basics' I'm talking about are the biological gifts we're born with that thrust us into the world as incredible learning organisms," he told me. "We are born with all the skills—all the basics—we need. Babies and very young children are incredibly intuitive, naturally creative, and deeply curious. When we were thinking about what to do about Grange, I was obsessed with whether we could find a way to harness that natural learning ability and understand what the system was doing to inhibit it. If we could work that out, we could create an unbelievable learning environment.

"So we said, 'Let's look at how kids learn. Let's really spend some time observing the kids in our nursery and early-years facility and see how we can take forward what they're doing.' It was clear that our kids had a natural predisposition to immerse themselves in role-play and highly experiehtial learning. There was a lot of mimicking and powerful learning when they could taste, smell, and see stuff. This is what I call three-dimensional learning." It was this desire to replicate these dynamic forms of learning in the less structured environment of preschools that sparked the creation of Grangeton.

"We created a town with TV and radio stations, because they were role-play environments that were cool for all of our kids, not just the preschoolers. If you're talking to preschool kids about looking after themselves, you build them a mocked-up doctor's surgery and they play at being doctors and nurses. We thought, 'If we were going to get our kids to understand the power of literacy and language development, let's build them a television station and a radio station so they could take those skills and play with them in a real context.' Eleven-year-olds would find that as cool as five-year-olds playing in a doctor's surgery. For us, everything then had to be about the richness of the experience and context."

The next thing was to appreciate the immense skills of the best early-years practitioners, who don't construct play environments just to encourage play. "Underlying the planning of those early-years environments are clear objectives in skills development. I wanted to explore how we could take that role-play-based experience to develop teamwork, resilience, self-confidence, and community responsibility."

The results of the Grangeton transformation were clear at every level. The students who had been mostly listless about going to school became deeply engaged and enthusiastic. And the school's overall results improved far beyond all expectations. In a little more than three years, Grange went from being one of the lowest-performing and least popular schools in the district to being at the top of every list.

"Our academic performance at Grange hit the top 5 percent. My kids and my staff worked harder than they would in a standard school, but there was no resentment, because they could see it was having real impact. The work levels were massive, but everyone was engaged in it a hundred percent."

The transformation at Grange illustrates three core themes that are at the heart of my argument: the room for radical innovation even within the education system as it is; the power of visionary leadership in effecting change; and the need for principals and teachers to create the conditions in schools in which students will flourish and give their best.

The examples we've looked at so far all demonstrate these themes. They also show that, for all that politicians sometimes treat it as one, education is not an industrial process at all; it is an organic one. Education is about living people, not inanimate things. If we think of students as products or data points, we misunderstand how education should be. Products, from screws to airplanes, have no opinions or feelings about how they are produced or what happens to them. People do. They have motivations, feelings, circumstances, and talents. They are affected by what happens to them, and they affect life right back. They can resist or cooperate, tune in or tune out. Understanding this points to an even closer analogy between mass education and industrialism.

So far, I've been comparing education to manufacturing. That's all well and good, you may be thinking, but no one seriously believes that students are widgets and schools are factories. Maybe. Maybe not. Either way, I think the proper analogy for industrial education is industrial farming.

The Industrial Revolution not only transformed the production of objects, it also transformed agriculture. I mentioned that, in preindustrial times, the vast majority of people lived in the countryside. Most worked on the land, raising crops and animals for their own use or for local consumption, and they used the same methods that had been used for generations before them. In the eighteenth century, all of that began to change. The invention of mechanical ploughs, threshing machines, and other devices for processing plant materials, such as cotton, sugarcane, and corn, brought about a revolution in the countryside that was as far-reaching as the industrial convulsions in the city. Industrialization produced vast efficiencies in planting, harvesting, and processing crops of every kind. In the twentieth century, the widespread use of chemical fertilizers and pesticides massively increased crop yields and productivity. These innovations in industrial agriculture and food production in turn supported the huge growth in human population.

One of the primary aims of industrial farming systems is to produce higher yields of crops and animals. They have achieved these results through developing huge, often monocultural farms growing large tracts of single crops, bolstered with chemical fertilizers and pesticides. They have been spectacularly successful in terms of yield and have bestowed immense benefits on humanity. As with many industrial processes, these successes have come at a high price.

The runoff of pesticides and fertilizers into rivers and oceans has created devastating pollution. The indiscriminate killing of insects has unbalanced entire ecosystems that depend on them and given rise to Rachel Carson's "silent spring."[6] For crop production, the price has been the degradation of topsoil around the world, to the point where the sustainability of these practices is now in serious question.

There are similar problems in the industrial production of animal products. Industrial factory farms replaced the open grazing of preindustrial times. Huge numbers of animals are now raised indoors in conditions that are intended to maximize production at minimal cost. These conditions include the widespread use of growth hormones to increase the size and value of the animals. Because the conditions in which they are kept are so unnatural, animal production increasingly depends on the widespread use of powerful antibiotics to control disease. All of these industrial techniques have had correspondingly adverse effects on human health.[7]

In the last thirty years especially, there has been a growing movement to implement alternative systems of organic farming. In organic crop farming, the emphasis is not primarily on the plants but on nurturing the soil itself. It differs fundamentally from industrial farming in seeing that all crop production depends upon the vitality of the soil and on its long-term sustainability. If the ecosystem is diverse and well managed, the health of plants will increase along with yields. The aim is to see agriculture as part of the larger web of life. The same approach is taken in the treatment of animals. Although organic agriculture covers a wide range of practices, at its heart, it is based on four principles:[8]

Health. The health of everything involved in the agricultural process—from the soil to the plants and animals to the entire planet—is equally critical, and any practice that compromises their health and well-being should be avoided.

Ecology. Agricultural processes have to be consistent with ecological systems and cycles, and it is vital to sustain the balance and interdependence of living systems.

Fairness. Every party involved in the process—from the farmer to the workers to the consumer—must be treated equitably.

Care. Before they are used, the effects of any new technology or technique on the living environment now and in the future must be fully considered.

As in farming, the emphasis in industrial education has been, and increasingly is, on outputs and yield: improving test results, dominating league tables, raising the number of graduates.

As with industrial farming, students and teachers alike are housed in conditions that inhibit their growth. Too often they are bored and disaffected, and increasingly they are kept with the program through drugs that artificially focus their attention. Meanwhile, the cost of the externalities is catastrophically high and rising every day. The industrial system of schooling worked for a while, but it is now exhausting itself and many people in it. The price we are paying is a damaging erosion of the culture of learning.

Education is really improved only when we understand that it too is a living system and that people thrive in certain conditions and not in others. The four principles of organic farming translate directly to the sorts of education we urgently need to cultivate. Paraphrased for education they might be:

Health. Organic education promotes the development and well-being of the whole student, intellectually, physically, spiritually, and socially.

Ecology. Organic education recognizes the vital interdependence of all of these aspects of development, within each student and the community as a whole.

Fairness. Organic education cultivates the individual talents and potential of all students, whatever their circumstances, and respects the roles and responsibilities of those who work with them.

Care. Organic education creates optimum conditions for students' development, based on compassion, experience, and practical wisdom.

The best schools have always practiced these principles. If all schools were to practice them, the revolution that we need would be well under way. Regardless, the task we face is not to increase yield in schools at the expense of engagement; it is to invigorate the living culture of schools themselves. That's what these principles are really about.

What basic purposes of education should the culture of schools fulfill? In my view, there are four: *economic, cultural, social,* and *personal.* Let's take them in reverse order.

ECONOMIC

Education should enable students to become economically responsible and independent.

It's sometimes argued that education is important just in itself, and that what goes on in schools shouldn't be affected by "external" interests, like the needs of business and the economy. This is a naïve idea. Mass education has always had economic purposes, and it is perfectly reasonable that it should. That is not to say that its purposes are only economic. We'll come to the others in a moment. But there is no denying the economic importance of education for individuals, communities, and countries.

Governments invest so heavily in education because they know that an educated workforce is essential for economic prosperity. Students and their families know that too. This is why in India 80 percent of families in poverty spend up to a third of their income on education, after food and shelter. Like parents everywhere, they expect that education will help their children find work and become economically independent. I expect that too. I can't tell you how much I want my children to be economically independent—and as soon as possible. Given how profoundly the world of work is changing, the question is, what sort of education do students need now to do that?

Many of the jobs that current systems of education were designed for are fast disappearing. Meanwhile, many new forms of work are emerging, especially from the transformative impact of digital technologies. It is almost impossible to predict what sorts of jobs today's students will be doing in five, ten, or fifteen years, assuming they have a job at all.

There is a lot of talk these days about the need for schools to promote "twenty-first-century skills." The U.S.-based Partnership for 21st Century Skills is a consortium of nineteen states and thirty-three corporate partners. It promotes a broad approach to curriculum and learning that includes the following categories: [9]

Interdisciplinary Themes
- global awareness
- financial, economic, business, and entrepreneurial literacy
- civic literacy
- health literacy
- environmental literacy

Learning Skills
- creativity and innovation
- critical thinking and problem solving
- communication and collaboration

Life and Career Skills
- flexibility and adaptability
- initiative and self-direction

- social and cross-cultural skills
- productivity and accountability
- leadership and responsibility

We'll talk more about some of these as we go on. It should immediately be clear, though, that they are not uniquely "twenty-first-century skills." Many schools and educators practiced and promoted them long before the twenty-first century got under way. They have always been important, and they are even more so now. The standards movement argues for them too, but the practices it has encouraged in schools largely denies them a place. The new and urgent challenge is to provide forms of education that encourage young people to engage with the global economic issues of sustainability and environmental well-being—to encourage them toward forms of economic activity that support the health and renewal of the world's natural resources rather than to those that deplete and despoil them.

To engage properly with their economic purposes, schools need to cultivate the great diversity of young people's talents and interests; to dissolve the divisions between academic and vocational programs, giving equal weight to both areas of study; and to foster practical partnerships with the world of work so that young people can experience different types of working environments firsthand.

CULTURAL

*Education should enable students to understand and
appreciate their own cultures and to respect the diversity of
others.*

When people live in regular contact, they deeply influence each
other's ways of thinking and behaving. Over time, every cohesive
human community evolves common conventions and values. They
develop a culture. I define culture as *the values and forms of behavior that characterize different social groups.* A shorter way of putting it is, "Culture is the way we do things around here."

A community's culture has many interweaving strands: belief
systems, legal practices, patterns of work, approved forms of relationships, food, dress, artistic practices, languages and dialects,
and so on. A culture lives in the interaction of all these elements
with each other. Cultures typically have many subcultures: individuals and groups who specialize in or stand apart from various
aspects of the overall culture, like Hell's Angels, who reject the
trappings of bourgeois society but still buy Harleys and use the
freeways.

Unless a community is physically isolated for a long time, as
some remote tribes are still, cultures are affected by their interactions with other cultures. As the world becomes more crowded
and connected, it is becoming more complex culturally. I recently
came across a riff on the Internet on what it means these days to
be British. It said, "Being British means driving home in a German car, stopping to buy an Indian curry or an Italian pizza, then
spending the evening sitting on Swedish furniture, drinking Bel-
gian beer, and watching American programs on a Japanese TV.
And the most British thing of all? Suspicion of anything foreign."

Adults and, more especially, children commonly move between various cultural and subcultural communities. With a population of seven hundred thousand students, for example, Los Angeles Unified School District (LAUSD) is the second largest in the United States, after New York City. The student body is roughly 73 percent Hispanic, 12 percent black, 9 percent white, 4 percent Asian, and 2 percent Filipino. Ninety-two languages are spoken in LAUSD schools; for more than two-thirds of students, English is a second language.

One of the supervisors for my doctoral dissertation at the University of London in the 1970s was Harold Rosen, an extraordinary teacher, activist, and distinguished professor of English. I remember talking with him after a conference on linguistic diversity in London schools. Someone had complained that their job was becoming very difficult because so many languages were spoken in schools—about eighty then, I think. Harold was amazed that language teachers should see linguistic diversity as a problem rather than an opportunity. Cultural diversity is one of the glories of human existence. The lives of all communities can be hugely enriched by celebrating their own cultures and the practices and traditions of other cultures.

There is a darker side to this diversity. Differences in values and beliefs can breed hatred and hostility. The history of human conflict has always been as much about culture as it has been about money, land, and power. Regional conflicts often center on deep cultural divisions—between Christians and Muslims, Sunni and Shia, Catholic and Protestant, Hutu and Tutsi, and the rest. Social antagonisms are commonly driven by perceived differences—between white and black, straight and gay, young and old. As humanity becomes more numerous and interwoven, living respectfully with diversity is not just an ethical choice, it is a practical imperative.

There are three cultural priorities for schools: to help students understand their own cultures, to understand other cultures, and to promote a sense of cultural tolerance and coexistence. To achieve these objectives, schools need a broad-based, rich curriculum, not a narrow, impoverished one. The standards movement doesn't begin to engage with these complexities.

SOCIAL

Education should enable young people to become active and compassionate citizens.

The promise of public schools has long been that they are the golden gateway to fulfillment and prosperity regardless of "social class or circumstances of birth."[10] For some people, the dream has come true; for many it has not. The gap between the rich and the poor has been growing yearly, and not only in America. So too has the achievement gap, especially for people of color.

For those in poverty, the ladder of education has become more and more rickety. Poorly focused resources, high rates of teacher turnover, and compounding social problems mean that schools are often not highways to further achievement but educational dead ends. The standards movement does nothing to address these inequities and everything to exacerbate them.

There is another issue. In democracies, education is meant to promote active citizenship. I currently live in Los Angeles. In June 2013, there was an election for mayor, the city's most important official. The eight candidates and their supporters spent about eighteen million dollars on their various campaigns. Yet only 16 percent of the 1.8 million registered voters in Los Angeles bothered to vote.[11] This is in a country where people have died for the right to vote, just as they have in other countries, including the U.K.

In 1913, a remarkable incident took place at the Epsom Derby, one of the premier events in the U.K.'s horse racing season. A horse belonging to King George was a prominent contender. As the pack approached the final furlongs of the race, a young woman, Emily Davison, ducked under the rail bordering the track and ran in front of the King's galloping horse. She was trampled to the ground, and three days later died in the hospital without regaining consciousness. Whether she intended to die is not known, though her reasons for confronting the King's horse are: Emily Davison was a campaigner for women's suffrage, and she died to promote women's right to vote.

Fifty years later, in 1963, Martin Luther King Jr. gave his historic "I Have a Dream" speech in Washington, D.C. He laid out a vision for democracy that, in spirit at least, would have won the enthusiastic approval of the nation's Founding Fathers. He called for a democracy that was "inclusive, substantive, and transformative." Fifty years later, many are still denied the vote, and many of those who have it choose not to use it.

Democratic societies depend for their strength on the majority of people being active citizens at the ballot box and in the community. The ballot box is democracy's sharpest tool. In many democracies, it is becoming dangerously blunted. Schools have vital roles in cultivating that sense of citizenship. They won't fulfill them by running academic courses on civics but by being the sorts of places that practice these principles in how they operate every day.

PERSONAL

Education should enable young people to engage with the world within them as well as the world around them.

Education is a global issue; it is also a deeply personal one. None of the other purposes can be met if we forget that education is about enriching the minds and hearts of living people. Many of the problems in current systems of education are rooted in the failure to understand this basic point. All students are unique individuals with their own hopes, talents, anxieties, fears, passions, and aspirations. Engaging them as individuals is the heart of raising achievement.

As human beings, we all live in two worlds. There is the world that exists whether or not you exist. It was there before you came into it, and it will be there when you have gone. This is the world of objects, events, and other people; it is the world around you. There is another world that exists only because you exist: the private world of your own thoughts, feelings, and perceptions, the world within you. This world came into being when you did, and it will cease when you do. We only know the world around us through the world within us, through the senses by which we perceive it and the ideas by which we make sense of it.

In Western cultures, we've become used to making firm distinctions between these two worlds, between thinking and feeling, objectivity and subjectivity, facts and values. As we'll discuss later, it turns out that these distinctions are not as reliable as they may seem. How we think about the world around us can be deeply affected by the feelings within us, and how we feel may be critically shaped by our knowledge, perceptions, and personal experiences. Our lives are formed by the constant interactions between these two worlds, each affecting how we see and act in the other.

The conventional academic curriculum is focused almost entirely on the world around us and pays little attention to the inner world. We see the results of that every day in boredom, disengagement, stress, bullying, anxiety, depression, and dropping out. These are human issues and they call for human responses.

As we argue in the Element books, what people contribute to

the world around them has everything to do with how they engage with the world within them. There are some things that we want all students to know, understand, and be able to do as a result of their education. But they also have their own unique patterns of aptitudes, interests, and dispositions. Education must attend to those too. Making education personal has implications for the curriculum, for teaching, and for assessment. It involves a transformation in the culture of schools. What does that look like in practice?

CHAPTER THREE

Changing Schools

"G UESS WHAT? Yesterday was your last day of school. What
 do you want to do?" This is something Ken Danford, co-
founder of North Star Self-Directed Learning for Teens in Had-
ley, Massachusetts, says regularly to kids who want to learn but
have found school frustrating, alienating, and uninspiring. How
do they react when Ken tells them that they don't need to go to
school any longer? "They're stunned," he told me. "They say
things like, 'Really? If you do that you can still go to college and
still get a job and the world will still like you?' No one has told
them that before."

Ken didn't start out as an iconoclast. He went to college to
become a teacher and got a job in a junior high school in Am-
herst, Massachusetts. He'd always liked school himself, so he
wasn't prepared for what he discovered when he began to stand
in front of the class. "It was dreadful. These kids didn't want to
be there. I was trying to sell them U.S. history that they didn't
want to learn. I was reading them the riot act: 'If you don't
learn U.S. history in eighth grade, you won't be able to do
whatever.' I thought I was an idiot listening to myself. I was
arguing with them about hats and tardiness and bathroom
passes—and if I wasn't mean about those things, the school
was getting on my case. I just couldn't do it. I just couldn't say
these things seriously to these kids and make such a mountain
out of a molehill.

"I read *The Teenage Liberation Handbook*, and that book described homeschooling and un-schooling as the land of nonconformist school people who just said, 'I'm gonna do something with my life. I don't have another day to waste. I'm not waiting until eighteen to get started—I'm going.' It turns out that people who do that and embrace living thrive. So I started wondering what it would take to not go to school. How about asking them what they want to learn? Do you want to be here today? Where do you want to go? With whom? For how long? They don't want to do history with me? OK, don't do history with me. They don't want to read? Then don't read. How do you do that? You do it by creating something that is not a school. You create a community center. You create a program. You tell people, 'I'm gonna help you and your parents be in charge of your life, and we're gonna have this cozy, happy place, and you can come here as much or as little as you want. You can do what you want while you're here, as long as you're nice. You can come and go as you please. And guess what? It'll probably turn out OK.'"

North Star is a center (Ken and his colleagues are very conscious about not calling it a school, because it is not accredited as one) that helps teenagers discover a passion for learning that has either been derailed or tamped down in a major way. While it is not a regular "school," it serves very effectively as one for many. "North Star is principally for teenagers who are in school and miserable, who don't want to go. Some are getting straight A's. Some of them have hobbies. Some of them don't know up from down and have all kinds of problems.

"There's a thing about letting people be—about letting them choose for themselves—that's so profound. There was no way to get that when we were teaching. What do you want to do and what do you want from me to help you? They don't know yet, so they have to try everything to figure it out. That might include saying no to everything and emptying out their lives and seeing what happens if they do nothing for a while. It's glorious fun."

While it might sound as though North Star is fast-tracking dropouts, the opposite is true. Most North Star participants go on to college, including MIT, Brown, Smith, UCLA, and Columbia, among others.[1] Participation in North Star is often seen as an asset by admissions directors, because North Star kids have a history of being self-directed and intellectually curious. Ken gave a particularly compelling example.

"We had a student who came when he was in seventh grade, after being homeschooled. He hung out, talked to people, tried to keep his life open. He'd trudge around with his math textbooks and he had a tutor here. At fifteen, he signed up for calculus at the community college and aced it. He had to go to the University of Massachusetts in order to take Calculus 2. He aced it. He took another couple of classes over the summer at UMass, two post-Calculus 2 courses. By this point, he'd turned sixteen. He could no longer get into the classes he wanted as an external student, so he goes to the admissions office and says, 'Look, I'm sixteen years old. I don't have four years of this, three years of that. I've never taken the SATs. All I know is I need to get enrolled in UMass so I can sign up for these advanced math classes.' So they put him in the Commonwealth program, which is supposed to be for valedictorians. By the time he was twenty, he graduated with a double major in math and Chinese."

Not all North Star students have experiences like this one, but they usually find a level of engagement that they never found in conventional school, and they regularly leave the center ready to do something positive with their lives. The North Star model has led to the creation of Liberated Learners, an outreach program helping others create centers based on the North Star model.[2]

Ken and North Star understand that learning comes in a wide

variety of shapes and sizes, that kids can't all be taught the same way, and that when students are taught in a way that best fits the way they learn and what interests them most, they can make enormous leaps. While it is an unconventional model, its success suggests a need for all schools to think in new ways about the way they serve their students.

Rules with Room

I often hear people say something like, "Our district would love to cater to the individual needs of our students, but the state/federal government won't let us." Certainly, as we've already noted, state and federal programs, with their focus on standardized curriculums and high-stakes testing, impose significant restrictions on the flexibility of local school systems. One of the actions we'll come to later is the need to press for radical changes in these policies. But it's also essential to make changes within the system as it is. As Laurie Barron, whom you met in chapter 1, showed at Smokey Road, and as many other examples in this book illustrate, there is room for maneuver and innovation already, based on the four principles of organic education.

Opportunities for change exist within every school, even where the emphasis on high-stakes testing has become extreme. Schools often do things simply because they've always done them. The culture of any given school includes habits and systems that the people in it act out every day. Many of these habits are voluntary rather than mandated—teaching by age groups, for example, or making every period the same length, using bells to signal the beginning and end of periods, having all of the students facing the same direction with the teacher in the front of the room, teaching math only in math class and history in history class, and so on. Many schools, a good number of which are dealing with adverse conditions and were once in considerable trouble, have used that space to innovate within the system, often with inspiring results. Innovation is possible because of the sort of system that education actually is.

A Tale of Two Systems

I said earlier that to transform any situation you need three forms of understanding: a *critique* of the way things are, a *vision* of how they should be, and *theory of change* for how to move from one to the other. Let me give you two examples of national reform movements that differ fundamentally on all three points and have had very different outcomes from each other.

In 1983, the U.S. Department of Education published a report on education that galvanized public and political debate. "A Nation at Risk" was written by a blue-ribbon panel of educators, politicians, and business leaders. The report warned that standards in American public education were disastrously low and continuing to fall. "We report to the American people," the authors wrote, "that while we can take justifiable pride in what our schools and colleges have historically accomplished and contributed to the United States and the well-being of its people, the educational foundations of our society are presently being eroded by a rising tide of mediocrity that threatens our very future as a Nation and a people. What was unimaginable a generation ago has begun to occur—others are matching and surpassing our educational attainments." In a startling comparison, the report went on, "If an unfriendly foreign power had attempted to impose on America the mediocre educational performance that exists today, we might well have viewed it as an act of war. As it stands, we have allowed this to happen to ourselves."[3]

The response was dramatic. President Reagan said, "This public awareness—and I hope public action—is long overdue. . . . This country was built on American respect for education. . . . Our challenge now is to create a resurgence of that thirst for education that typifies our Nation's history."[4] In the years that followed, hundreds of millions of dollars were spent on initiatives to raise standards in U.S. schools. Following his election, President Clinton picked up the education gauntlet and announced the centerpiece of his reform strategy, Goals 2000. This was a national initiative to build consensus on what should be taught in schools, in what disciplines, and by what age. Under the leadership of Education Secretary Richard Riley, a program was put in place to develop national standards that states could adopt at their own discretion. For all its ambitions and some significant achievements, Goals 2000 withered in the face of opposition from many states who argued that the federal government had no place telling them what their schools should do.

Following his election in 2000, George W. Bush enacted No Child Left Behind, which gave rise to a massive expenditure of money, time, effort, and a pervasive culture of national testing and standardization. This strategy has been largely adopted by the Obama administration too. Overall, the results have often been dismal. As I write this, the United States is still battling high rates of nongraduation, largely unchanged levels of literacy and numeracy, and widespread disaffection among students, teachers, parents, business leaders, and policymakers alike. Whatever their best intentions, many of the reform initiatives in the United States have not worked even on their own terms. And they won't, not for as long as they are rooted in the wrong story.

The *critique* that underlies the standards-based reform movement is that traditional academic standards are too low and have to be raised. The *vision* is of a world in which academic standards are very high and as many people as possible have college degrees, and there is full employment as a result. The *theory of change* is that the best way to do this is to specify exactly what the standards are and to focus relentlessly on them through an insistent process of standardized testing.

The story in Finland could hardly be more different. Finland regularly appears at or close to the top of the PISA rankings for mathematics, reading, and science, and it has done so since the tests were first administered in 2000. It was not always like this. Forty years ago, the Finnish system was in crisis too. But Finland chose not to go down the route of standardization and testing. Instead, the reforms were based on a completely different set of principles.

All Finnish schools are required to follow a broad and balanced curriculum that includes the arts, sciences, mathematics, languages, humanities, and physical education, but schools and districts have considerable latitude in how they do so. Finnish schools give a high priority to practical and vocational programs and the development of creativity in schools. Finland has invested heavily in the training and development of teachers, and as a result teaching is a high-status, secure profession. School principals are given wide discretion in how they run their schools and considerable professional support. Finland encourages schools and teachers to collaborate rather than compete by sharing resources, ideas, and expertise with each other. Schools are encouraged to have close links with their communities and with the parents and other family members of their students.[5]

Finland has consistently high standards of achievement on all international measures, but there is no standardized testing apart from a single examination at the end of high school. Finnish schools do not do these things in addition to achieving high standards—they achieve high standards precisely because they do these things. The system is so successful that visitors from around the world make pilgrimages to Finland to understand the education miracle that seems to have happened there. Is the system in Finland perfect? Of course not. It's evolving, as organic systems do. But overall, education in Finland is succeeding where many other systems are falling disastrously short.

You may say that we can't make realistic comparisons between Finland and the United States. Finland has a population of 5.5 million; the population of the United States is 314 million. Finland is a small country of 130,000 square miles; America takes up nearly 4 million square miles. This is all true. But the comparison still holds.

In America, education is mainly organized at the state level. Of the fifty states in America, thirty have populations equal to or smaller than Finland. Oklahoma has a population closing in on four million, Vermont has a little more than six hundred thousand, and so on. I was in Wyoming recently. From what I could tell, I was the only person there. Even in the more populous states, the real action happens at the district level. There are nearly sixteen thousand school districts in the United States and approximately fifty million school-age children. That averages out to a little more than three thousand students per district—which means they have far fewer students than Finland.

The point is not that U.S. policymakers should learn to speak Finnish and rename their state capitals New Helsinki. In other ways, there are major differences between Finland and the United States. Culturally, Finland is much more homogeneous than some (though by no means all) U.S. states. The two countries have very different political cultures and different attitudes about taxation and social welfare. Nonetheless, the principles that Finland has embraced to transform education can and do transfer to other cultural settings, including the United States. Studies of high-performing education systems around the world confirm that these are the only principles and conditions that really do work.

Living with Complexity

I said that education is best seen not as an industrial system but as an organic one. More specifically, it is what is known as a "complex, adaptive system." Let me develop this idea before we move forward.

A system is a set of related processes that have a combined effect. There are various sorts of systems, from simple to complex. A lever is a simple system. It's a rigid bar with a pivot closer to one end. It converts a force that's applied at the long end into a greater force at the shorter end. A switch is a simple system that turns a flow of electricity on or off. A microprocessor does the same.

There are complicated systems, which consist of many simple systems that are orchestrated to work together. Computers, automobiles, televisions, and nuclear reactors are all complicated systems that are composed of hundreds, maybe thousands, of simple systems.

Living systems like plants, animals, and people are not only complicated, they are *complex*. In a living organism, all the apparently separate systems that compose it are intimately related and depend on each other for the health of the organism as a whole. Plants with diseased roots don't flourish and have perfectly healthy flowers or fruit; if the roots are in trouble, the whole plant is in trouble. Animals don't thrive for long if only some of their organs are functioning properly; to get along, they need everything to be in working order to some degree.

Living systems also adapt and evolve. They have a *dynamic* and synergistic relationship with their physical environment. Organisms have all kinds of latent potential that may emerge depending on the conditions. If the environment changes in the wrong way, an organism may suffer and possibly die, or it may adapt to the changes over time and even evolve into something else.

You are a complex, adaptive system. Your body is an intricate web of physical processes, all of which are essential to your health and survival. Like the rest of life, we human beings depend on the world around us for the nutrients we need to live. When the physical environment changes too quickly or in the wrong way, we put ourselves at risk. Otherwise, we may adapt to it and change how we live.[5] Human life is more than physical, and our capacity to adapt is more than metabolic. As conscious beings, we may choose to change our outlook and do things differently.

Education systems too are complex and adapting. They are *complex* in several ways. They consist of numerous interest groups: students, parents, educators, employers, professional and commercial organizations, publishers, testing agencies, politicians, and on and on. There are multiple systems within the system, which constantly interact with each other. They include social services, counseling and psychological services, health care, and examinations and testing agencies. They all have their own special interests, which may overlap or conflict and affect each other with varying degrees of influence. Employers and politicians may be parents. Parents may be educators or students themselves.

There is great *diversity* within and between education systems. Although many national systems have similar industrial characteristics, there are different levels of prescription and control. There are many types of schools: faith-based, independent, and selective schools, and schools that specialize in particular disciplines. Some countries have few private schools; others have many.

Wherever and whatever they are, every school is a living community of people with unique relationships, biographies, and sensibilities. Each school has its own "feel," its rituals and routines, its own cast of personalities, its own myths, stories, in-jokes, and codes of behavior, and its many subcultures of friends and factions. Schools are not sanctuaries that are set apart from the turmoil of everyday life. They are embroiled in the world around them in every way. A vibrant school can nourish an entire community by becoming a source of hope and creative energy. I've seen whole neighborhoods thrive through the enlivening presence of a great school. Poor schools can drain the optimism from all the students and families who depend on it by diminishing their opportunities for growth and development.

The culture of schools is also affected by the general climate for education—by national and state laws, by economic circumstances, and by conditions and traditions in the dominant culture.

In all of these ways, education is a living system that manifests itself in myriad ways every day in the actions of real people and institutions. It's precisely because the education system is so complex and diverse that it can be changed and that it *does* change.

All living systems have a tendency to develop new characteristics in response to changing circumstances. They may have "emergent features," through "the interaction of small elements forming together to make a larger one."[6] In education, there's an abundance of emergent features right now that are changing the context in which schools work and the cultures within them.

For example, the spread of digital technologies is already transforming teaching and learning in many schools.[7] In 2014, there were roughly 7 billion networked devices on Earth, the same as the world population. In 2015, there are twice that many. It was estimated in 2014 that in *one minute* on the Internet 204 million emails were sent, 47,000 apps were downloaded, there were 6 million Facebook views, 2 million new searches on Google, 3,000 photo uploads, 100,000 Tweets, 1.3 million video views on You-Tube, and thirty hours of new videos uploaded.[8] Every minute. It would take you five years to watch all the videos crossing the network every second.

As Dave Price shows in his fascinating and wide-ranging book, *Open*, the growing availability and sophistication of digital technology is transforming both the world in which students learn and the means by which they do it.[9] Virtually every day there are new tools for learning and creative work in all sorts of disciplines, and new programs and platforms that can help to customize education for every learner. These technologies are also facilitating new partnerships between students, teachers, and professionals in many other fields.

As Marc Prensky, Jane McGonigal, and others have convincingly shown, the dynamics and aesthetics of digital gaming can be harnessed with powerful results to energize and enliven learning across the whole curriculum.[10] Meanwhile, mobile technologies are also bringing education to populations that previously had no access to it at all, including rural areas of Africa, Australasia, and South America. Later, you'll see how Silvina Gvirtz has used netbooks to help impoverished kids in Buenos Aires become excited about learning.

The changes are more than technological. As disaffection spreads with the numbing effects of standardized testing, schools and their communities are starting to push back against it. Parents who are anxious about the effects of the industrial education of their children are increasingly taking matters into their own hands. There is a still small but significant movement in homeschooling and un-schooling. Later, you'll hear from Logan LaPlante about what homeschooling has done for him.

As college graduates find that their degrees have less value than they thought, students are questioning whether to go to college at all and are looking hard at other options. As potential students turn away, colleges and universities are discovering that their old allure is fading. As a result, they are developing new models. Later in this book, you'll learn how Clark University in Massachusetts is mastering this challenge.

These are just a few examples of how education is changing and adapting as technologies and cultural values continuously interact with each other. There are many others. For all these reasons, the best place to start thinking about how to change education is exactly where you are in it. If you change the experiences of education for those you work with, you can change the world for them and in doing so become part of a wider, more complex process of change in education as a whole. That was the principle that inspired Ken Danford to found North Star, and it applies in all the other examples we feature in this book. It was also the principle behind the success of the Arts in Schools project, which I directed in the U.K. Let me elaborate briefly on that process, because it may help to identify the conditions of change in your school or local system.

A Tale of Two Projects

Earlier in my career, I was involved with two projects that had similar aims but very different impacts.

My first proper—that is, paid—job in education was in the midseventies as one of three members of the core team of a national research project on the role of drama in schools, called Drama 10-16. My doctoral studies were on this very theme, so this was a dream job, especially since I was offered actual money to do it. The project was funded by the Schools Council, which was then the main national agency for curriculum development in the U.K.

In the previous twenty years, there had been a rapid expansion of drama in schools. Many schools had their own drama departments, specialist teachers, studios, and theaters. Most school districts had full-time drama advisers, some of whom had teams of advisory teachers. Specialist college and university departments offered full-time teacher training programs in drama. There was also a lot of debate about the real value of drama education and about best practices. Our job was to take a close look at what drama teachers were actually doing in schools and to make recommendations for future development.

We selected six school districts with well-developed drama programs and worked closely with three schools and the local drama advisers in each district. In the first year, we made regular visits to our schools and made detailed case studies of the drama teachers' work with their students. We hosted regional and national meetings on issues in drama education, and we ran a series of residential workshops for all the advisers and teachers in the project to share practices and perspectives.

In the second year, we worked on a book, *Learning Through Drama*, that set out a conceptual framework for drama in schools and a series of practical recommendations. The Schools Council funded us for a third year to disseminate our findings through a national program of workshops, courses, and conferences. After the third year, the funding ended, we all moved on to other things, and the activities of the project died down.

The drama project followed a classic process of research, development, and dissemination. We went into the schools to find out what was going on, we developed our proposals, and then we published them to the world. Our work had considerable influence in schools throughout the U.K., and its effects continued to spread after we closed the office. Although we helped to establish several professional associations to support drama teachers, there was no specific agency to continue the work of the project itself. It was a limited program and it had limited impact as a result.

The Arts in Schools project was different.

In the late eighties, the conservative government of Margaret Thatcher passed a law that introduced a national curriculum for schools in England. The 1988 Education Reform Act (ERA) was an earthquake in British education. Until then, schools could teach whatever they liked. In practice, they often had similar curricula, but in theory they were free agents. The ERA put an end to all that. A national curriculum had been coming for a while and was originally mooted by the previous Labor government. That was until 1984, when the oil crisis in the Middle East sent shock waves through Western economies. That, combined with high levels of unemployment, led then Prime Minister James Callaghan (Labor) to give notice that schools could no longer just go their own way. He insisted that some agreement on national priorities in education would have to be thrashed out.

In the run-up to 1988, many people feared that the new national curriculum would be too narrow and utilitarian. Some worried that the arts in particular would be pushed to the margins. As a preemptive strike, the independent Calouste Gulbenkian Foundation convened a nationwide commission to review the place of the arts in education. With others, I researched and wrote the report of the commission, *The Arts in Schools: Principles, Practice and Provision.*

We wrote the report with four objectives in mind. One was to make the arts a fundamental part of the debate that was raging in the U.K. on the future of education. Up to this point, the arts were barely being discussed as the national curriculum was being shaped. The second was to make the case for the arts as clearly as possible to policymakers at all levels. Our third objective was to identify the problems, practical and otherwise, that faced the development of the arts in schools, and the fourth was to propose a workable plan of action for schools and policymakers.

The publication of *The Arts in Schools* generated a wide variety of projects, including conferences, pilot programs, and in-service courses. It even fostered a new understanding of the importance of the arts as part of social policy outside of school, especially for young people. Given the impact of the report, I was asked to design, and then direct, a national project to help schools implement the recommendations.

In doing so, I was mindful of the important but limited impact of the Drama 10-16 project. Consequently, I based the Arts in Schools project on an entirely different model of change. The aim was not just to promulgate the report's recommendations, but to empower schools to put them into practice by transforming what they were doing in their own classrooms with their own students, staff, and communities. Over the next four years, the project facilitated a national network of school-based innovation that included more than sixty school districts, three hundred schools, and two thousand teachers and other professionals. The benefits for schools were immediate, widespread, and, most important, sustained. Three decades later, I still hear from people who talk about the impact of the project on their schools and on their own practice.

Drama 10-16 was a good program that effected limited change. The Arts in Schools project generated more widespread and lasting change. Why was one project more effective than the other? It had to do with how the programs were designed and how they worked in practice. In the latter, we treated schools as the complex, adaptive systems that they are. That meant addressing the various, interdependent components of the system.

Each school district in the Arts in Schools project identified a group of participating schools as the main sites for innovation.

They each convened a local advisory group to support and guide the work in schools, to advocate on behalf of the local project, and to create the best climate for it to succeed. The advisory groups included education policymakers, members of local cultural organizations, funding agencies, and business leaders.

The Arts in Schools project didn't solve the problem of the marginalization of arts education. Arts education is still under fire in the standards movement, as much so in the U.K. as it is in the United States. By appreciating the complexity of the education system and appealing to that system at multiple levels simultaneously, the project did effect lasting change in the many schools and districts that took part in it. I strongly believe that any attempt at systemic transformation in education must take a similar approach.

Taking responsibility for change begins by accepting that change is within your power. One of the things I found so rewarding about the Arts in Schools project was that schools took our suggestions and created courses of action appropriate to their particular situations. Over time, hundreds of schools in the U.K. put our recommendations into action in their own way.

As we go on, we'll look at more schools that are transforming education for their students based on personalized approaches to learning that are customized to both the student and the community. These schools go beyond the ritual forms of organization (teaching by age group, fixed teaching periods, sharp subject divisions, and linear assessment patterns) that many schools follow. They do so because they know that the fundamental work of schools is not to increase test results but to facilitate learning.

THE ROOT OF THE MATTER

In my book *Out of Our Minds*, I quoted the work of theater director Peter Brook. Over a long lifetime of work, his driving passion has been to make theater the most transformative experience it can be.[11] He acknowledges that a lot of theater doesn't have this sort of impact; it's a night out to pass the time that would have passed anyway. To heighten its power, he says, it's critical to understand what the essence of theater is. To do that, he asks what can be taken away from a typical theater event for it still to be theater.

You can take away the curtains and the lights, he says, along with the costumes. They're not essential. You can take away the script—a lot of theater is unscripted. You can get rid of the director and dispense with the stage, the crew, and the building. A lot of theater happens without any of these things and always has.

The only thing you can't lose is an actor in a space and an audience watching. It may be just one actor and one person watching, but these are the essential and irreducible elements of theater. The actor performs a drama that the audience experiences. "Theater" is the whole relationship between the audience and the drama. For theater to have its most transformative effects, it's essential to focus on that relationship and make it as powerful as possible. Nothing should be added, Brook says, unless it deepens it. He has demonstrated this conviction in a series of groundbreaking, internationally acclaimed productions.

For me, the analogy with education is exact. I made a distinction in the introduction between learning and education. The fundamental purpose of education is to help students learn. Doing that is the role of the teacher. But modern education systems are cluttered with every sort of distraction. There are political agendas, national priorities, union bargaining positions, building codes, job descriptions, parental ambitions, peer pressures. The list goes on. But the heart of education is the relationship between the student and the teacher. Everything else depends on how productive and successful that relationship is. If that is not working, then the system is not working. If students are not learning, education is not happening. Something else may be going on, but it's not education.

A great deal of learning—and education—goes on outside the formal setting of schools and national curricula. It happens anywhere there are willing learners and engaging teachers. The challenge is to create and sustain those experiences within schools. The root task is to create the conditions in which the relationship between students and teachers can flourish. This is what I mean by revolutionizing education from the ground up. In doing this, there is a natural ecosystem of responsibilities.

- At the most fundamental level, the focus of education has to be on creating the conditions in which students will want and be able to learn. Everything else has to be arranged on that basis.
- Next, the role of teachers is to facilitate students' learning. Doing this properly is an art form in itself, and that's what we'll be focusing on in chapter 5.
- The role of principals is to create the conditions in their schools in which teachers can fulfill these roles. Doing this has implications for leadership and school culture.
- The role of policymakers is to create conditions—whether at the local, state, or national levels for which they are responsible—in which principals and schools can fulfill these responsibilities.

In a publicly funded system of education, there has to be some agreement on what students should learn and why, and ways of holding teachers and schools accountable for how well they're doing. We will look at these issues as well. But first, let's go to the heart of the matter by looking at learning. For schools to improve, there must be an understanding of the nature of learning itself—how students learn best and the many different ways in which they do so. If schools and educational policies get this wrong, everything else is noise.

CHAPTER FOUR

Natural Born Learners

NEWBORN BABIES have a voracious appetite to learn about the world around them. Take language. In ordinary circumstances, by the time they are two or three years old, most children learn to speak with remarkable fluency. If you are a parent, you know that you don't teach your children how to speak. You couldn't. You don't have the time and they wouldn't have the patience. Young children absorb language just by being exposed to it. You may correct, encourage, and congratulate them along the way, but you don't reach a point when you sit them down and say, "Look, we need to talk. Or, more specifically, you do." This is not how it works, and language is just one example of the vast capacity that we all have for learning.

In chapter 2, I described the transformation that Richard Gerver helped to bring about at Grange Primary School in the U.K. As successful as his idea was, Richard isn't saying that districts all around the world should turn their schools into towns. Instead, he suggests they take the back-to-basics approach that led to the creation of Grangeton. "As a starting point, we should be getting all educators—whether at the university, school, or professional development level—to find the best early-years facilities they can in their region and spend time learning from what they do," he told me. "Then ask, how can we take some of what they're doing and translate it to a level that works for our students? That is the greatest celebration of natural learning that is practical and demonstrable."

The Ecstasy and Agony of Learning

Just how much are children natural learners? Sugata Mitra tested that question when he ran an experiment in a New Delhi slum in 1999. He installed a computer in a wall, turned it on, connected it to the Internet, and watched how children reacted to it. Not only had none of these kids ever seen a computer before, but the Web browser was in English, a language none of them knew. Very quickly they learned what they could do with the computer and then started teaching it to each other. Within hours, they were playing games, recording their own music, and surfing the Net like pros.[1] If Twitter had been around back then, they probably would have had half a million followers by the end of the month.

Sugata decided to try a more ambitious experiment. He connected a computer to a speech-to-text program and gave it to a group of Indian children who spoke English with a very strong Telugu accent. The computer couldn't make out their accents, so the speech-to-text program typed gibberish. The kids didn't know how to make the computer decipher what they were saying, and Mitra admitted that he didn't either. So he left the machine with the kids for two months, and when he came back the children had refined their accents to the neutral British accent the computer had been programmed to understand.

A short while later, Sugata tried to find out if twelve-year-old, Tamil-speaking children could teach themselves biotechnology in English on their own. Again, he gave them two months, and even he didn't expect much from the results. "I'll test them, they'll get a zero," he said. "I'll give the materials, I'll come back and test them—they get another zero. I'll go back and say, 'Yes, we need teachers for certain things.'

"I came back after two months, and the twenty-six children marched in looking very, very quiet. I said, 'Well, did you look at any of the stuff?' They said, 'Yes, we did.' 'Did you understand anything?' 'No, nothing.' So I said, 'Well, how long did you practice on it before you decided you understood nothing?' They said, 'We look at it every day.' So I said, 'For two months, you were looking at stuff you didn't understand?' So a girl raises her hand and says, literally, 'Apart from the fact that improper replication of the DNA molecule causes genetic disease, we've understood nothing else.' "[2]

Sugata continues to discover how much children can learn on their own if given effective tools. He recently launched a "granny cloud," a group of retired teachers who help students learn and explore via a Skype connection,[3] and at the end of 2013, he launched the first School in the Cloud, "where children can embark on intellectual adventures by engaging and connecting with information and mentoring online."[4]

His experiments have shone a light on the immense capacities that children have to learn.[5] So if children are such natural learners, why do so many of them struggle at school? Why are so many bored by the whole process? In many ways, it's a function of the system itself and of the conventions that pervade it.

In the conventional high school classroom, students sit at desks, facing the front, while the teacher instructs, explains, and sets assignments. The mode of learning is predominantly verbal or mathematical; that is, students mainly write, calculate, or discuss with the teacher. The curriculum is a body of material to be learned. It is arranged into various subjects, usually taught by different teachers. There are frequent tests and a lot of time spent in preparing for them. Inevitably students grasp some material more quickly than others, but the class is intended to get through the material at the same rate and over the same amount of time. Whether individuals keep up with or fall behind the class as a whole is taken as one indication of their general ability.

The school day is typically divided into regular blocks of time of forty minutes or so, which are allocated to different activities in a repetitive weekly schedule. At the end of each period, there's a signal—often a bell or buzzer—for everyone to stop what they're doing and move on to the next activity with a different teacher in another room.

Why are schools so often run this way? The main reason is that mass education was built on two pillars, which are still evident in the behavior of modern systems. You can think of these as the *organizational* culture and the *intellectual* culture of schools. As I argued in chapter 2, the organizational culture of mass education is rooted in the manufacturing processes of industrialism. The intellectual culture has much deeper roots that stretch back to antiquity and of Plato's Academy (the origin of our word "academic").

I said earlier that education is dominated by the idea of academic ability. For many people, it seems "academic" is a synonym for "intelligent" and "academic success" for "educational achievement." Properly conceived, "academic" has a more limited meaning. It refers to intellectual work that is mainly theoretical or scholarly rather than practical or applied. (It's for this reason that the word "academic" is sometimes also used to describe ideas—and people—that are thought to be impractical or purely theoretical.)

There are three principal elements in academic work. The first is a focus on what philosophers call propositional knowledge—facts about what is the case, for example, that the Declaration of Independence was signed in 1776. Second, there is a focus in academic work on theoretical analysis—of concepts, procedures, assumptions, and hypotheses, for example, the nature of democracy and liberty, the laws of motion, the structures of sonnets. The third element follows from these. It is an emphasis on desk studies that mainly involve reading, writing, and mathematics rather than on technical, practical, and applied work that involves manual dexterity, physical skills, hand-eye coordination, and the use of tools.

Propositional knowledge is sometimes called knowing *that* and is distinguished from procedural knowledge, or knowing *how*. Procedural knowledge is what we use in making things and getting practical work done. It's possible to study art history academically without knowing how to paint and music theory without being able to play an instrument. Making art or music—so that there is actually something there to study—involves knowing *how* as well as knowing *that*. Procedural knowledge is vital in all practical fields, from engineering to medicine to dance. Some people flourish in academic work and find that they have passions for specific fields of study. Others find that their real interests in the practical application of ideas and techniques and have passions for specific fields of practice.

Of course, academic work is important in itself, and theory can and should inform practice in all areas of life. But in the conventional academic curriculum, the emphasis is squarely on the former rather than the latter. Academic studies are unquestionably essential and should form part of every student's education. But they are not enough. They are necessary but not sufficient to the sort of education that all students now need.

Human intelligence embraces much more than academic ability: it suffuses all the achievements that are manifest in the arts, sports, technology, business, engineering, and the host of other vocations to which people who are alert to them may devote their time and lives. All our lives and futures depend on people mastering a vast range of practical abilities and skills. While schools can hardly be expected to teach all of them to all students, they should at least lay the foundations for their development by giving them the equal status and place they deserve in general education.

It might strike you as curious that despite the manifest wealth of human intelligence, our schools have come to focus on such a specific aspect of it. The reasons, as I argue in *Out of Our Minds*, are enmeshed in the impact of the European Enlightenment on higher education and on the evolution of the scientific method and its applications in industrialism. I won't go into that again here, but the upshot is that our school systems are now a matrix of organizational rituals and intellectual habits that do not adequately reflect the great variety of talents of the students who attend them.

Because they conflict with these systems, too many students think that they are the problem, that they are not really intelligent, or must have difficulties in learning. Some people do have learning challenges and may need special support. For many others, the problem is not that they cannot learn but how they are required to learn.

WHOSE PROBLEM IS THIS?

I said earlier that education is both a global issue and a deeply personal one. It is for all of us. I was born into a large working-class family in Liverpool, England. I have five brothers and a sister. I told some of their stories in the Element series. We grew up with our parents—and often our extended family—in a small terraced house on Spellow Lane, in the stadium shadows of Everton, one of the top soccer teams in the country. Ironically, I was fortunate in my education, because I had polio as a child and was sent to a special school.

While I was there I had various mentors and eventually passed the 11+, a test that determined who went to the high-status, academic "grammar schools" rather than the lower-status "secondary moderns." Going to grammar school was the route to college, and out of service and blue-collar work to potential jobs in business and the professions. If not for that, I would not have had the life I've had and would not be doing what I do now. Two of my brothers passed their test and went on to grammar schools too. Although they were every bit as able, my other brothers and my sister Lena did not.

Lena loved her time at Gwladys Street Elementary School in the early fifties. She loved the relaxed atmosphere and the opportunities to read, write, do arts and crafts, play sports—and just play. The 11+ came as a cold shower. The children all knew it was a big deal but weren't quite sure why. On the day of the test, they were bused to an unfamiliar school and crowded in a hall with children they didn't know from other schools.

They sat separately at individual desks and were told not to talk. They were given a booklet of questions and puzzles that they had to complete in a set time. At the end of the test, the booklets were collected, and the students were sent back to their schools. Several weeks later, a manila envelope from the Liverpool Education Committee dropped through the letter box at home. Our parents opened it and told Lena quietly that she'd failed the test. She wasn't surprised. She'd had no preparation for it and had no idea what was expected. The next letter they received said she was to go to Stanley Park Secondary Modern School for Girls.

She was there for four years, from the age of eleven until she left school at fifteen. She hated almost all of it. There was a set curriculum with no choices. She spent most of her time in classes of forty or more other girls of the same age, facing the front, doing as they were told. They had classes in history, geography, mathematics, English, and sciences. She got on quietly, doing what was expected. Naturally shy, she never put her hand up for fear of attracting attention.

The lessons she liked best were when she got to move around and make things: domestic science, where she cooked actual food; chemistry, where she could do experiments; needlework, where she could cut and sew fabrics; and sports, where she could breathe and run. But these bright spots felt few and far between the hours of sitting, writing, and not talking.

In the final year of school, the class met as a group with the visiting careers officer who explained that, according to their suitability, they might consider jobs as secretaries, personal assistants, nurses, hairdressers, or factory workers. And so they did. Of all of the options, Lena and four or five others thought that hairdressing sounded most interesting. It involved a three-year apprenticeship in a salon; one day a week at college studying art, chemistry, cutting, and styling; and, above all, working with people on something that mattered to them personally. She was pleased with her choice and so were my parents. They weren't completely focused on her work prospects just then. My father had just had an industrial accident in which he had broken his neck, and was now a quadriplegic. So Lena made her choice with the family's blessing but without its full attention.

On the last day of school, the headmistress visited every class to offer some words of advice. She also asked the pupils to stand up as she called out their various job options. She congratulated the would-be nurses, secretaries, and factory workers. Then she asked if anyone was thinking of being a hairdresser. Five girls, including Lena, stood up. "Well," the headmistress said, "I might have known that the lazy ones would choose a lazy job." They'd stood up proud and expectant, and sat down baffled and embarrassed. Lena had always worked hard and had never been told she was lazy by anyone. She went to Stanley Park at eleven feeling she'd failed, and now she was leaving it at fifteen feeling that she'd failed again. But then, this was the first time the headmistress had ever spoken to her.

As it happens, she became a successful hairdresser with her own business. She realized later, though, that if the school had known her, it might have helped her take a different route. She has learned that she is highly organized, with a gift for working with people, and she thinks now that she should have gone into a profession that drew more deeply on those talents.

But she left secondary modern school in the sixties when there were no great expectations of those kids, especially girls. As Lena says, "When you spend your time in school as part of a crowd, being judged in the same way, how is anyone supposed to know who you are or what you can really do?" Exactly.

Then as now, many of the problems that young people experience in motivation and learning are caused by the system itself. Change the system, and many of these problems tend to disappear. Let me give you another example of what happens when the frame that is normally placed on learning is taken away.

FREE TO LEARN

After a long tenure as senior artistic director at the BRIT School for the Performing Arts & Technology, Adrian Packer was offered the opportunity to become the first principal of Everton Free School, an alternative educational institution for teens created by the Everton Football Club, one of the U.K.'s most popular soccer teams. By an extraordinary coincidence, for me at least, the school is being built on waste ground on Spellow Lane, the street I grew up in as a child, and almost exactly opposite the house where we lived. Partly for that reason, I was moved to see that Everton Free School aims to "institutionalize opportunity" for every student regardless of their circumstances.

Free schools are new in the U.K. Like charter schools in the United States, they are funded by the national government, but they are allowed to operate outside the strictures of the national curriculum, and they have more freedom in terms of standards for the school day, staff hiring practices, and budgets.[6] Everton Free School was set up to offer personalized opportunities to teenagers for whom traditional education simply wasn't working.

Callum Mains was one such teenager. Callum loved going to school early on, but when he reached his teens he found his school too big and too impersonal, so he stopped attending about half the time. Life at home had become difficult after his father died when Callum was thirteen, and school offered no relief, putting him in programs that failed to match his interests or inspire new ones. For him, Everton Free School was a lifeline, a chance to connect with an institution that was actually paying attention to him and his ambitions.

"Being here is like you're working with the teachers, not against them," he told me. "Here, you feel like they notice you and they will take what you think into account. I think it if wasn't for the Free School, I'd just be one of those kids smoking weed. This really helped me not to go down that path. This showed me you can do whatever you want." The Everton Free School and all the others we've looked at demonstrate two critical points: First, all students have great natural abilities. Second, the key to developing them is to move beyond the narrow confines of academicism and conformity to systems that are personalized to the real abilities of every student.

This Time, It's Personal

A few years ago I bought a new car. It took a long time. Once I'd decided on the basic model, I was offered an endless series of choices to customize it to my personal tastes and needs: color, finish, fabrics, sound systems, trims, number of doors, engine size, and so on. It was like filling out a tax return. I asked the salesman how many versions of this car there actually were. He didn't know, but guessed that mine would be unique, just like all the others he'd sold. In contrast, I got my first car when I was twenty-three. Back then, there was only one question: "Do you want it or not?"

Nowadays, we take for granted that we can personalize just about anything, from the apps on our smart phones, to the clothes we wear, to our pages on Facebook. The same is true of health care. As technology and the understanding of biology continue to develop, the medicines you take will become ever more tailored to your individual body type.

This process of personalization seems to be everywhere, but it has yet to take root in education. This is ironic, because it is in education that personalization is most urgently needed. So what does that mean? It means:

- Recognizing that intelligence is diverse and multifaceted
- Enabling students to pursue their particular interests and strengths
- Adapting the schedule to the different rates at which students learn
- Assessing students in ways that support their personal progress and achievement

The Diversity of Intelligence

I said that children are natural learners, and they are. In the first years of life, they learn prodigiously about the world and the people around them and begin to develop some of the most remarkable capacities within them. Of course, other species learn quickly too. There is an increasing understanding of how intelligent many other animals are, and of the subtlety of their behavior, abilities, and relationships.

There's also a fair amount of debate out there over whether other animals truly learn in the way we define it, but there are many compelling examples. For instance, in *The Pig Who Sang to the Moon*, author Jeffrey Moussaieff Masson tells the story of Piglet, a pig who goes swimming every morning, enjoys the company of children (as long as they rub her belly), and seems to sing to the sky during full moons.[7]

Then there is the case of 007, the problem-solving crow, who, during an experiment conducted by Dr. Alex Taylor, made his way through eight obstacles—all of which needed to be addressed in a specific way—to get to food nestled deep within a container.[8] Perhaps best known is the case of Koko, the gorilla to whom the Gorilla Foundation taught American Sign Language. Koko learned more than a thousand signs, created compound signs to convey new information, and showed a significant understanding of spoken English.[9]

For a time, some animals can outperform human babies in some ways. Koko was certainly more effective at getting his point across than most infants. Quickly, though, humans demonstrate a power that sets us apart from all other creatures: the power of symbolic thought, of which language is the most obvious example. In at least one fundamental respect, human beings are different from the rest of life on Earth: we do not live in the world directly, as other species seem to do. Instead, we see it through frameworks of ideas and values. We not only exist in the world, we have ideas and theories about it that affect what we make of it all and we see ourselves and each other. These powers of imagination and creativity are among the few things that set us apart from the rest of life on Earth. But they make all the difference.

As they grow up, children learn as we all do that they live not in one world but two. As I noted earlier, there is the world that exists whether or not you exist: the world of other people, of material objects and events. There is also a world that exists only because you exist: the world of your private consciousness. One of the challenges of being alive is making sense of both of these worlds and of the relationship between them.

When we live closely with other people, we affect each other's ways of thinking and feeling. We develop common ways of being together, shared values and behavior. As children grow, they absorb the ways of seeing and thinking that are embedded in the languages they speak and the values and lifestyles of their communities. Collectively, we have created sophisticated languages and organized systems of thought, abstract theories and practical technologies, complex art forms, and intricate cultural practices. In these ways, we literally create the worlds that we live in, and the worlds that different cultures inhabit are often strikingly opposed.

In *Out of Our Minds*, I discuss the many different senses (more than five) that we have and how they compare with other species, some of which can perceive aspects of the world around them that we can't even detect. Nonetheless, we are endowed with immense capacities to think about and act in the world that are different in kind from the rest of life around us. We think and communicate about the world in all the ways we experience it. We think in sounds and images, in movement, in words and numbers, and in all the ways these various modes make possible. We think in metaphors and analogies: we reason and empathize, speculate and suppose, imagine and create.

One of the features of human life is the variety of individual talents, interests, and temperaments. Psychologists and others in the human sciences are naturally drawn to trying to define and classify them. The most influential theory of intelligence in the last hundred years or so is IQ—the idea that we each have a set amount of innate intelligence, which can be quickly tested and given a number. I've written elsewhere about the shortcomings of this idea and won't go into it again here for fear of straining your patience.[10] I will only say that it presents a narrow and misleading conception of how rich and diverse human intelligence really is.

There have been various attempts at broader theories of intelligence. One of the most influential is Howard Gardner's theory of multiple intelligences. He describes MI as "a critique of the standard psychological view of intellect: there is a single intelligence, adequately measured by IQ or other short-answer tests." On the basis of evidence from disparate sources, he argues that human beings have a number of relatively discrete intellectual capacities. He identifies eight modes of intelligence and suggests that we all have a unique blend of all of them.[11]

The theory of MI has been widely debated and alternative conceptions have been proposed. These and other theories about the diversity of intelligence have all attracted criticism. Theories generally do. Some critics challenge the structure of the theories— are there three forms of intelligence or should it be four or eight or ten? Others argue that these are only theories for which there is no scientific proof and until there is we should treat them as speculative and provisional. Both forms of criticism are reasonable and proper. The progress of science, as Karl Popper argued, is not linear.[12] It is based on "conjectures and refutations." Any theory, however appealing, awaits the emergence of better ones or of evidence that supports, doubts, or refutes it.

What I find curious in this case is that some critics have concluded that since these particular theories of multiple intelligence have not been scientifically proven, there is no substance to what they are attempting to explain. Well, there plainly is. A few years ago I was at a meeting in the office of a senior government official in northern Europe. He was skeptical about intelligence being diverse and asked what proof there was of it. We were sitting at a beautifully carved mahogany table in an oak-paneled room in a seventeenth-century building. There were striking modernist paintings on the walls, a large flat-screen television tuned to a twenty-four-hour news channel, two Apple computers on his glass-and-steel desk, and an intricately hand-woven traditional carpet on the floor. Behind him, there were shelves of novels, poetry, and leather-bound books. A recording of Mozart was playing quietly in the background. All of these are products and evidence of the extraordinary diversity of human intelligence and ability. "Look around," I said, "and listen. The diversity of intelligence is everywhere." He seemed struck by a new thought.

The evidence is in the multiple cultures and achievements that characterize human life on Earth, in science and the arts, philosophy and religion, technology and engineering, sports and athleticism, and all the many ways in which these human activities cross-pollinate and enrich each other.

If we're serious about meeting the four main purposes of education, we need to provide for the different ways in which our intelligence allows us to act in the world around us and to fathom the world within us. It's essential that all students have proper opportunities to explore the range of their abilities and sensibilities in school, including but going well beyond their capacities for conventional academic work. This has fundamental implications for the structure and balance of the curriculum for everyone.

ENABLING STUDENTS TO PURSUE THEIR OWN INTERESTS AND STRENGTHS

We all have a wide range of natural aptitudes, and we all have them differently. Personalization means teachers taking account of these differences in how they teach different students. It also means allowing for flexibility within the curriculum so that in addition to what all students need to learn in common, there are opportunities for them to pursue their individual interests and strengths as well.

In the Element books, I argue that being in your element is where talent meets passion. We all have different strengths and weaknesses, different talents. There are some things for which I have a natural feel. I can express myself reasonably well in words and always could. Try as I did, I never felt so much at home with numbers. I had friends at school who relished math lessons. They just got it. I was competent and passed the tests, but for me it was often an effort to grasp some of the concepts and techniques that seemed to come easily to others. Of course, any aptitude, however weak, can be developed through practice. And any talent, however prodigious, can be honed through practice. But the same amount of practice by two people with different levels of aptitude will almost certainly take them to different levels of achievement. It's easy to see those differences, even in your own household.

Bring a new piece of electronics into your home, and ask each member of your family to figure out how to get it to work. Your partner might go directly to the owner's manual, while one of your children goes online to access some YouTube videos about the device, and another just turns the thing on to see what happens. Each of them approaches learning about this new thing differently—because each is a different person. If that's the case, then teaching everyone the same way is inefficient, to say the least.

Being in your element is not only about finding your talents. Some people are good at things they don't really care for. To be in your element, you have to love it. It's also about passion. Our view of the outer world is shaped in part by our physical characteristics and by our cultures. But we each have our own personalities, talents, interests, hopes, motivations, anxieties, and dispositions. Profound things can happen when students are given room to explore their own interests and capacities. Laurie Barron wasn't able to make headway with her middle school students until she acknowledged that what they felt was most important to them *was* the most important thing. Football or art or music (or, for that matter, science or literature or history) got them through the rest of the day, and made the classes that didn't engage them tolerable.

All learning depends in part on memorizing information and ideas. The assumption in schools seems to be that you either have a good memory or a bad memory, and that if you have the latter, you're probably not very bright and are just going to have to work harder. And yet the students who struggle to memorize historical dates or multiplication tables often have no trouble memorizing the lyrics to hundreds of songs or referencing a particular play from a sporting event that took place ten years earlier. Their "bad" memories in school may be a lack of engagement, not lack of capacity.[13]

ADAPTING THE SCHEDULE TO THE RATES AT WHICH
INDIVIDUAL STUDENTS LEARN

If different people learn best in different ways, they also learn at different rates. Whole-class teaching and set programs can make it difficult for teachers to recognize and accommodate these differences. The result is that some students do less well than they could. Low achievement can lead to low expectations, which can have a debilitating effect on a student's entire school career. Raising individual achievement in schools means engaging students as individuals and not prescribing a standard steeplechase for everyone to complete at the same time and in the same way.

One of the steadfast traditions in education is the grouping of students by age. Some parents will hold their children out of kindergarten for a year if they feel they aren't ready for school, but once they are in the system, they move along year by year with their same-age peers. Eight-year-olds share their classrooms with other eight-year-olds. A fourteen-year-old might take an elective class with a seventeen-year-old, but will be taking language arts with other fourteen-year-olds.

If you look at any first-grade class, you'll probably find a handful of kids who are reading comfortably, another handful who are sounding out each word, a couple who are struggling to make sense of it all, and one or two who have already moved on to John Green. Most will eventually be fluent readers, but at this point they're on different tracks. Some learners just get math quickly and would probably be comfortable with an introduction to algebra in third grade. Others see math as a party to which they have not been invited and would probably be best served getting a refresher on fractions in ninth grade.

And then there is the incongruous conventional conveyor belt schedule in schools. Think about applying this approach to the business world. If every forty or so minutes, the whole workforce had to stop what it was doing, move to different rooms, do something else entirely, and rinse and repeat six times a day, the business would rapidly grind to a halt and it would probably be bankrupt within a few months. Different activities need more or less time than others. A group project may need several hours of uninterrupted work; a personal writing assignment may be better done in a series of shorter sessions. If the schedule is flexible and more personalized, it is more likely to facilitate the kind of dynamic curriculum that students now need. One of the most exasperating features of the conveyor belt schedule is having to stop an activity before it's completed. That's where someone like Joe Harrison comes in.

Joe wasn't trained as a teacher when he started working on a music education program in a school in Manchester, in the U.K. He saw how the frenetic pace of a normal school day makes it exceedingly difficult for students to ever get truly engaged in a project or a subject. "It was interesting work," he told me, speaking about the job in Manchester. "It was engaging and exciting. The young people enjoyed it and the teachers enjoyed it, and we had some interesting ideas with it. But no matter what we imagined possible with this music project, it always had to be limited to one hour every Monday morning. The whole project then becomes not about education anymore. All of the educational possibilities, all of the power of something like that is diminished, because you've gotta get them to the next lesson. The options for getting really engrossed weren't there. That's when I came to understand about a deficiency in the education system."

Joe then began to work with Creative Partnerships, a U.K. government program for developing creativity in schools that was one of the recommended outcomes of the *All Our Futures* report that I chaired. He started to realize that his primary role was to address the problem he'd identified while in that school in Manchester. "I was trying to provide space and time for the young people to find their own creative process. All of the projects I did were about trying to carve time out of the notoriously hectic school day."

While he was working with Creative Partnerships, he came upon Carl Honoré's book *In Praise of Slowness*,[14] a paean to the value of taking time to do things at the right speed. The book launched the Slow Movement around the world, and it seemed to speak directly to an obvious need Joe saw in the education system. When he researched the Slow Movement, Joe was surprised that there was no discussion of education, the field that mattered most to him. Spurred by this, he started Slow Education, launching a website for global conversation and offering his services on a local scale. He began working with schools on a new model. One of those schools was Holy Trinity Primary School in Darwen, Lancashire.

"Darwen is a deprived area. Lots of the children have behavioral or emotional difficulties and well above the national average are on free school meals. The results they were getting weren't great at all. The process they went through to deal with this is where we really start to see the idea of Slow Education coming into play. They spent a lot of time looking at the relationships and understanding the community and the children they were working with. Rather than banging their head against a brick wall trying to get grades up, they started breakfast clubs. They did projects that involved shifts. Lots of the town became involved. This engagement on a more personal level meant that the teaching and learning became much more grounded. At least once a term, teachers have one-to-one sessions with every child."

Joe saw at Holy Trinity what could be accomplished when the school and the community devoted time to learn who each individual student was and what they were about, and to create programs geared to specific interests, and capacities. They put less emphasis on grades and increased the emphasis on personal interaction between students, teachers, and the community. The result, unsurprisingly, was that the students gained a vastly improved appreciation of the education experience. Students started referring to Holy Trinity as a second home, and instances of problem behaviors declined. At the same time, grades did improve, and the Office for Standards in Education gave the school a higher rating.[15]

Joe is quick to point out that there is no one ideal model of Slow Education—and that is precisely the point. Slow Education is always about individualizing the process, about allowing learners the space and the time to discover their passions and their strengths. "Slow Education is about deep learning for meaningful results." Joe told me, "At the heart of it is the quality of the engagement between the teacher and the learner being more important that simply judging students by ability and tests."

ASSESSMENT THAT SUPPORTS PERSONAL PROGRESS
AND ACHIEVEMENT

We're going to be looking at the pressure created by high-stakes testing in chapter 7. The ubiquity and limitations of standardized testing call into question the entire approach to assessment in most education systems. For now, I'll just offer this message from Monty Neill, executive director of the National Center for Fair and Open Testing (FairTest). "Assessments should include multiple kinds of evidence, from multiple-choice questions to essays and projects, teacher observations and student self-evaluations," Monty wrote in an article for *Root and Branch* magazine. "Good teachers know how to use a broad range of assessments and that one can use many different tools to assess knowledge. Unfortunately, pressure to boost scores on standardized tests has reduced the range of assessments teachers use. For example, one teacher, in a FairTest report on NCLB, described how she had to reduce the number of book reports she assigned because of the time required for test prep. These kinds of stories have been told thousands of times across the nation."[16]

IT'S CHILD'S PLAY

The increasing standardization of education—and the sheer amount of education that's going on—also runs against the grain of the most natural way in which people of all ages learn, and especially young children: through play. Play in its many forms has fundamental roles in all phases of life and especially in the physical, social, emotional, and intellectual development of children. The importance of play has been recognized in all cultures; it has been widely studied and endorsed in the human sciences and demonstrated in practice in enlightened schools throughout the world. And yet the standards movement in many countries treats play as a trivial and expendable extra in schools—a distraction from the serious business of studying and passing tests. The exile of play is one of the great tragedies of standardized education.

Peter Gray is a research professor of psychology at Boston College. He has been studying play from a biological evolutionary perspective, and he notes that human young, when they are unencumbered by other responsibilities, play much more than other mammals, and that they benefit from this tremendously. A few years back, he embarked on a survey of anthropologists who had been studying hunter-gatherer cultures. All of the anthropologists surveyed pointed out that children in these cultures were allowed to play without adult guidance all day. The adults considered unsupervised play essential to learning skills that lead to becoming responsible grown-ups. "Some of these anthropologists told us that the children they observed in these cultures are among the brightest, happiest, most cooperative, most well-adjusted, most resilient children that they had ever observed anywhere," Dr. Gray said. "So from a biological evolutionary perspective, play is nature's means of insuring that young mammals, including young human beings, acquire the skills that they need to acquire to develop successfully into adulthood."[17]

Compare this with how most developed cultures organize their children's education. As Dr. Gray points out in his book *Free to Learn*, children start school at ever-younger ages. "We now have not only kindergarten, but prekindergarten in some districts. And preschools, which precede kindergarten or prekindergarten, are structured more and more like elementary schools—with adult-assigned tasks replacing play." The school day has grown longer, and now there are renewed calls to extend the school year. Along the way, opportunities for free play within the school day have largely been eliminated. "Not only has the school day grown longer and less playful, but school has intruded ever more into home and family life. Assigned homework has increased, eating into time that would otherwise be available for play."[18]

Peter Gray considers this a tragic loss for our children. He stands in a long tradition of psychologists, philosophers, anthropologists, and educators who argue that children "are designed, by nature, to play and explore on their own, independently of adults. They need freedom in order to develop; without it they suffer. The drive to play freely is a basic, biological drive."

Lack of free play may not kill the physical body, says Dr. Gray, as would lack of food, air, or water, but it kills the spirit and stunts mental growth. "Free play is the means by which children learn to make friends, overcome their fears, solve their own problems, and generally take control of their own lives. It is also the primary means by which children practice and acquire the physical and intellectual skills that are essential for success in the culture in which they are growing. Nothing that we do, no amount of toys we buy or 'quality time' or special training we give our children, can compensate for the freedom we take away. The things that children learn through their own initiatives, in free play, cannot be taught in other ways."

I couldn't agree with him more. Children have a powerful, innate ability to learn. Left to their own devices, they will explore options and make choices that we can't, and shouldn't, make for them. Play is absolutely fundamental to learning: it is the natural fruit of curiosity and imagination. And yet the standards movement is actively eliminating opportunities for play in schools.

When I was a child, we had regular breaks in the school day where we could play on our own and with each other, indulge our imaginations, and experiment with a range of practical skills and social roles. Now, perhaps a fifteen-minute recess is shoehorned into the elementary school schedule and is the first thing to go if the schedule is disrupted. Meanwhile, politicians lobby for longer school days and longer school years.

Many of the problems in raising achievement in schools are rooted in how school is done and the extent to which the conventions conflict with the rhythms of natural learning. If your shoes hurt, you don't polish them or blame your feet; you take the shoes off and wear different ones. If the system doesn't work, don't blame the people in it. Work with them to change it so that it does work. The people who are best placed to make the change are those who, in the right conditions, can have the most impact on the quality of learning: the teachers.

CHAPTER FIVE

The Art of Teaching

R AFE ESQUITH has taught for thirty years in the same class-room, Room 56 at Hobart Elementary School, in Korea-town, a Los Angeles neighborhood. Most students at Hobart are from immigrant Asian and Latino families, and many do not speak English when they start school. This is a low-income area where overall achievement and graduation rates are low. Most of Rafe's students qualify for free breakfast and lunch at the school. But most of the students who have passed through Rafe's class-room have gone on to graduate from high school, speaking perfect English. Many have gone on to Ivy League and other top-ranked universities and to successful professional careers. Some of his alumni have even come together to create a foundation to support his work with the generations of students that have followed them.

All of this would be impressive and surprising enough. But even more remarkably, Rafe does all of this by teaching his stu-dents Shakespeare. Every year, he takes one of Shakespeare's plays and he and the class study it from every perspective—its story, characters, language, history, and performance. Few if any of the "Hobart Shakespeareans" had even heard of Shakespeare before they entered Rafe's classroom, but they come to inhabit the Bard in ways that would be surprising for people three times their age.

I had the privilege of seeing a performance of *The Tempest*, huddled on the same crowded bleachers in Room 56 that have held enthralled audiences from around the world for the last thirty years. We watched an excited, accomplished group of thirty-five nine- and ten-year-olds give a virtuoso ensemble performance of what many critics consider one of Shakespeare's greatest works. The children not only spoke the text beautifully, they played live music on more than a dozen instruments, which they had also learned to play during the year, and sang three- and four-part harmonies. When she wasn't onstage, I noticed that the young Korean girl who was playing Ariel was mouthing the words of all the other characters. During intermission, I mentioned to Rafe that she seemed to know the whole play by heart. He smiled and said, "Of course. They all do." Before the second act started, he told the cast what I'd said and asked if they all knew the whole play. They smiled too and nodded. Rafe asked them collectively to speak Miranda's first speech. They did, perfectly.

This wasn't some uncomprehending trick of memory. They clearly understood, and loved, the play. One of the regular attendees at Hobart Shakespeareans' performances is Sir Ian McKellen, one of the world's most distinguished classical actors. He said of them, "They understand every single word. That couldn't be said of all actors who do Shakespeare."[1] But Shakespeare is only a small part of the curriculum in Room 56 at Hobart, and work on the play doesn't begin until after the regular school day ends. The rest of the time, they're doing things like reading way above grade level and contending with math topics more often suited to high school kids. The walls of Room 56 are adorned with pennants from universities like Yale, Stanford, and Notre Dame—schools that Rafe's former students have attended, often as the first people in their families to go to college.

Rafe has managed to engage his students' hunger for learning to such a degree that they arrive at school early, they come during vacations, and they agree to swear off television for the entire year they are with him. His class motto is "There Are No Shortcuts," and his kids work ridiculously hard. But he's right there with them. "If I want those children to work hard, then I better be the hardest worker they ever saw," he told the *CBS Evening News*.[2] He manifests this by working long hours, six days a week, returning to the school on Saturdays to offer SAT prep to former students.

In his book *Teach Like Your Hair's on Fire*, he tells about a transformative moment for him. It involved helping a girl who "was one of those kids who always seem to be the last one picked for the team, a quiet girl who appeared to have accepted the idea that she could never be special." The class was doing a chemistry lesson and working with alcohol lamps. As tended to happen with this student, her lamp wouldn't light, and this brought her to tears. Though she urged him to go on with the rest of the class, Rafe refused to leave her behind. He realized that the problem was with the lamp itself, and he set about to fix it:

> For some reason, the wick was not as long as it should have been—I could barely see it. I leaned as close as I could, and with a long kitchen match tried to reach it. I was so close to the match that I could feel the flame as I tried to ignite the lamp. I was determined to get the lamp working. And it started working! The wick caught fire, and I looked up triumphantly to see the smile I expected on the girl's face.
>
> Instead, she took one look at me and began screaming in fear. Other kids started yelling as well. I did not understand why they were all pointing at me, until I realized that while I was lighting the lamp, the flame had touched my hair; it was now smoldering and scaring the hell out of the children.[3]

Rafe got the fire out fairly easily—the kids helped by smacking him in the head repeatedly—and the experiment continued without further incident. But the experience resonated deep within him:

> For the first time in weeks, I felt great about being a teacher. I had been able to ignore the crap that all teachers on the front lines face. I had done everything I could to help someone. I didn't do it particularly well, but the effort was there. I thought to myself that if I could care so much about teaching that I didn't even realize my hair was burning, I was moving in the right direction. From that moment, I resolved to always teach like my hair was on fire.

Rafe Esquith knows that teaching is not just a job or a profession. Properly conceived, teaching is an art form. This point was underscored when Rafe became the first teacher to receive the National Medal of the Arts, and it is one that I see reinforced whenever I see great teachers at work.

What Are Teachers For?

Formal education has three main elements: curriculum, teaching, and assessment. Typically, the standards movement is focused on curriculum and assessment. Teaching is seen as a way of delivering the standards. These priorities are entirely back to front. It doesn't matter how detailed the curriculum is or how expensive the tests are; the real key to transforming education is the quality of teaching. More than class size, social class, the physical environment, and other factors, the heart of educational improvement is inspiring students to learn, which is what great teachers do.

John Hattie, professor of education at Auckland University in New Zealand, has compared studies from around the world of the factors that influence student achievement. He has a list of

140 of them.[4] At the top are students' expectations of themselves. One of the most important factors is teachers' expectations of them.[5]

The core role of a teacher is to facilitate learning. It may seem unnecessary to say that, but much of what teachers are expected to do is something other than teaching. A great deal of their time is taken up with administering tests, doing clerical tasks, attending meetings, writing reports, and taking disciplinary action. You may say that these are all part of the job, and they are, but the job they are meant to be part of is helping students to learn. When those other tasks distract from that job, the real character of the teaching profession is obscured.

Too often the standards movement casts teachers in the role of service workers, whose job is to "deliver" the standards, as if they were a branch of FedEx. I'm not sure when this concept first crept into education, but it demeans teachers and their profession. Tragically, not all education officials act as though teachers are real professionals who need to be supported. Some take a hard line on teachers, suggesting that their employment be tied directly to student performance—even though it's clear that many factors affect how well children do in school, including the very nature of the tests they take. Michael Gove, a former British secretary of state for education, described academics who run university departments of education and teacher training courses as "the New Enemies of Promise,"[6] suggesting that they are regularly turning out teachers who are indoctrinated in left-wing theories and not up to the job practically.[7]

Unsurprisingly, teachers in the U.K. did not take well to this. At its annual conference in 2013, the National Union of Teachers (NUT) passed a unanimous, unprecedented vote of no confidence in the secretary of state for education, followed by the chant "Gove must go."[8] Christine Blower, the general secretary of the NUT, said that Gove "should now recognize that morale in the teaching profession is at dangerously low levels." A month later, the National Association of Head Teachers delivered its own no-confidence vote, with the president of the union remarking that teachers and students had "never had it so bad."[9]

In contrast, the world's high-performing systems of education, by the PISA criteria at least, put huge value on the importance of well-trained, highly motivated, and well-compensated teachers. Singapore, South Korea, and Finland set a very high bar for their teachers. It's an extremely rigorous process to become a part of the profession, requiring extensive training not only in a teacher's particular discipline, but also in connecting with students, mentoring, managing a classroom, assessing aptitudes, and so on.[10]

But if children are natural learners, why do they need teachers at all?

The Power of Teaching

I've said that education is a living process that can best be compared to agriculture. Gardeners know that they don't make plants grow. They don't attach the roots, glue the leaves, and paint the petals. Plants grow themselves. The job of the gardener is to create the best conditions for that to happen. Good gardeners create those conditions, and poor ones don't. It's the same with teaching. Good teachers create the conditions for learning, and poor ones don't. Good teachers also know that they are not always in control of these conditions.

There is a continuing and often antagonistic debate in education between traditional and progressive methods of teaching and learning. In the usual caricatures, traditional teaching is focused on teaching facts and information through direct instruction to the whole class; progressive teaching is based on learning by discovery, self-expression, and small group activities. In my experience, the apparently sharp divide between progressive and traditional approaches is more theoretical than real in many schools. In practice, teachers in all disciplines usually do—and should—use a wide repertory of approaches, sometimes teaching facts and information through direct instruction, sometimes facilitating exploratory group activities and projects. Getting that balance right is what the art of teaching is all about.

Because of my advocacy of creativity in schools, it's been assumed by some critics that I am squarely in the progressive camp and oppose all forms of traditional teaching methods— that I am even against students learning facts at all. None of this is true. I'm always happy to defend what I do think, but naturally find it exasperating to be told I think something I do not and then be criticized for it. I have consistently argued throughout my professional life that creative work in any domain involves increasing control of the knowledge, concepts, and practices that have shaped that domain and a deepening understanding of the traditions and achievements in which it is based.

In 1977, for example, we published *Learning Through Drama*, one of the outcomes of the Drama 10-16 project for the Schools Council. We argued in detail there that children's own exploratory and improvised work in drama should be deepened by a growing understanding of the traditions, practices, and literature of world theater.

In the reports of the Arts in Schools project, we argued that there are two complementary ways of engaging students in the arts: "making"—the production of their own work; and "appraising"— understanding and appreciating the work of others. Both are vital to a dynamic and balanced education in the arts. Making involves the reciprocal development of the individual's *creative voice* and of the *technical skills* through which to express it. Appraising involves a deepening *contextual knowledge* of other people's work—of how, when, and why they were made—and growing powers of *critical judgment*—both artistic and aesthetic—in responding to them.

These four areas of creative, technical, contextual, and critical development apply equally well in all the other disciplines of the curriculum, including sciences, humanities, and physical education. This is exactly the argument that was made in 1999 in *All Our Futures: Creativity, Culture and Education*, where we looked at the balance and dynamics of the whole school curriculum. The abiding problem in conceiving of teaching in terms of either traditional or progressive approaches is that it misconceives the essential need for balance between all of these elements.

To achieve this balance, expert teachers fulfill four main roles: they *engage*, *enable*, *expect*, and *empower*.

ENGAGE

Great teachers understand that it's not enough to know their disciplines. Their job is not to teach subjects; it is to teach students. They need to engage, inspire, and enthuse students by creating conditions in which those students will want to learn. When they do that, their students will almost certainly exceed their own expectations and everyone else's too. Great teachers achieve results by bringing the best out in their students. They do this through a variety of methods. Maybe they do it by going the extra mile, as Rafe Esquith regularly does for the Hobart Shakespeareans. Or maybe they do it the way Thomas Friedman's journalism teacher did it.

Friedman grew up outside of Minneapolis and went to St. Louis Park High School. There, he enrolled in Hattie Steinberg's journalism class in Room 313. As he reports it, it was the only journalism class Friedman—the world-renowned columnist for

The New York Times and best-selling author—ever took or needed. In a piece for the *Times*, Friedman called Steinberg his favorite teacher, and explained that he benefited in innumerable ways from her cajoling, commitment to fundamentals, and tough love (he also referred to her as the toughest teacher he ever had). He describes the dramatic effect Steinberg had on him and his fellow reporters on the school's paper this way:

> Those of us on the paper, and the yearbook that she also supervised, lived in Hattie's classroom. We hung out there before and after school. . . . None of us could have articulated it then, but it was because we enjoyed being harangued by her, disciplined by her, and taught by her.[11]

"These fundamentals cannot be downloaded," Friedman added. "You can only upload them, the old-fashioned way, one by one." Would Thomas Friedman have become the standard-bearer he has become if he had never met Hattie Steinberg? Maybe. Clearly the man teems with talent, and there's the real chance that this talent would have emerged even without expert instruction. Maybe he would have underperformed, failed to make the most of his natural resources, covering the local city hall beat instead of writing articles and books we discuss a decade and more after they were published. We'll never find out, because Thomas Friedman had the good fortune to be inspired by an extraordinary teacher.

ENABLE

It's sometimes assumed that the main role of a teacher is direct instruction. There's an essential place for direct instruction in teaching. Sometimes it's with a whole class, sometimes with smaller groups, and sometimes one-on-one with individual students. But expert teachers have a repertory of skills and techniques. Direct instruction is only one of them, and knowing how and when to use the appropriate technique is what great teaching is all about. Like all genuine professions, it takes judgment and connoisseurship to know what works best here and now.

You expect your doctor to know a lot about medicine in general as well as having some specific area of expertise. But you also expect her to apply what she knows to you in particular and to treat you as an individual with specific needs. Teaching is the same. Expert teachers constantly adapt their strategies to the needs and opportunities of the moment. Effective teaching is a constant process of adjustment, judgment, and responding to the energy and engagement of the students.

In her book, *Artistry Unleashed*, Hilary Austen explores great performances in work and life. In one example, she looks at the work of Eric Thomas, a former philosophy student at Berkeley, who now teaches horsemanship. The essence for the rider, he says, is to become one with the horse, a living animal with its own energy and moods. Dr. Austen describes one class where things aren't going so well for the student, who reins the horse in while Eric offers some coaching.

He tells the student that she's putting a lot of effort into trying to get the horse to turn better, but that every third or fourth turn she drops the ball and doesn't do anything. What's that about? he asks. The student says, "I'm too early and then too late, and then he reacts and I can't tell what to do." Eric pauses and then says, "You're trying to do too much. Stop thinking, and pay attention to your horse. It's about trying to feel what is happening underneath you right now. *You can't ride yesterday's horse* [my italics]. You can't ride what might happen. Everybody who rides has the same problem: we're hoping what we learned yesterday will always apply. You often ride the problem you had a minute ago, all for the goal you want to achieve. But this is not a recipe. It changes every second, and you've got to change with it."[12]

Good teachers know that however much they have learned in the past, today is a different day and you cannot ride yesterday's horse. This sort of responsiveness can rarely be achieved by standing in the front of a room talking at a group of twenty-five or thirty kids for lesson after lesson. It's virtually impossible to sustain real engagement that way, especially with younger children. Such an approach to teaching by its very nature limits the possibility of connecting with each student individually. Rafe Esquith has no teacher's desk in his classroom. If the desk were there, he might sit behind it, and he thinks that his role is to be moving among his students all the time.

Children are naturally curious. Stimulating learning means keeping their curiosity alive. This is why practical, inquiry-based teaching can be so powerful. In place of offering answers to questions they haven't asked, expert teachers provoke questions in students so that they are inspired to explore them. Jeffrey Wright is a gifted science teacher from Louisville, Kentucky. He uses a wide variety of techniques, such as blowing up pumpkins, helping students build hovercraft, and shooting things out of long tubes to entertain his students and, more important, to cause them to want to learn more about science.

"You see a huge fireball burning in my hand and go up to the ceiling," he said, "and I'm not going to have any kids sleeping, and every one of those people are out there asking how—how, how, how. As soon as you get the kid asking how or why, I can rope them in and get that intrigue going."[13]

Wright understands that an essential part of the process of enabling his students and piquing their curiosity is understanding where they come from and what is going on in their lives during all of the hours when they aren't in school. "What I went home to when I was young is very different from what some of these kids go home to. Some of these kids—I hear them talk about it all the time—hear gunshots at night. I'd have a hard time sleeping or studying if I knew there were gunshots outside." Students tell him about pregnancies, abortions, abusive parents, and other things affecting their lives, which has led Wright to understand that "'One size fits all' doesn't work." If he's going to have an effect on their lives, he needs to do it at an individual level.

"Mr. Wright has the key to the city," said Denaz Taylor, one of his students. "He said, 'I couldn't care less about Newton's Third Law. I want to teach you something you can take outside of school.' It makes me feel like he really cares about me, and I know he does."[14]

It's pretty clear that Jeffrey Wright does care about Newton. His gift as a teacher is to find ways of helping his diverse group of students to understand and care about Newton too.

EXPECT

Teachers' expectations have radical implications for the achievements of their students. If teachers convey to students that they expect them to do well, it's much more likely that they will. If they expect them to do badly, that's more likely too.

Rita F. Pierson was a professional educator in America for more than forty years, starting in 1972. Her mother and grandmother were educators before her. Rita taught in elementary school, junior high, and special education classes. She was a counselor, a testing coordinator, and an assistant principal. She brought a special energy to each of these roles—a desire to get to know her students, show them how much they matter, and support them in their growth. In the last ten years of her career, she led professional development workshops for thousands of educators on themes that included "Helping Under-Resourced Learners," "Meeting the Educational Needs of African American Boys," and "Preventing Dropouts."

In 2013, I had the honor of sharing the platform with Dr. Pierson at the Brooklyn Academy of Music in New York City for a PBS special, *TED Talks Education*. In a captivating presentation, she said that she had spent her entire life "either at the schoolhouse, on the way to the schoolhouse, or talking about what happens in the schoolhouse."[15] In her time in education, she had seen a lot of reforms—some good, some not so good—to try to alleviate the dropout problem. But the fact is, she said, "We know why kids drop out. We know why kids don't learn. It's poverty, low attendance, negative peer influences. We know why. But one of the things that we rarely discuss is the value and importance of human connection, relationships."

The key to raising achievement is to recognize that teaching and learning is a relationship. Students need teachers who connect with them. And above all, they need teachers who believe in them. Rita talked about marking failing papers with the number of correct answers rather than the number of incorrect ones (plus-two with a smiley face instead of minus-eighteen, for instance). Her students still knew that they'd underachieved, but by focusing on the positive, Rita gave them something to build from and an incentive to keep trying. Most important, she made it clear that she was rooting for them.

EMPOWER

The best teachers are not only instructors. They are mentors and guides who can raise the confidence of their students, help them find a sense of direction, and empower them to believe in themselves. Sergio Juárez Correa understands this better than most.[16] He teaches fifth grade at José Urbina López Primary School in Matamoros, Mexico, a destitute town not far from the U.S. border that regularly serves as a backdrop for drug wars. Juárez Correa spent the first five years of his teaching career standing in front of the classroom trying to impart some information to his students so they might have a chance at better lives. This task felt futile, and the results were not encouraging. The students at José Urbina commonly failed on ENLACE, Mexico's national achievement examination.

Then in 2011, Juárez Correa decided that he was going to change things. He was convinced that teaching *at* his students would continue to accomplish little. He'd been reading about children's innate abilities to learn, and he'd studied the work of those who were setting out to prove it, including Sugata Mitra. Juárez Correa decided that the only way he could truly help his students to grow was to empower them to learn for themselves.

He started having students work in groups, and he encouraged them to believe in their extraordinary levels of potential. He guided them through a process of discovery, showing them, for example, how to make the concept of fractions real in their lives and to make geometry more practical and tangible. He built his lessons on open-ended questions, urging his students to learn by reasoning rather than by memorizing information and spitting it back out during tests. He encouraged conversation and collaboration, and he wasn't worried that his classroom seemed unruly. His students were feeling empowered, and this sense of empowerment gave them an unprecedented passion for learning.

One girl in this class, Paloma Noyola Bueno, turned out to be a math prodigy. She understood, at an instinctual level, mathematical concepts that postgraduate students have trouble reconciling. When Juárez Correa asked Paloma why she'd never expressed much interest in math before, she told him that no one had made it seem as interesting as he had made it. When it was time to take the ENLACE again, Paloma, a girl who lived beside a dump in a poverty-devastated town, delivered the highest math score of anyone in all of Mexico. She was celebrated on a national television show.

Paloma's test scores were extraordinary, but they were not completely unique. Ten kids from Juárez Correa's class scored in the 99th percentile in math on the test. Juárez Correa was conflicted over these accomplishments—after all, the kids had achieved success on a standardized test that assessed rote knowledge rather than the kind of collaborative, creative, discovery-based learning he promoted to generate this breakthrough. Still, it was inarguable that he'd shown in resounding fashion what kids can do when you empower them to learn.

It's exactly this understanding of the relationship of teaching and learning that underpins the concept of "Learning Power." One of the originators and key proponents of Learning Power is the British academic and author, Guy Claxton. He argues that Building Learning Power (BLP) is about "helping young people to become better learners, both in school and out. It is about creating a culture in classrooms—and in the school more widely—that systematically cultivates habits and attitudes that enable young people to face difficulty and uncertainty calmly, confidently and creatively." Students who are more confident of their own learning ability "learn faster and learn better. They concentrate more, think harder and find learning more enjoyable. They do better in their tests and external examinations. And they are easier and more satisfying to teach."[17]

Building Learning Power is based on three fundamental beliefs, which resonate exactly with what I'm arguing for throughout this book:

- The core purpose of education is to prepare young people for life after school; helping them to build up the mental, emotional, social, and strategic resources to enjoy challenge and cope well with uncertainty and complexity.
- This purpose for education is valuable for all young people and involves helping them to discover the things that they would really love to be great at, and strengthening their will and skill to pursue them.
- This confidence, capability, and passion can be developed since real-world intelligence is something that people can be helped to build up.

Claxton sees these three core beliefs as being "particularly relevant in societies that are full of change, complexity, risk, opportunity and individual opportunity for making your own way in life." Putting them into practice "involves a gradual, sometimes challenging but hugely worthwhile process of culture change by schools and habit change by teachers."

I mentioned that Rita Pierson's mother was also a teacher. For years, Rita watched her mother use her break times to meet with students. She would make home visits in the afternoon, "buy combs and brushes, and peanut butter and crackers to put in her desk drawer for kids that needed to eat, and a washcloth and some soap for the kids who didn't smell so good."

Years after her mother retired, Rita watched some of those kids come through and say to her, "You know, Ms. Walker, you made a difference in my life. You made it work for me. You made me feel like I was somebody, when I knew, at the bottom, I wasn't. And I want you to see what I've become."

How powerful would our world be, asks Dr. Pierson, "if we had kids who were not afraid to take risks, who were not afraid to think, and who had a champion? Every child deserves a champion, an adult who will never give up on them, who understands the power of connection, and insists that they become the best that they can possibly be."

The Flipped Classroom

One of the reasons I became so interested in drama teaching earlier in my career is that good drama teachers are experts in setting questions for students to explore and in facilitating the complex processes of collaborative inquiry and personal questioning upon which deep learning so often rests. Drama depends on group work and inquiry, often on the teacher standing to the side coaching and mentoring, guiding questions that the students explore as they learn from each other. In recent years, some of these techniques have become widely adopted in other disciplines in a movement that's known as the Flipped Classroom. One of the inspirations for this movement is Salman Khan, accidental founder of the Khan Academy.

Sal Khan didn't intend to revolutionize the curricula. He already had a very full life as an analyst at a hedge fund. At first, all he wanted to do was respond to the request of one of his younger cousins, who lived in another part of the country. She was having trouble with math, something that Sal was quite good at, and she asked for his help. He said he would tutor her when his workday was over. It turned out that the tutoring went very well, so well that other cousins asked him to do the same thing.

Soon Sal was running the "Khan Academy" for school-age relatives and others. "It was almost a joke at the time. In 2006, I found myself working with fifteen of my family, friends, and cousins every day after work. It was a friend who suggested that I make some videos to help me scale up a little bit. I gave it a shot, and I used YouTube as a hosting platform."

Once Sal started putting his instructional videos on YouTube, people he didn't know stumbled upon the videos and started using them to aid in their own learning. He began getting comments from viewers all over the world, telling him how his videos made a particular subject understandable and even entertaining for the first time. The more videos he made, the more followers he acquired, and something that had started as a purely personal thing began to take on dramatic new global dimensions. By 2009, more than sixty thousand people were using the Khan Academy every month.

By the end of that year, some major supporters, including Bill Gates and Google, had rallied behind Khan Academy. "They asked where I thought this could go, and I told them we could hire a team and we could build out the software platform that I had started building. I imagined a tool where everyone could learn at their own pace. It could be used by teachers for differentiated instruction. Then a lot of pieces started to fall into place."

What became clear to Sal, and to the more than seven million people who now visit Khan Academy regularly, is that the site could be used to take learning in surprising new directions. The videos and other instructional materials on the Khan Academy site allow learners to work at their own speed and to go as deep into a subject as their interest and their mastery allows. Sal notes that what he's encouraging is mastery, not a brushing acquaintance with a topic or skill. For instance, a young learner being introduced to fractions watches a couple of videos and then needs to answer five basic questions correctly before moving on to the next set of videos and another exercise. Eventually, the learner needs to answer a higher number of questions in a row before being able to move on. This encourages the learner to understand the topic properly and to have a genuine facility with it rather than simply studying to spit back answers during a test.

To Sal Khan, learning this way allows for the most effective use of both homework time and classroom time. "Classrooms shouldn't be built around passivity, and around listening to someone and taking notes. It should be around learning at your pace. Then, when you go into a room with human beings, you should interact with them. Khan Academy can guarantee that you have a good academic scaffold, but if you're still bumping into things, that's where a physical classroom is there for you to ask questions, or for you to answer other people's questions, or do more project-based things."

This is a form of pedagogy that began to gain followers when Eric Mazur, a Harvard physics professor, started using it instead of the traditional university lecture. What Mazur saw was that his students learned and understood how to apply what they were learning considerably more effectively when he served as the "guide on the side" as opposed to the "sage on the stage." He'll have his students read from a course book, watch one of his lectures online, or watch something else on the topic before coming into the class. When class starts, he offers a bit of introduction, lets students think about what he's just said, and then polls responses. Invariably, different students come to different conclusions, some of which are closer to the right answers than others. He then has the students with the right answers convince students near them with the wrong answers.

"Imagine you have two students sitting next to each other, Mary and John. Mary had the right answer because she understands it. Mary is more likely to convince John than Professor Mazur in the front of the class. Why? Because she has only recently learned it. She still knows what the difficulties are that John has. Whereas Professor Mazur learned it such a long time ago, and to him it is so clear that he no longer understands the difficulties that a beginning learner has."[18]

In the flipped classroom, rather than having a teacher stand in front of a group of students and lecture on a topic, the students get this form of instruction online at home. The class time is then used by the teacher for peer instruction (the method Mazur just described) to help students individually if they are having trouble, to engage students in conversation about the topic, and to challenge students who are already showing mastery. Essentially, the classwork becomes the homework, and the homework becomes the classwork, with the advantage that each allows the student to progress at a personalized pace.

There's strong evidence that flipped classrooms can be very effective. A study in the late nineties showed that students who were taught using peer instruction "exhibited learning gains almost two standard deviations higher than those observed in the traditional courses"[19] Other studies have shown similarly dramatic improvements.

In 2013, four dozen Idaho public schools began a pilot program to flip some of their classrooms using Khan Academy programs. One of the teachers involved in the program is Shelby Harris, a seventh-grade math teacher at Kuna Middle School who was featured in the Davis Guggenheim documentary, *Teach.* "I was so nervous it was going to be about pushing the teacher out of the way and bringing the computer in," she said. "I thought that it would distance me from the kids. It's been completely the opposite. I teach better now than I have in thirteen years. I get so much more personal time with the kids. I get to teach them what they need, when they need it."[20]

She considers the immediate feedback offered by Khan programs, together with having a teacher available to provide personalized aid where necessary, to be hugely beneficial. "They think they're doing it right, and they feel great about it," she said of the experience of traditional homework, "and then they come to correct it in class and it's all wrong—and they had no idea. On Khan, when they do one problem, they find out immediately if they got it right or got it wrong. If they got it wrong, they're able to click through the solution steps and find out exactly where their error was, so they know how to fix it better the next time. They're able to do powerful learning on their own. I'm there to support them when that doesn't work."

Sal Khan sees what Shelby Harris is talking about as reflective of his own experience with education. "When I was in school, I saw how little learning happens when people are passively sitting in a lecture. This is true whether you're in first grade or you're a graduate student. When I think about the experiences when I really got something out of it, it really was something like the math team where there were thirty kids all trying to mentor each other and learn from each other. The teacher was there to guide us but not to lecture at us. I learned a lot in journalism class, which was again a lot of students collaborating on something and having a shared goal. I was on the wrestling team in high school. We were pushed hard, but we wanted to do it because it was a collaborative environment where kids are helping each other and the coaches were there to mentor you.

"The classroom should not be about direct instruction. None of us liked it, and none of us felt particularly engaged. The teachers don't like it, either. They feel like they're just shooting information into a vacuum. Human beings should not be passive. When they get together, they should be interacting with each other. They should be solving problems, or they should be making things."

Creative Teaching

Let me say a few words about creativity. I've written a lot about this theme in other publications. Rather than test your patience here with repetition of those ideas, let me refer you to them if you have a special interest. In *Out of Our Minds: Learning to Be Creative*, I look in some detail at the nature of creativity and how it relates to the idea of intelligence in the arts, the sciences, and other areas of human achievement. In 1997, I was asked by the U.K. government to convene a national commission to advise on how creativity can be developed throughout the school system from ages five through eighteen. That group brought together scientists, artists, educators, and business leaders in a common mission to explain the nature and critical importance of creativity in education. Our report, *All Our Futures: Creativity, Culture and Education*, set our detailed proposals for how to make this happen in practice and was addressed to people working at all levels of education, from schools to government.

It's sometimes said that creativity cannot be defined. I think it can. Here's my definition, based on the work of the *All Our Futures* group: *Creativity is the process of having original ideas that have value.*

There are two other concepts to keep in mind: imagination and innovation. Imagination is the root of creativity. It is the ability to bring to mind things that aren't present to our senses. Creativity is putting your imagination to work. It is applied imagination. Innovation is putting new ideas into practice.

There are various myths about creativity. One is that only special people are creative, another is that creativity is only about the arts, a third is that creativity cannot be taught, and a fourth is that it's all to do with uninhibited "self-expression." None of these is true. Creativity draws from many powers that we all have by virtue of being human. Creativity is possible in all areas of human life, in science, the arts, mathematics, technology, cuisine, teaching, politics, business, you name it. And like many human capacities, our creative powers can be cultivated and refined. Doing that involves an increasing mastery of skills, knowledge, and ideas.

Creativity is about fresh thinking. It doesn't have to be new to the whole of humanity—though that's always a bonus—but certainly to the person whose work it is. Creativity also involves making critical judgments about whether what you're working on is any good, be it a theorem, a design, or a poem. Creative work often passes through typical phases. Sometimes what you end up with is not what you had in mind when you started. It's a dynamic process that often involves making new connections, crossing disciplines, and using metaphors and analogies.

Being creative is not just about having off-the-wall ideas and letting your imagination run free. It may involve all of that, but it also involves refining, testing, and focusing what you're doing. It's about original thinking on the part of the individual, and it's also about judging critically whether the work in process is taking the right shape and is worthwhile, at least for the person producing it.

Creativity is not the opposite of discipline and control. On the contrary, creativity in any field may involve deep factual knowledge and high levels of practical skill. Cultivating creativity is one of the most interesting challenges for any teacher. It involves understanding the real dynamics of creative work.[21]

Creativity is not a linear process, in which you have to learn all the necessary skills before you get started. It is true that creative work in any field involves a growing mastery of skills and concepts. It is not true that they have to be mastered before the creative work can begin. Focusing on skills in isolation can kill interest in any discipline. Many people have been put off by mathematics for life by endless rote tasks that did nothing to inspire them with the beauty of numbers. Many have spent years grudgingly practicing scales for music examinations only to abandon the instrument altogether once they've made the grade.

The real driver of creativity is an appetite for discovery and a passion for the work itself. When students are motivated to learn, they naturally acquire the skills they need to get the work done. Their mastery of them grows as their creative ambitions expand. You'll find evidence of this process in great teaching in every discipline from football to chemistry.[22]

Teaching in a Different Key

There are many people who work in other professions who can work alongside teachers and bring their energy, enthusiasm, and specific expertise to education, To do that, they don't have to be trained as teachers. They do need to have dual passions: a passion for a particular discipline and a passion for sharing their enthusiasm with children. Neil Johnston is one such person. While he was still in college, he started his company Store Van Music as a vehicle for his musical compositions and productions. To generate the extra income a start-up always needs, he began teaching music in a nearby school two days a week.

"The school was in quite a deprived area," he told me. "There were two kids out of a school of six hundred learning guitar. That was the only one-to-one music program the school had.

"I love the way digital changed the music industry," Neil said, "but the love and passion I had for the music industry wasn't reflected at all by what I saw in the classroom. The bit that really struck me was that the groups of learners we had the most difficulty with were the same groups of learners that would sit during break time and lunchtime with their phones out listening to music. They all loved music, but they hated music lessons."

With limited time and limited resources, Neil tried to bring a fresher and more relevant approach to music to his students. He was working on commercials and doing scores for video games, and would bring his work into the classroom to get his kids involved in the process. Those who could not see the point in learning about a centuries-old composition began to perk up at the idea of brainstorming for something that might show up on their PlayStation or Xbox.

At the same time, he started talking to the kids about music from their perspective, by using the songs they were listening to on their phones during breaks. "Everyone has an opinion about music, whether they love it or hate it. I'll play Britney Spears in a classroom and there might be thirty kids who adore it. And there will be however many that hate it—and they're prepared to voice their opinion about it. But it gets the conversation started. They're engaged. They're not desperate to go on their phone and look at Facebook while we're in class. They're not getting distracted."

Seeing the connection he was beginning to forge between the kids and music education, Neil started bringing bands into schools for one-day rock and pop workshops. Predictably (at least at this point), the workshops were hugely popular, and this drew the attention of a number of corporations fascinated with what he was doing. Apple contacted Store Van Music to begin a conversation about how they might be able to work together, but while there was mutual interest, there wasn't a clear opportunity.

Then Apple released the iPad and everything changed. "It really caught my eye when the iPad came out. I thought that this was brilliant and just what I needed to teach music—a touchable interface with some great apps so the kids don't need to know a musical instrument to take part. When the iPad 2 launched, they launched a GarageBand app, and I got straight on the phone to Apple and said, 'Can I borrow a ton of these? I want to try something.' "

Neil wanted to try a program designed around teaching students music from the inside of the experience by having them play songs rather than simply study songs. Prior to this, such a program would only have been available to students who had access to instruments and had the interest and discipline to learn the rudiments. With GarageBand on the iPad, this was no longer necessary. The tablet and the app turned students into guitarists, drummers, saxophonists, and more, with just a few clicks.

"The thing about using tablets is that there are no barriers to entry for kids. We can get a group of kids who don't play anything to exercise the listening skills that a band needs to succeed. They don't need to know a scale. We can set the scale on the iPad, and they only need to use the same skills a kid would use to tap on a triangle to keep in time. It doesn't exclude the kids that are doing great, either. You can give them a lot of challenging tasks as well."

The students responded to the program with great enthusiasm, much more than Neil had anticipated. Soon, Store Van was doing workshops with a large number of schools in the south of the U.K. "We made a video in June 2011 demonstrating the use of this as a teaching tool. Up until then, we had had a relationship with fifty to sixty schools in a focused area. When the video went up, we started getting invited all over the world. Education is 60 percent of our business now. We did a U.S. tour back in 2012."

While the success of the program might have been part of Store Van's expansion plan, there were some considerable surprises as well, maybe none more than seeing a song he recorded with the four hundred students at Gaywood Primary School hit

No. 1 on the iTunes charts. Meanwhile, a video of Neil creating the song "You Make Me So Electric" with a group of students has been viewed hundreds of thousands of times on YouTube.

Neil is quick to note that he has certain advantages with his one-day workshops over the teachers that work with students every single day. It's a bit like the divorced dad who sees his child once a week and showers the kid with treats. When Store Van Music is around, every day is a holiday.

"Because we don't come from a straight teaching background, we probably throw things at kids that others might not. We'll challenge them. We'll give them forty minutes to come up with a piece of music for a TV commercial." However, he notes that "We're also there for the teacher. What we've learned is that we're inspiring teachers as much as we're working with kids." By giving his workshops practical relevance—showing kids how to play a song, write a jingle, and release a tune into the world—Neil engages students, whether they are interested in music as a profession or not, at an entirely different level than if he were simply trying to get them to appreciate the great masters.

"Linking industry to education makes learning relevant. Things have moved on so much from the textbook. Information is just as relevant as it always was, but it needs to be put across in a more up-to-date way. If kids can see this in a real-life example, that's what makes a difference."

Teaching as Entertainment

Where Neil Johnston uses entertainment as a teaching tool, Mitch Moffit and Greg Brown use teaching as an entertainment tool. They've created a hugely popular YouTube video channel called AsapSCIENCE that turns teaching into performance art. Which came first, the chicken or the egg? What would happen to you if you stopped sleeping? What's going on in your brain when you fall in love? AsapSCIENCE uses a combination of real science and clever graphics to answer these and many other questions, leading tens of millions of people, largely students, to seek them out.

"Sometimes, coming from the education system, you don't always get the interesting tidbit first," Mitch said to me. "It's very information-based, and you have to learn the back end before you get the interesting stuff. This was a chance for us to flip it on its head and say, 'Here's the thing you already like, and now we'll talk about it while teaching you what's happening. Let's learn the science angle from the opposite way.'"

Greg is a trained teacher who found the traditional approach to teaching to be regularly frustrating for him. "The curriculum was so driven by standards and by a specific curriculum that we had to deliver in science," he told me. "For me, all I could see was that the education system was not effective for these kids at all. Trying to get them interested was the hardest part. It was just so interesting to be able to put on a YouTube video that I'd made and see their response. As soon as YouTube was put on the screen, they'd all pay attention, because it represented things they were doing in their free time. They were listening, they were attentive, they would ask questions. It would spark discussions that none of the lessons that I had to teach would do. It was interesting to use it as a little experiment and it was amazing to see that these kids were curious and they had questions about the world, but when you have to start by teaching them what an atom is, their eyes gloss over. They're not interested in that.

"The main issue I had when I was trying to teach was that all of the things I was trying to teach were not relating to the students. The students had no idea why they were learning it, what they were learning it for. One of the reasons our channel does so well is that we're answering questions that people of all ages and varieties and backgrounds want to know. They can relate to them."

AsapSCIENCE shows that teachers can be a "big draw" if they present the material in a way that excites learners. They've also shown that, much like home cooks who sneak vegetables into desserts, it's possible to get students to absorb more of what is good for them if you give them something sweet to go along with it. "Our videos aren't a substitute for a real teacher, but they are a catalyst," Greg said. " 'Hey, farts are funny; let's talk about farts. And then we're going to learn about gasses.' Our videos can work as a spark that interests someone in the topic."

Learning to Teach

So what kind of training does it take to be a truly great teacher? Does it require any training at all? As we've seen, Neil Johnston has done an excellent job of bringing the love of music to kids who had never picked up an instrument before, although he has no formal training as a teacher. We've included various other ex-amples of people without teaching qualifications who have en-gaged students at extraordinary levels. I would guess that every one of these people would acknowledge that they can do so be-cause of the narrow scope of what they're trying to accomplish. Michael Stevens excites huge numbers of kids to learn more about science on his excellent YouTube channel, Vsauce, but he readily admits, "Teaching is so different. I get to do an episode about whatever I want, however I want to do it, once a week, whereas a teacher has to come in every day and fulfill state requirements and be a disciplinarian and a friend and all this other stuff. What I do on Vsauce is an independent study."

There's a view among some politicians that if you have a good degree in a particular discipline, you can teach. Do you have a master's degree in molecular chemistry? Then of course you can be a science teacher. The notion is that, if you possess the expertise, you can effectively pass that expertise on to others. That's all you need to know. The rest of it is just mechanics. It's not. Certainly, knowing what you're teaching is usually important. I say *usually*, because it isn't always, as we'll see. In some domains, it's obviously essential. I can't speak Romanian, so there's not much hope of my teaching it well. There's no point saying, "Oh, go on. How hard can it be?" I can't do it. Subject expertise is often essential for great teaching, but it's never enough. The other half of great teaching is knowing how to inspire students with the material so that they actively want to, and do, learn it. This is precisely why all high-performing school systems invest so heavily in the selection and extensive training of teachers, and why in those systems teaching is a well-respected and well-rewarded profession.

One of the best accounts of the need for effective training and development is by Andy Hargreaves and Michael Fullan in their groundbreaking analysis, *Professional Capital: Transforming Teaching in Every School*. They argue conclusively that short-term, cost-cutting approaches to teacher recruitment and training inevitably result in a teaching force that is "inexperienced, inexpensive, and exhausted in short order." The price we pay is the impoverishment of learning and the degradation of our children's opportunities for success.

Initial training for teaching should involve extensive practice in schools, guided by expert practicing teachers. But it should also include the study of the practice and ideological history of education, and of the various movements and schools of thought that have driven it. Since the main business of teaching is to facilitate learning, it should include the serious study of theories of learning and research in psychology and, crucially now, in the cognitive sciences. And it should include some understanding of how education systems work in different countries and with what results and effects. Initial training is essential, but once in the profession, effective practitioners need continuing opportunities for professional development to refresh their own creative practices and to keep pace with related development policy practice and research more generally.

Great teachers are the heart of great schools. In their various roles, they can fulfill three essential purposes for students:

- **Inspiration:** They inspire their students with their own passion for their disciplines and to achieve at their highest levels within them.
- **Confidence:** They help their students to *acquire* the skills and knowledge they need to become confident, independent learners who can continue to develop their understanding and expertise.
- **Creativity:** They enable their students to experiment, *inquire*, ask questions, and develop the skills and disposition of original thinking.

These benefits should derive from all teaching, across the whole curriculum. So what should the curriculum include?

CHAPTER SIX

What's Worth Knowing?

HIGH TECH HIGH near San Diego, California, was founded in 2000 as a charter high school designed to integrate technical and academic education. It is now a collection of five high schools, four middle schools, and three elementary schools serving more than five thousand students a year.[1] A school day at High Tech High is very different from the day in most schools. High Tech High builds its curriculum around project-based learning. "Project-based learning goes something like this," says art teacher Jeff Robin. "You figure out what you want the students to learn—it could be the standards, or it could be your own creation—and you develop a project. You reverse-engineer the content into the project."[2]

Larry Rosenstock is the founding principal of High Tech High. He puts it this way: "You're taking the methodology of tech—which is group-performed, team-taught, experiential, applied, expeditionary—and the content of academics—literacy, numeracy, the humanities, all the things kids need to know—and you're trying to wed the pedagogy of tech with the content of academics."

The students cover the whole curriculum effectively because they integrate one discipline into another. Art and biology might be combined, for instance, or humanities and math. The students are publishing texts, making documentary films, and creating a wide variety of projects. They might learn about ecosystems—

along with photography and graphic design—by writing and producing a book about the ecology of San Diego Bay. In addition, they're taking their work out into the real world, creating projects that serve their local community and beyond. Recently, a section on DNA bar coding generated a tool used in African markets to discover whether meat was being sourced from poachers.

Unlike most schools, the students don't spill into the corridors every forty minutes to change classrooms to study separate subjects. High Tech High divides the day into fewer blocks of time. The aim is to allow for a more sustained and immersive experience in different sorts of projects. "There are no bells," Larry told me. "If you want to go to the bathroom, you go to the bathroom. There's no public address system. There's a lot of *doing* going on. It's like *uncovering* the subject rather than covering the subject. Doing fieldwork, not memorizing biology words. Our kids do internships in the public and private sectors. It's loose, but it's tight in a different type of way.

"Students work with teachers who are working in teams. You're not going from subject to subject that much. You're making and creating a lot of things. You're expected to have public exhibitions of your work on a fairly regular basis. You're standing up and presenting quite frequently. You have to have fun."

Organizing curriculum in such a dramatically different way from most high schools requires the buy-in of many groups, including parents, who didn't immediately align with the High Tech High method. "When High Tech High first opened, we had parents questioning our approach. But they would say that they couldn't take their kids out because they love coming too much. Then we started getting kids into great colleges."

Nearly all High Tech High students go to college, and 70 percent of them go to four-year colleges. "Our college completion numbers are extraordinarily good. I know there are people who say that everyone doesn't need to go to college. I get that. NBA players don't, and rock stars don't, and brilliant programmers don't. Our hypothesis is that even those kids who might not go to college are better served if they are not segregated from those kids who are in programs that will prepare them and expect that they will be."

More than half of these college attendees are the first generation in their family to get a postsecondary education. That's because High Tech High puts a premium on cutting across social strata. They choose their students through blind lottery, and they replenish their school population during transitional periods— elementary school to middle school, middle school to high school—by selecting from underrepresented zip codes.

"Although pedagogy is what we are all about," Larry said. "I think what beats it by a nose is social class integration. In terms of social capital, the country is failing. There's a systematic misprediction. We mispredict who can and who can't do what based on ethnicity, socioeconomic status, and gender. Now standardized testing has given us another methodology for mispredicting. What we're trying to do is not slip into the trap of the misprediction and getting launch velocity, as we like to call it, with kids you're not accustomed to achieving that with. . . . When you're working with these kids, you realize how bright they all are. You just have to reach all of them in different ways."

Reaching all students is exactly what is at stake in the transformation of education. As we've seen, that means focusing on the quality of learning and teaching. It also means having the sort of curriculum that makes it possible.

What Is the Curriculum For?

The curriculum is a framework for what students should know, understand, and be able to do. In most schools, some parts of the curriculum are compulsory, some are optional, and some are voluntary, like clubs and after-school programs. There's a difference between the *formal* curriculum and the *informal* curriculum. The formal curriculum is the compulsory part, which includes what is assessed and tested. The informal part is whatever is voluntary. The formal and informal parts together are the *whole* curriculum.

The obvious purpose is to provide a map of what students are meant to learn. But the curriculum has another purpose. Schools need a curriculum so they can work out how to use their resources and how to arrange everyone's use of time and space. Typically, schools divide the day into units of time and allocate them to each of the subjects. This may seem like common sense. The school day needs to be organized, after all, and students and teachers need to know what's happening when and where. In principle, the curriculum should shape the schedule. In practice, it often works the other way around.

When she was in the tenth grade, our daughter wanted to continue studying dance but could not, because of conflicts in the schedule. When I was fourteen I had to drop art because it clashed with German, which the school felt was more important for me to study. It wasn't, but there it is. Many high school students have had similar experiences. If the schedule is flexible and more personalized, it is more likely to facilitate the kind of dynamic curriculum that students now need.

A Constant Controversy

Some of the fiercest debates in education are about what should be taught and who should decide. It's not my intention here to go into the details of the content of the curriculum—the facts, ideas, skills, and other materials that should be covered in various disciplines. That's another book or library of its own, as E. D. Hirsch[3] and others, including governments of all sorts, have shown in their attempts to do just that. Every such attempt courts controversy. As I write, the most heated controversy in education in the United States concerns the introduction of the Common Core Standards, which set out basic curriculum content for literacy, math, and science. According to the architects of the standards, they are designed to define "the knowledge and skills students should gain throughout their K–12 education in order to graduate high school prepared to succeed in entry-level careers, introductory academic college courses, and workforce training programs" and are informed "by the highest, most effective standards from states across the United States and countries around the world."

Whatever their intrinsic merits may be, the Common Core Standards are dividing the nation as policymakers, teachers, parents, and whole communities in state after state rebel against them as being a bridge too far in the perceived federal takeover of education.

My aim here is more modest, but just as important, I believe. It is to look at what the curriculum as a whole is meant to achieve in relationship to the four purposes I set out earlier, and to ask what sort of curriculum that has to be. Even that is controversial enough. Debates about what subjects should be taught in schools have rumbled through education from its earliest days, and the curriculum has changed radically along the way.

In ancient Rome, education was based on the seven liberal arts or sciences: grammar, the formal structures of language; rhetoric, composition, and presentation of argument; dialectic, formal logic; arithmetic; geometry; music; and astronomy. This vision of the curriculum dominated education in Europe up to and throughout the Middle Ages.

During the Renaissance, in the fifteenth and sixteenth centuries, some schools brought in other subjects, including spelling and drama, and argued for more practical methods of teaching and learning. Some began to teach music and dancing, drawing, and sports, including wrestling, fencing, shooting, handball, and soccer. In the eighteenth century, some schools began to include history, geography, mathematics, and foreign languages in the curriculum. That met with strong resistance from traditionalists who believed that a classical education was all that counted. For the most part, the classical curriculum continued to dominate education in Europe until the mid-nineteenth century.[4]

Then, three seismic social changes reshaped the school curriculum. The growing impact of science and technology was changing the intellectual climate. The spread of industrialism was changing the economic landscape. And the new science of psychology was proposing new theories about intelligence and learning. Each of these developments radically challenged accepted ideas about benefits of a strictly classical education.[5]

As mass education expanded, a new type of curriculum began to take shape, which still dominates education now.[6] It's useful to think of the curriculum in terms of *structure, content, mode,* and *ethos.*

By *structure* I mean how the whole curriculum is conceived, as well as the relationships between the various elements. National curricula are usually organized around discrete subjects: math, science, history, and so on. There is usually a hierarchy to these subjects, especially in high schools, which you can identify by the amount of time and resources given to them, and by whether they are compulsory or optional, or formally assessed.

At the top are math, languages, and sciences. Next are the humanities—history, geography, and sometimes social studies and religion. At the bottom are the arts and physical education. "The arts" usually mean music and visual arts. Drama, when it is taught at all, is usually deemed the lowliest art, except for dance, which is a rarity in most systems.

By *content* I mean the material that has to be learned. Because of the preoccupation with academic learning, the emphasis is usually on theory and analysis rather than on practical or vocational skills.

By *mode* I mean how students engage with the curriculum: whether it is mainly desk based or project based, individual or collaborative. In most systems, the emphasis is on desk-based academic tasks and on individual rather than group activities.

By *ethos* I mean the general atmosphere and character of schooling: the silent messages about priorities and values that the curriculum conveys. These aspects of education are sometimes called the *hidden curriculum*. The dominant ethos of the standards movement is that school is a kind of steeplechase, the purpose of which is to clear the frequent obstacles of tests and assessments in which there are always winners and losers. As we've seen, many students think school is boring or distressing as a result, an experience to be endured rather than enjoyed. So what sort of curriculum should schools have? To answer that we need to keep in mind the four basic purposes of education, which I outlined in chapter 1: *economic, cultural, social,* and *personal.*

Where to Begin?

The conventional curriculum is based on a collection of separate subjects, which are thought to be self-evidently important. That's one of the problems. The proper starting point is to ask what students should know and be able to do as a result of their education. This question has led to various attempts to reframe the curriculum in terms of competencies. I think this is a good idea. As I see it, the four basic purposes suggest eight core competencies that schools should facilitate if they really are going to help students succeed in their lives. Each competency is relevant to all four purposes. You'll see that all eight competencies begin with the letter C, which has no intrinsic significance other than being a good way for me, and hopefully you, to remember them. They are:

CURIOSITY—THE ABILITY TO ASK QUESTIONS AND EXPLORE HOW THE WORLD WORKS

Human achievement in every field is driven by the desire to explore, to test and prod, to see what happens, to question how things work, and to wonder why and ask, what if?

Young children have a ready appetite to explore whatever draws their interest. When their curiosity is engaged, they will learn for themselves, from each other, and from any source they can lay their hands on. Knowing how to nurture and guide students' curiosity is the gift of all great teachers. They do that by encouraging students to investigate and inquire for themselves, by posing questions rather than only giving answers, and by challenging them to push their thinking deeper by looking further.

For some of us, curiosity about some things may be short-lived and quickly satisfied. For others, it may become a sustaining passion on which whole lives and careers are spent. In any case, a lifelong sense of curiosity is one of the greatest gifts that schools can give their students.

CREATIVITY—THE ABILITY TO GENERATE NEW IDEAS AND TO APPLY THEM IN PRACTICE

As individuals, we all create our own lives through the perspectives we develop, the choices we make, and the talents and passions we may discover and pursue. Developing young people's creative abilities is central to meeting all four purposes of education. Being creative is at the heart of being human and of all cultural progress. Ironically, our powers of creativity may also be our undoing. Many of the challenges we face as a species are the product of our creativity—in the conflicts between different cultures and our collective abuse of the natural environment. In that respect, it's not lemurs or dolphins, with their poor imaginations, who are putting the climate at risk by how they choose to live—it's us, with our much richer imaginations and powers of creativity.

The answer now is not to suppress our creativity but to cultivate it more seriously and with a greater sense of purpose. As the challenges that face students become more complex, it's essential that schools help them all to develop their unique capacities for creative thought and action.

CRITICISM—THE ABILITY TO ANALYZE INFORMATION AND IDEAS AND TO FORM REASONED ARGUMENTS AND JUDGMENTS

The ability to think clearly, to consider arguments logically, and to weigh evidence dispassionately is one of the hallmarks of human intelligence. Of all the lessons history has to teach us, this one is evidently one of the hardest to practice.

Critical thinking involves more than formal logic. It involves interpreting what's intended, understanding the context, fathoming hidden values and feelings, discerning motives, detecting bias, and presenting concise conclusions in the most appropriate forms. All of that takes practice and coaching.

Critical thinking always was important to human flourishing; it is becoming even more so. We are now bombarded from every direction with information, opinions, ideas, and pitches for our attention. The Internet alone is the most ubiquitous source of information that humanity has devised, and it is growing exponentially. So too are the risks of confusion and obfuscation.

There are immense benefits in the digital revolution for the education of all young people. At the same time, the need has never been greater for them to separate fact from opinion, sense from nonsense, and honesty from deception. Clear, critical thinking should be at the heart of every discipline in school and a cultivated habit outside it too.

COMMUNICATION—THE ABILITY TO EXPRESS THOUGHTS
AND FEELINGS CLEARLY AND CONFIDENTLY IN A RANGE
OF MEDIA AND FORMS

Fluency in reading, writing, and mathematics are accepted imperatives in education, and so they should be. It's just as important to promote clear and confident speech—what is sometimes called "oracy."[7] The development of skills in spoken language is now, sadly and wrongly, neglected in schools.

Verbal communication is not only about literal meanings; it's also about appreciating metaphor, analogy, allusion, and other poetic and literary forms of language. Communication is not only about words and numbers. Some thoughts can't be properly expressed in these ways at all. We also think in sounds and images, in movement and gesture, which gives rise to our capacities for music, visual arts, dance, and theater in all their variations. The ability to form and communicate our thoughts and feelings in all these ways is fundamental to personal well-being and to collective achievement.

COLLABORATION—THE ABILITY TO WORK
CONSTRUCTIVELY WITH OTHERS

We are social beings. We live and learn in the company of others. Outside schools, the ability to work with others is critical to the strength of communities and to meeting the challenges we collectively face. Yet, in many schools, young people largely work on their own; they learn *in* groups but not *as* groups.

Enabling young people to work together can enhance self-esteem, stimulate curiosity, heighten creativity, raise achievement, and foster positive social behavior.[8] Through group work, students can learn to cooperate with others in solving problems and meeting common goals, to draw on each other's strengths and mitigate weaknesses, and to share and develop ideas. They can learn to negotiate, to resolve conflicts, and to support agreed solutions.

Through working together in schools, young people can come to realize the fundamental truth of Helen Keller's maxim that "Alone we can do so little; together we can do so much."

COMPASSION—THE ABILITY TO EMPATHIZE WITH OTHERS AND TO ACT ACCORDINGLY

Compassion is identifying with the feelings of others and especially with their suffering. Compassion is rooted in empathy. It begins by recognizing in ourselves the emotions that others are feeling and how we would feel in the same circumstances. Compassion is more than empathy; it is the living expression of the Golden Rule, to treat others as you would have them treat you. Compassion is the practice of empathy.

Many of the problems that young people face are rooted in lack of compassion. Bullying, violence, emotional abuse, social exclusion, and prejudices based on ethnicity, culture, or sexuality are all fueled by failures of empathy. In the wider adult world, cultural conflicts and toxic social divisions are ignited and inflamed by these failures too.

As the world becomes more interdependent, cultivating compassion is a moral and a practical imperative. It is also a spiritual one. Practicing compassion is the truest expression of our common humanity and a deep source of happiness in ourselves and others. In schools, as elsewhere, compassion has to be practiced, not preached.

COMPOSURE—THE ABILITY TO CONNECT WITH THE INNER LIFE OF FEELING AND DEVELOP A SENSE OF PERSONAL HARMONY AND BALANCE

We live in two worlds: the world within us and the world around us. The standards-driven curriculum is full of the outer world. It does little to help young people fathom the world within them. Yet how we act in the world around us is deeply affected by how we see and feel about ourselves. As the writer Anaïs Nin once said, "I do not see the world as it is, I see it as I am."

Many young people now suffer from stress, anxiety, and depression in school. For some, these feelings are caused by school itself and, for some, by their lives outside. In all cases, these feelings can lead to boredom, disengagement, anger, and worse. Schools can mitigate the effects by changing their cultures in all the ways we have discussed. They can also give students the time and techniques to explore their inner worlds through the daily practice of meditation. A growing number of schools are doing this now, and both students and faculty are experiencing the personal and community benefits of the regular practice of cultivating mindfulness and composure.

CITIZENSHIP—THE ABILITY TO ENGAGE CONSTRUCTIVELY WITH SOCIETY AND TO PARTICIPATE IN THE PROCESSES THAT SUSTAIN IT

Democratic societies depend on informed citizens being actively involved in how they are run and led. For that to happen, it's essential that young people leave school knowing how society works and in particular how the legal, economic, and political systems operate and affect them.

Active citizens are people who are aware of their rights and responsibilities, informed about how social and political systems work, concerned about the welfare of others, articulate in their opinions and arguments, capable of having an influence on the world, active in their communities, and responsible for their own actions.[9]

Citizenship education is not about promoting conformity and the status quo. It is about championing the need for equal rights, the value of dissent, and the need to balance personal freedoms with the rights of others to live in peace.

The skills of citizenship need to be learned and practiced. They also need to be continually renewed. This may be what John Dewey had in mind when he said, "Democracy has to be born anew every generation, and education is its midwife." For that to happen, it's essential that schools do not just talk about citizenship. As with each of these competencies, schools need to exemplify it in how they actually work.

These competencies don't come online at distinct stages of students' time in school. They should evolve from the beginning of education and be practiced and refined throughout their lives with increasing confidence and sophistication. Students who leave school feeling confident in these eight areas will be well equipped to engage in the economic, cultural, social, and personal challenges that they will inevitably face in their lives. What sort of curriculum do schools need to promote these eight competencies?

Proposing a Structure

As I argued in chapter 4, human intelligence includes but takes in much more than academic ability. For all of the reasons I gave there, I find the conventional idea of academic subjects too limiting as a basis for planning the school curriculum. "Subjects" also suggests discrete areas of knowledge, edged by clear, permanent boundaries. In practice, knowledge in all its forms continues to evolve; outside schools, the boundaries between different subjects constantly overlap. There is another problem.

In a sense, there is really no such thing as an academic subject. There are only academic ways of looking at things. Academic work is a mode of analysis and it can be applied to anything: foreign languages or particle physics, poetry or geology. Schools have evolved to place great emphasis on this mode of study, but it is not the subjects as such that are inherently academic but how they are looked at.

In planning the school curriculum, I much prefer the idea of *disciplines*. A discipline is a mixture of theory and practice. Mathematics, for example, is a combination of methods and processes *and* of propositional knowledge. The student is not only learning about mathematics, but also how to do mathematics. The same is true of disciplines that involve physical skills and the control of materials and tools, including music, art, design, engineering, technology, theater, dance, and the rest.

Conceiving of the curriculum in terms of disciplines also opens up all the possibilities of interdisciplinary activities—as they are doing in High Tech High—in which issues and ideas can be explored collaboratively from different perspectives, drawing on concepts and skills from several disciplines. In the world outside schools, a great deal of what goes in is essentially interdisciplinary. So what disciplines should the curriculum include?

In my view, a balanced curriculum should give equal status and resources to the following: the arts, humanities, language arts, mathematics, physical education, and science. Each addresses major areas of intelligence, cultural knowledge, and personal development. As well as providing a framework for what all students should learn in common, the right balance of these disciplines allows schools to cater to the personal strengths and interests of students as individuals.

THE ARTS

The arts are about the qualities of human experiences. Through music, dance, visual arts, drama, and the rest, we give form to our feelings and thoughts about ourselves, and how we experience the world around us. Learning in and about the arts is essential to intellectual development. The arts illustrate the diversity of intelligence and provide practical ways of promoting it. The arts are among the most vivid expressions of human culture. To understand the experience of other cultures, we need to engage with their music, visual art, dance, and verbal and performing arts. Music and images, poems and plays are manifestations of some of our deepest talents and passions. Engaging with the arts of others is the most vibrant way of seeing and feeling the world as they do.

HUMANITIES

The humanities are concerned with the study of human culture. These include history, the study of languages, philosophy, religious education, and aspects of geography and social studies. Humanities education broadens and deepens students' understanding of the world around us—its diversity, complexity, and traditions. It aims to enlarge our knowledge of what we share with other human beings, including those removed in time and culture, and to develop a critical awareness of our own times and cultures.

LANGUAGE ARTS

Articulate language is one of the hallmarks of human intelligence. As children learn to speak, they learn how to think, reason, and communicate. They also learn the cultural values and ways of thinking that are embedded in their languages. Language learning in schools includes oracy, literacy, and literature. Oracy is the ability to speak clearly, fluently, and with confidence. Literacy is knowing the skills and conventions of reading and writing. Literature is among humanity's most important art forms. The study and practice of the literary arts gives students intimate access to the insights and sensibilities of other lives, times, and traditions.

MATHEMATICS

Mathematics is the abstract science of number, size, quantity, and space and the relationships between them. Systems of mathematics date back to the beginnings of human civilization and are among the greatest achievements of human culture. Numeracy is essential in itself. It is also the gateway to learning in many disciplines. Mathematics in its many forms has an essential place in the practice of all of the sciences, in technology, in the arts, and in many aspects of daily life.

PHYSICAL EDUCATION

We are not brains on legs. We are embodied beings, and our mental, emotional, and physical well-being are intimately connected. Physical education and sports are bound up in many different cultural traditions and practices and evoke powerful feelings and values, both in relation to the games themselves and through the sense of collective activity and belonging they can generate. They provide important opportunities to develop individual and team skills and to share success and failure in controlled environments. In these and other ways, physical education has essential and equal roles with other disciplines in a balanced approach to creative and cultural education.

SCIENCE

Science is the systematic search to understand the world around us. The natural sciences, including physics, chemistry, biology, earth sciences, and astronomy are focused on exploring and predicting phenomena of the natural world. The social sciences, including psychology, sociology, and economics, are focused on the behavior of individuals and societies. Science education has an essential role in the education of all students. Science education encourages an understanding of evidence and the skills of objective analysis, gives access to existing scientific understanding of the processes of the natural world and the laws that govern them, and provides opportunities for practical and theoretical inquiry, by which existing knowledge can be verified or challenged. Science education also promotes an appreciation of the scientific concepts and achievements that have shaped the modern world and of their significance and limitations.

The idea of *disciplines* opens up the dynamics of interdisciplinary work, which is the basis of the curriculum at High Tech High and other schools. It is because of these dynamics that disciplines keep shifting and evolving. Outside of schools, all of these disciplines are dynamic fields of inquiry. They should be in schools too. It's commonly assumed, for example, that the arts and the sciences are polar opposites in education. The sciences are thought to be about hard facts, truth, and objectivity; the arts are about feelings, creativity, and subjectivity. While there's some truth in both of these caricatures, they are still caricatures.

In practice, the arts and sciences overlap in all kinds of ways. Imagination and creativity, properly conceived, are as much a part of science as of the arts. Learning in science includes engaging with existing scientific knowledge, using the methods of scientific inquiry to investigate hypotheses, and exploring the interactions of science with other fields, including technology. The great discoveries and theories that have driven science forward depend on profound leaps of imagination and practical ingenuity in the design and interpretation of experiments.

The arts are also highly disciplined forms of practice that call on refined skills, critical judgment, and cultural sensibility. The humanities overlap in many ways with the sciences and the arts, sharing with the arts the primary concern for understanding the human dimension of experience and with the sciences a concern for theoretical analysis, evidence, and explanation.

Finding the Right Mode

Many students learn best when they are actively doing things and not only studying ideas in the abstract: when their curiosity is aroused, when they are asking questions, discovering new ideas, and feeling for themselves the excitement of these disciplines. The truth of this has been illustrated in all of the examples so far, at Grange, at North Star, and at High Tech High. Larry Rosenstock comments that "Elementary schools get it right in the first place—they're multidisciplinary and use fuzzy logic, and you're making and doing things. So are doctoral studies. You enter as a question mark and leave as a question mark."

Effective learning in any field is often a process of trial and error, of breakthroughs punctuated by failed attempts to find a solution. This dynamic is at the heart of the curriculum and a key to the success of High Tech High. "Failure is an important part of the process. We celebrate the failure: 'Great, now you know something that doesn't work. You can cross it off the list and go somewhere else.' This critical part of the learning experience the learning that comes from failure—is far too often pro-grammed out of the academic curriculum."

One of the most interesting recent innovations in teaching and learning is what has now become known as design thinking. This is an approach that is now used in many organizations and in a growing number of schools too. It draws on the creative and ana-lytic techniques of professional designers in identifying and solv-ing problems and in conceiving of new products and services. Design thinking is usually cross-disciplinary and highly collabo-rative. One of the best accounts of the principles and practices involved is Tim Brown's *Change by Design: How Design Thinking Transforms Organizations and Inspires Innovation.*

Design thinking and many of the other strategies for learning that we've looked at in this book show that the common divide in schools between academic and vocational programs is miscon-ceived and can be disastrous. It also marginalizes students whose real talents and enthusiasms are for the practical application of knowledge. Fostering that dynamic should be at the center, not at the edges, of the curriculum.

Alison Wolf is a professor of public sector management at King's College London and the author of *The Wolf Report*, a re-view of vocational education prepared for the British government. She sees enormous benefits in vocational education in preparing students to be successful, contributing adults, but believes that this kind of education can flourish only if it is treated with simi-lar but different rigor in school systems that academic programs receive.

"You just have to break the walls down," she told me. "The more you have other people going into schools who have not gone from going to school, going to college, and becoming a teacher—not just for a one-off assembly, but actually as part of the furniture—the more you build into the system some space for people to breathe. You need to make it an official part of your curriculum, part of the accountability people have to put a tick by, to get people out of the classroom and doing things that are intrinsically variable and therefore cannot have their own curriculum attached to them. I feel that you need to build the nonstandard bit into the traditional structure so that it becomes a box to tick in its own right and that you then need to make sure that the box itself cannot be standardized."

Big Picture Learning is a powerful example of how connecting schools with the world around them and integrating academic and vocational programs can lead to much higher levels of engagement and achievement. Big Picture Learning is a growing network of more than a hundred schools around the world that was founded in 1995 by Elliot Washor and Dennis Littky, two educators involved in all aspects of developing schools, programs, and policy. The core idea behind Big Picture schools is that education is the responsibility of everyone in the community. Big Picture schools foster the kind of learning that can happen only when education is allowed to extend beyond the walls of the school. Students spend considerable stretches of time working in the community under the guidance of volunteer mentors, learning in real-world situations.

"Communities must build their schools and neighborhoods together," Washor said, "bringing together all municipal departments to reform high schools and to build the structures for learning communities need. Only by establishing true community learning places can cities restore to high schools a sense of place and give students a sense that they have an important contribution to make in their communities."[10]

Washor and long-time colleague Charles Mojkowski talk about the value of this in their book *Leaving to Learn*:[11]

Traditional instructional processes and assessments cannot bring all students to competence, much less craftsmanship and mastery. To keep students in school and engaged as productive learners through to graduation, schools must provide many experiences in which all students do some of their learning outside school. All students need to leave school—frequently, regularly, and, of course, temporarily— to stay in school and persist in their learning. To accomplish this, schools must take down the walls that separate the learning that students do, and could do, in school from the learning they do, and could do, outside. The learning in both settings and contexts must be seamlessly integrated.[12]

A few pages later, the authors explain why they feel this approach is so important:

Most young people find school hard to use. Indeed, many young people find school a negative learning environment. Not only do schools fail to help students become competent in important life skills, they provide a warped image of learning as something that takes place only in schools, segregated from the real world, organized by disciplines and school bells, and assessed by multiple-choice, paper-and-pencil tests. Schools have scores of written and unwritten rules that stifle young people's innate drive for learning and restrict their choices about at what they want to excel, when to practice, from whom to learn, and how to learn. It is no wonder that so many creative and entrepreneurial youth disengage from productive learning. They recognize that staying in the schools we offer them constitutes dropping out from the real world.

Over the past two decades, Big Picture Learning has amassed a laudable record of success through their one-student-at-a-time,

personalized, community-driven approach. The first Big Picture
school was Metropolitan Regional Career and Technical Center in
Providence, Rhode Island. The initial freshman class was com-
prised mostly of African American and Latino kids who'd had
trouble fitting into traditional school environments. These kids
were at high risk of dropping out if they'd been kept in their regular schools, and most came from homes where education beyond
high school was little more than a dream. Four years later, this first
class had a 96 percent graduation rate, with 98 percent of graduates admitted to postsecondary schools. Overall, the U.S. Big Picture schools have a graduation rate of 92 percent, compared to the
national average of 66 percent.[13]

The basic premise of the book is that many reform policies are
tackling the problems of education from entirely the wrong perspective. Elliot Washor and Charles Mojkowski agree, and their
Big Picture schools demonstrate the principles and methods on
which the real solutions to those problems should be based.

A Different Ethos

In chapter 4, you read about what Joe Harrison was doing with
Slow Education. A flagship example for Slow Education is Matthew Moss High School in Rochdale, about thirty-five miles
northeast of Liverpool. The Matthew Moss website includes the
header "We Are Different," and clicking on it takes you to the
following statement:

> What makes Matthew Moss very different from other schools
> is its Learning Agenda. Strange as it may seem, most schools
> do not have this; they concentrate on teaching, assuming
> that learning will follow. It has been proven so often that
> this is not so. Anyone recalling their own school experiences

will know that the teacher taught them many things but they did not actually learn most of them.

At MMHS we wanted to put the learner at the center of what we do and so set about researching how to help them develop into effective learners. Effective learners will be happy and successful in life because they are self-dependent and can adapt to demanding situations—they will know what to do when they don't know what to do.[14]

At the center of the Matthew Moss learning agenda is a program called My World, which involves four double sessions a week. "It's very much project-based learning," Joe told me. "It focuses on processes, and teachers are there as facilitators and guides and coaches. They even actually stand at the front and teach sometimes. But more often the process is directed by the young people in the class. One project they ran there looked at family trees. Each person created their own family tree and they got genealogists in to support that process and to critique them about the family trees they were creating. Having done that, each of the people were able to take an aspect of their family tree that interested them and just go with it. One young person was really into football. The head teacher was having a learning conversation with this pupil and asked him, 'Well, really, what's the point of this? Sure, you like football, but what's the point of this?' The student stopped for a moment and he really thought about it and he said, 'When I'm playing football, I feel completely different.' At that point, the penny dropped for the head teacher. He ended up developing a project about sports psychology and going into real depth. The kind of depth that any standard curriculum could never provide because you're never going to be able to find that many people who are interested in it.

"They're always very keen to provide a deep sense of purpose with these projects. They'll bring in outside agencies to treat the work as real work. What they find is that sometimes a pupil will not really find their motivation for maybe a couple of years or so. But they've just gotta go with that and when they do, it's always going to be a more powerful educational experience of real value to that one person.

"All of these things just take time. What they're starting to see now is that the results are a by-product and not the focus of the entire education experience. But the results are getting better and exceeding the expectations. Colleges will take students with lower grades from Matthew Moss because they understand them to be better learners."

Living Democracy

Some schools are involving students at an even more essential level. In 1987, Yaacov Hecht started a school in Israel in which every decision related to curriculum came through a vote involving students, teachers, and parents. The Democratic School of Hadera was the first school in the world to call itself democratic.[15] Today, there are hundreds of democratic schools throughout the world, nearly a hundred of which are in the United States, including Brooklyn Free School in Brooklyn, New York, the Farm School in Summertown, Tennessee, and Youth Initiative High School in Viroqua, Wisconsin, just to name a few.

"What we're saying is that everyone can be excellent if we let them choose the areas in which to develop themselves," Yaacov said during a recent presentation. "We take the student in democratic education outside of the box and look for the area where they can be successful."[16]

In "Democratic Education," Yaacov lays out the primary components of a democratic school:

- A choice of areas of learning: the students choose what they want to learn and how
- Democratic self-management
- Evaluation focusing on the individual—without comparison with others and without tests and grades
- A school where children grow from age four to adulthood[17]

Yaacov went on to found the Institute for Democratic Education and the Institute for Democratic Education Conference (IDEC), which involves educators from all over the world.

Jerry Mintz is one of the leading voices in support of democratic process in schools. He founded the Alternative Education Resource Organization, was the first executive director of the National Coalition of Alternative Community Schools, and, with Yaacov, was a founding member of IDEC.[18] Most American democratic schools are private schools, though a few of them are charter schools within public school systems. However, Jerry thinks these schools can point out the direction toward change in all public schools.

"I think the best way to change the public school system is to create models outside of it," he told me. "If you take California, for example, there are so many homeschoolers that in self-defense every California school district has created programs for independent study—which is homeschooling. Every district has as part of their public education a homeschool program. That is the way that alternatives are affecting the system.

"There are two opposite paradigms involved with this that have to do with the way people look at learning. The one that we're involved with is that kids are natural learners. That's the paradigm we know is true, and modern brain research reinforces that at every step. But the one that schools operate under almost everywhere is that kids are naturally lazy and need to be forced to learn. What happens over the course of seven or eight years is that this becomes self-fulfilling. If you force kids to learn things they're not interested in for seven or eight years, after a while you tend to extinguish that natural ability to learn."

Jerry travels extensively to demonstrate the democratic education process. Even though he's been doing so for more than three decades, he still finds each experience energizing and inspiring. "I continue to be shocked at the power of it. For example, I went to an at-risk public school out on Long Island. This school started after the other schools ended, so the kids would come in at 3:30 and go until 7:30. The kids felt that they had been dumped into this thing. What happened when I started to demonstrate democratic process was very interesting. At first, I could see by the body language how skeptical the kids were. But by the time we were done, they were *so* engaged in it. One of the kids brought up that he thought he should be allowed to wear a hat in school. A teacher responded that this sounded reasonable, but it violated a district rule. The teacher said that if the kid wanted to, the teacher would go to the school board and try to get that rule changed for their group. You could feel the change that took place in the relationship between the teachers and the students just in that meeting because, all of a sudden, instead of being on the opposite side of the fence, they were on the same side. After I did that session, the school decided they were going to do meetings every week, so it became a democratic program.

"At the end of that year, the school district was doing its usual cost-cutting, and they were going to cut some things in the whole district. The only kids that went to protest the cuts were kids from that democratic program—because they had become empowered." Jerry believes that extraordinary learning can take place when students choose what they want to learn, and when the school environment is one of adventure and discovery rather than stricture. Jerry even titled one of his books, *No Homework and Recess All Day*.

"I ran a school for seventeen years that was based on pure democracy. It had noncompulsory class attendance. Most of the kids were low income. Only about a quarter of our income came from tuition; we did fundraising for the rest of it. In that school, the kids had a rule—and it was a serious one—that you couldn't stay after school unless you were good. Kids would fight for their right to stay after school. They would stay there for as long as there was a staff member willing to be there. They also passed a rule that under no circumstances should there ever be a snow day. They knew that I lived at the school, so if they could get there, there could be school. The kids successfully voted out some vacations. They tried to vote out summer vacation and they passed a thing where we would go at least once a week until the staff said they wouldn't do that anymore. That's how they felt about school. People have trouble understanding this because they have been indoctrinated to think that school is something that kids don't like."

Jerry is convinced that the democratic process can thrive in any school environment, regardless of the age of the students. This was recently reinforced for him when a school in New Jersey asked him to demonstrate the process with preschoolers.

"I'm thinking as I'm driving there, 'Wow, the oldest kid there is five. Is this going to work?' I was sure that I was going to have to give them the agenda or something like that. They all sat in a circle and I started to explain to them that there were two main things you bring up at a democratic meeting. One is something you think is a problem in the school, and the other is something you think is a good idea. I no sooner got the words out of my mouth than all of the students' hands went up. It was amazing. One little four-year-old girl said that she heard that there was something like caffeine in chocolate and that maybe people shouldn't be able to eat chocolate in the afternoon. That was voted on and passed. There was another kid who said that it probably wasn't a good idea for kids to go outside if they had a cold. They discussed that, and it was passed."

Obviously, the nature of the discussion—and the curriculum and policies put in place—varies dramatically by age. Jerry is firmly convinced, though, that democratic process has a role in every school at every level. "You can't change state laws, and you can't change federal laws, but it's all applicable to public schools. One of the biggest revolutions would be if individual teachers democratized their classrooms. The problem in most schools is that most people have no idea how to do something like this, because they didn't grow up like this and there's no training program for it. We have an online course for people who are starting new schools, and in some cases for people who want to change their existing schools."

For Jerry, there is only one true impediment to this sort of change. "If you don't trust kids to be natural learners, you're not going to get there."

The Principles of Curriculum

All of the disciplines I've touched on here have an equal place at all stages of education, from prekindergarten through to the end of high school and beyond. Of course, they should be provided for in ways that take account of children's ages and levels of development. In terms of personalization, it's also essential that as they grow, students should be able to focus more on some disciplines than others as their interests start to become more focused. That's what choice and diversity mean.[19]

If schools are to meet the four purposes we've outlined and various competencies they imply, it's important that the curriculum as a whole has these characteristics.

- **Diversity:** It should be broadly based to cover the sorts of understanding that we want for all students and to provide proper opportunities for them as individuals to discover their personal strengths and interests.
- **Depth:** It should provide appropriate choices so that as they develop, students can pursue their own interests in proper depth.
- **Dynamism:** The curriculum should be designed to allow for collaboration and interaction between students of different ages and teachers with different specialties. It should build bridges with the wider community, and it should evolve and develop in the process.

One of the forces that can stifle the diversity, depth, and dynamism of the curriculum is the wrong sort of assessment, and especially the demands of standardized testing. Let's turn now to that.

CHAPTER SEVEN

Testing, Testing

O F ALL THE TOPICS we're covering in this book, I don't think any generates such an emotional response as high-stakes, standardized testing. The Internet is filled with videos of teachers crying and parents steaming (and the other way around) when discussing the subject. Millions of words have traveled through the blogosphere detailing the stress, anxiety, frustration, and collateral damage inflicted by high-stakes tests. The uproar against the proliferation of standardized tests has never been louder—and yet they continue to dominate the education land-scape in America and all over the world. Take fifth-grade teacher, Rhonda Matthews.

"I'm going to tell you what testing looks like in fifth grade," she said.[1] "I would say we lose about a month of teaching to these tests. The tests are six days total, spanning over two weeks. And I feel it would be unfair to my students if I didn't spend some time giving them a chance on practice tests and trying to impart some testing strategy. So there goes another two weeks. This is about as pared-down as you can get in the testing world. I know that the amount of time lost in other schools is far greater than one month.

"State tests stop all the thinking, discussing, and community-building. Once we get into test prep, there's no real conversation. Because of time constraints during the testing, I tell my students, 'Please *don't* think too much about the text. Just focus on answering the questions. The test prep I intend to do this year will not be around content—I actually feel confident that my students can read and think. Test prep this year will be around speed and how to work effectively under pressure."

Before the George W. Bush administration introduced NCLB in 2001, the federal government required students to take six tests over the course of their K–12 careers: one each in reading and math in elementary school, middle school, and high school. Now, to qualify for federal funding, school systems must administer fourteen standardized tests in reading and math to public school students, and, as of 2014, all students are required to be performing at a level deemed proficient or higher. Some school districts somehow don't believe this is enough and require even more tests. Schools that fail to meet these standards are subject to widespread staff dismissal or even closure.

States were allowed to apply for waivers of the 2014 deadline, but one of the conditions was adoption of Common Core. In April 2014, Washington became the first state to lose its waiver, because it didn't require school districts to use statewide test scores in teacher evaluations. The loss of the waiver puts severe restrictions on how the state can use federal money, leading one school official to say, "I don't think there's any way that it's not going to hurt kids."[2]

So what are the real problems here, and what are the possible solutions?

Standards and Standardization

I'm not against all forms of standardization. In some areas, it has brought huge benefits. I spoke recently at the annual conference of the organization responsible for bar codes—yes, there is one. Bar codes are those small patterns of black lines and numbers that are now attached to every sort of product. The first bar code was invented in 1948 by Norman Joseph Woodland, an American graduate student in mechanical engineering. The idea was stimulated by a conversation he overheard between the dean of students and a supermarket executive who was looking for a better way to keep track of stock. One day, while Woodland was sitting on the beach musing on this problem, he marked out the dots and dashes of Morse code in the sand. He pulled his fingers toward him in the sand, scoring it with parallel lines, and the idea was born.

Bar codes are everywhere now, enabling organizations to track every individual item to which they are attached. They have revolutionized supply-chain management and facilitated international quality standards in food production, importing, manufacturing, medicine, and innumerable other fields. Bar codes have helped to ensure that, wherever they originate, products are held to common standards of quality. There is no doubt that our lives have been improved immeasurably, as it were, as a result.

In some areas, it's good to set standards, and that's true of education too. There are two problems, though. The first, as I keep saying, is that people don't come in standard versions. For personalized education to work, it has to be sensitive to all the differences we've discussed. That means that standards have to be applied with proper care. The second problem is that only some areas of education lend themselves to being standardized. Many of the most important developments that schools should be encouraging do not. Both of these problems have been dramatically illustrated in the way the standards movement has affected schools in practice. There have been two disastrous consequences.

Instead of being a means of educational improvement, standardized testing has become an obsession in itself. Even young children now spend much of their time at school sitting at their desks preparing for, taking, or debriefing from tests. "There's been an incredible proliferation of testing," Monty Neill, executive director of FairTest, told me. "Not so much by states, but mostly by districts. They buy cheap, badly made tests that are supposed to predict how well the kids are going to do on the big test at the end of the year, and the kids who aren't doing well on that get more test prep. In most big cities, you have at least three interim benchmark tests being used. In some cases, they will go to one a month and in some cases we've heard of more than that."

Because so much hangs on them, the pressure is everywhere to teach to the tests and give scant attention to what is not tested. Second, because they have to be administered on such a large scale, the tests focus on limited forms of response, often through multiple-choice formats that can be quickly processed with optical scanners. All sense of nuance and complexity is usually lost in the process. The tests take little or no account of contextual factors that can affect student performance.

"The tests don't measure very much of what's important, and they measure in a very narrow way," Monty said. "The testing requirements and the data derived from that is essentially colonizing the classroom and making it very hard for teachers to spend time on things that are important for students to know or be able to do, or to engage their interest and attention." When standardized tests are the primary factor in accountability, the temptation is to use the tests to define curriculum and focus instruction. "How the subject is tested becomes a model for how to teach the subject. At the extreme, school becomes a test-prep program."

Pressure to boost scores on standardized tests has reduced the range of assessments teachers use. For example, in a FairTest report on NCLB, one teacher described how she had to reduce the number of book reports she assigned because of the time required for test prep. These kinds of stories have been told thousands of times across the nation. One of the most eloquent and well-informed critics of standards and standardization in its various forms is Alfie Kohn. A former classroom teacher and now an author, trainer, and adviser, he too shows in a series of books and case studies how this approach to assessment has had many negative effects on the quality of teaching and learning.[3]

The University of Oregon's Yong Zhao observes that, in developed countries, attempts to standardize curriculum and teaching methods fail students there on two fronts. The first is in emphasizing skills that students from less developed areas can sell for far less. "If all children are asked to master the same knowledge and skills" he said, "those whose time costs less will be much more competitive than those with higher costs. There are many poor and hungry people in the developing world willing to work for a fraction of what workers in developed countries need. To be globally competitive, developed countries must offer something qualitatively different, that is, something that cannot be obtained at a lower cost in developing countries. And that something is certainly not great test scores in a few subjects or the so-called basic skills."[4]

Second, the emphasis on testing comes at the expense of teaching children how to employ their natural creativity and entrepreneurial talents—the precise talents that might insulate them against the unpredictability of the future in all parts of the world. FairTest makes the same point in its "National Resolution on High-Stakes Testing": "The over-reliance on high-stakes standardized testing in state and federal accountability systems is undermining educational quality and equity in U.S. public schools by hampering educators' efforts to focus on the broad range of learning experiences that promote the innovation, creativity, problem solving, collaboration, communication, critical thinking, and deep subject-matter knowledge that will allow students to thrive in a democracy and an increasingly global society and economy," the organization states.[5]

There is another problem here. Because test results weigh so heavily in school funding and teacher evaluations, some schools, districts, and states are led into massaging the figures in various ways. Often schools pay attention "only to those students near the cutoff point in the hope of nudging them into the passing column, and that, in turn, often means neglecting both the low achievers and the high achievers," observes FairTest. Students who might not do well in the test may be dropped from the program so as not to depress the overall results. I've often been told that some parents ask for their children to be diagnosed with attention problems and to be medicated, because the diagnosis allows the children to be given more time to complete the tests. For some people at least, ADHD has become a strategic condition.

Raising the Stakes Even Higher

State-administered K–12 tests are not the only stress point for students and parents. Perhaps the most worried-over standardized test of all is the SAT. For most of the past nine decades, the SAT has been the primary hurdle students must clear on their way to college. The SAT has caused such anxiety in the lives of American high schoolers that it has spawned a test-prep industry that generates nearly a billion dollars in yearly revenue.[6]

Still in his teens, Nikhil Goyal has established himself as a strong voice for education reform through public speaking, advocacy, and his books. When in high school, Nikhil moved with his family from a middle-class neighborhood to an upper-middle-class one, and the stress caused by the SAT came into focus for him. "In my new school, there was a big competition for college admissions," he told me. "I just noticed that kids were stressed out; they were very unhealthy. They were basically robots, in my opinion. They were very compliant, could easily follow direction, and their creativity and curiosity were just about drained by that point. A lot of kids are suffering from Stockholm Syndrome. These are some of the most privileged kids in America, and they're actually the strongest defenders of this system the way it is, because they're succeeding. They're getting high grades, they're going to Harvard and Yale and Princeton."

Interestingly, one of the major players in the test-prep industry now has a huge contempt for the tests. "These tests measure nothing of value," said John Katzman, co-founder of Princeton Review. "It's just an utter disrespect for educators and kids married to an utter incompetence."[7] Studies support Katzman's point of view, including multiple reports that show that high school GPA is a far stronger predictor of college success than SAT scores are.

Since 1985, FairTest has been advocating for assessment that is neutral on the basis of race, gender, class, and culture and has been pushing hard to minimize the use of standardized tests and the influence they have on students and school systems. "Our ideal outcome," Monty said to me, "is that no standardized test is used in a high-stakes manner for college admissions or university admission, including graduate school. Passing a standardized test should never be a sole hurdle for graduation, grade promotion, tracking decisions, and so on."

The American Federation of Teachers agrees. "It's time to restore balance in our schools so that teaching and learning, not testing, are at the center of education," said AFT President Randi Weingarten in 2012.[8] "Test-driven education policies continue to force educators to sacrifice time needed to help students learn to critically analyze content and, instead, focus on teaching to the test." During the AFT national convention that year, the organization issued a resolution that said, in part, "We believe in assessments that support teaching and learning, and align with the curriculum rather than narrow it; that are developed through collaborative efforts, not picked off a shelf."

American universities are beginning to catch on, as more than 150 schools ranked in the top tiers of their respective categories have reduced the importance given to the information gleaned from the SAT and similar tests, such as the ACT.[9] Meanwhile, even the College Board (creators of the SAT) understands the need to change and have announced a comprehensive revision of the test to be released in 2016.

If there is such strong opposition to standardized tests, why are students still taking so many of them? To understand that, we need to look at the testing industry.

High Stakes and a High Bottom Line

The testing and educational support industry is booming. In 2013 it had combined revenues in the United States alone of $16.5 billion.[10] To put that in context, the entire U.S. domestic cinema box office gross in 2013 was a little less than $11 billion[11] and the National Football League is currently a $9 billion business.[12]

The testing industry is dominated by four major players: Pearson, CTB McGraw-Hill, Riverside Publishing, and Education Testing Services. As I write this, Pearson has deals to produce testing materials in eighteen U.S. states and is the leading scorer of standardized tests in the country. CTB McGraw-Hill holds several state contracts for its TerraNova and California Achievement Test. Riverside creates the Iowa Tests of Basic Skills, among others, while the GRE is one of the offerings of Education Testing Services.[13]

Each of these companies has had their share of hiccups over the years. In 2013, McGraw-Hill encountered a significant problem scoring their Regents exams for a group of New York City high school seniors, resulting in a delay in these students receiving their diplomas.[14] ETS had their immigration language tests suspended in the U.K. because of what was deemed "systemic fraud."[15]

And then there's "Pineapplegate." For several years, Pearson included in some of their state tests a reading passage entitled "The Pineapple and the Hare" that involved a magical hare and a talking pineapple in a race that ends tragically for the pineapple. Students were then asked multiple-choice questions about this nonsense story, where the choices were nearly as confusing as the passage itself. Parents who heard about the passage became so dismayed about it that a few even created a Facebook page called "The moral of the story is, pineapples don't have sleeves," referring to a detail in the story about what the pineapple was wearing.

"Why put a reading passage with questions so nonsensical on a state standardized exam, either as a 'field test' question or for any other purpose?" asked Leonie Haimson, a New York City–based parent and writer. "Especially given the high-stakes nature of these exams, which will be used in New York City to decide which students to hold back, the school's grade on the progress reports, and in the near future, as an integral part of the new statewide teacher evaluation system. A story that makes no sense and with questions that apparently have no right answer could wreck the confidence of any student on the first day of a strenuous, three-day ELA [English Language Arts] exam—was this what it was designed to do?"[16]

Whatever it and the many other tests are apparently designed to do, there is no doubt that one of their functions, from the perspective of the industry, is profit—and a lot of it. Testing on the scale that we see it now is one more example of the increasing commercialization of education.

The Mother of All Tests

The drive to standardize assessment is strongly influenced by international competition, which is now driven by the PISA league tables of the OECD. In 2012, Shanghai scored at the top in reading, math, and science. All of the top five scorers in reading and math were Asian countries/economies, while the top four in science were Asian, with Finland at number five. Countries such as the United States, the U.K., and France found themselves in the middle of the pack.[17] U.S. performance on recent league tables has contributed directly to the federal government's push for Common Core.

The intentions of the OECD are honorable enough. The aim is to offer a regular, objective guide to international standards in education. No one could object to that. The problem is not in the intention but in the effects. We regularly hear politicians—especially in the West—declaiming their country's world rankings in reading, math, and science and using these rankings to support the need for tougher standards in schools and to dictate to school systems exactly what should be emphasized and how. Yet some of the school systems that rank highest on the PISA league tables do less standardized testing than the United States does. At age twelve, students in Singapore take the Primary School Leaving Examination, which has admittedly high stakes, as it determines which lower secondary schools those students will go to. Admission into post-secondary schools is based on their performance on the Cambridge General Certificate of Education O Level or N Level exam.[18] Meanwhile, Finland has only one standardized test, the national Matriculation Exam, which comes at the end of upper secondary school (essentially equivalent to high school in the United States).[19]

Among the top PISA systems, the one significant exception to this pattern is Shanghai, as Shanghai students receive a steady diet of standardized tests. As we saw earlier, though, Shanghai is thinking of stepping away from the PISA tests. Vietnam is also experimenting with forms of assessment and accountability that move away from the narrow strictures of standardized tests in elementary schools to making greater use of teacher judgment.[20]

PISA itself understands that the testing conversation needs to be more nuanced, especially if education as a whole is to become more relevant to the lives that students will ultimately lead.

Andreas Schleicher is director for education and skills and special adviser on education policy to the secretary-general at the OECD. "The world economy no longer pays you for what you know; Google knows everything," he told me. "The world economy pays you for what you can do with what you know. If you want to learn if someone can think scientifically or translate a real-world problem into a mathematical context, those things are harder to assess, but they're also more important in today's world. We see a rapid decline in the demand for routine cognitive skills in our world and the kinds of things that are easy to test and easy to teach are also the kinds of things that are easy to digitize, automate, and outsource."

He acknowledges that there are inherent limits to what can be assessed through multiple-choice tests and that one of the challenges for the United States in getting assessment right is scale. "We try to test fewer people fewer times, and therefore invest in the quality of the assessment. The number of students involved is reasonable, so we can afford to include, for example, open-ended tasks and computer-designed and computer-delivered instruments.

"We always have to balance what is important to assess and

what is feasible to assess. In 2000, we started with reading, math, and science. In 2003, we started to add social and emotional sorts of components. In 2012, we have a very interesting assessment of creative problem-solving skills. People ask us why we didn't do that from the start, but at that time, we didn't have the kind of computer-delivered assessment systems that we now have.

"It's very hard to assess creative skills if you give a student a problem that is already written out on paper and you ask them to write their responses on the paper. Creative problem-solving skills really have to do with you interacting with the problem and the nature of the problem changing as you interact with it. That is only possible in a computer-simulated environment."

While firmly committed to expanding PISA's efforts in this kind of testing, Andreas noted that more gray areas emerge when doing so. "Open-ended tasks are less reliable. You need more of them, you need human raters, you need multiple raters. You have the issue of inter-rater reliability. People don't like it, because it's more expensive and it's a bit more contestable, but on balance you get a lot more relevant information. People make very different statements on an extended open-ended task than they do on a multiple-choice one."

As is so often the case, the complications come not from the collection of the data, but with what is done with it. In May 2014, a large collection of academics from around the world published an open letter to Andreas Schleicher asking, among other things, that PISA consider offering an alternative to the league tables and skipping a testing cycle to allow school systems time to absorb what they've already learned.

"PISA results are anxiously awaited by governments, education ministers, and the editorial boards of newspapers, and are cited authoritatively in countless policy reports," the letter states. "They have begun to deeply influence educational practices in many countries. As a result of PISA, countries are overhauling their education systems in the hopes of improving their rankings. Lack of progress on PISA has led to declarations of crisis and 'PISA shock' in many countries, followed by calls for resignations, and far-reaching reforms according to PISA precepts."[21]

Among the greatest concerns the authors of the letter express is that PISA results tend to lead to increased standardized testing within countries and efforts to make short-term fixes designed to move a country up in the rankings rather than actually improve conditions for students.

Neither I nor many other critics of high-stakes testing are questioning the need for assessment, which is a vital part of education, but the form it now takes and the harm it is causing. So what is assessment, and what is it for?

The Need for Assessment (and Testing)

Assessment is the process of making judgments about students' progress and attainment. As I argue in *Out of Our Minds*, an assessment has two components: a description and an assessment. If you say that someone can run a mile in four minutes or can speak French, these are neutral descriptions of what someone can do. If you say that she is the best athlete in the district or speaks French like a native, these are assessments. The difference is that assessments compare individual performances with others and rate them against particular criteria.

Assessment has several roles. The first is *diagnostic*, to help teachers understand students' aptitude and levels of development. The second is *formative*, to gather information on students' work and activities and to support their progress. The third is *summative*, which is about making judgments on overall performance at the end of a program of work.

One problem with the systems of assessment that use letters and grades is that they are usually light on description and heavy on comparison. Students are sometimes given grades without really knowing what they mean, and teachers sometimes give grades without being completely sure why. A second problem is that a single letter or number cannot convey the complexities of the process that it is meant to summarize. And some outcomes cannot be adequately expressed in this way at all. As the noted educator Elliot Eisner once put it, "Not everything important is measurable and not everything measurable is important."

One way to enhance the value of assessment is to separate these elements of description and comparison. Student assessments can draw on many forms of evidence, including class participation, portfolios of work, written essays, and assignments in other media. Portfolios allow for detailed descriptions of the work that students have done, with examples and reflective comments from themselves and others.

In peer group assessment, students contribute to the judgments of each other's work and to the criteria by which it is assessed. These approaches can be especially valuable in assessing creative work.

Some teachers have always used a range of assessment methods in class. The rise of testing has made that more difficult, but some teachers are pushing back in their own classrooms. There are challenges, but there can be enormous benefits too. For example, Joe Bower is a science and language arts teacher in Alberta, Canada, who, six years into his teaching career, decided that he could no longer abide by using grades as his primary form of assessment.

"I have come to see grades as schools' drug of choice, and we are all addicted. . . . Grades were originally tools used by teachers, but today teachers are tools used by grades."[22]

What Bower discovered was that the reliance on grading made him less effective as a teacher and had a negative effect on students. He points out that when many students are asked what they got out of a class, they'll respond with something like, "I got an A." While his school insisted that he give grades on report cards, he abolished all other grades in his classroom and delivered the report card grade only after asking his students to assess their own work and recommend the grade they should receive. The students' suggestions usually aligned with his, and there were far more cases where students would have recommended a lower grade than a higher one. The result of doing away with grading was that he eased the pressure on his students and allowed them to focus on the content of their assignments and their classwork rather than on the rubric to score them.

"When we try to reduce something that is as magnificently messy as real learning, we always conceal far more than we ever reveal. Ultimately, grading gets assessment wrong because assessment is not a spreadsheet—it is a conversation. I am a very active teacher who assesses students every day, but I threw out my grade book years ago. If we are to find our way and make learning, not grading, the primary focus of school, then we need to abandon our mania for reducing learning and people to numbers."

Real Instead of Symbolic—At Least for a Moment

Given the uproar against and problems with standardized tests, are there any other models for large-scale assessment that work better? Sometimes the best way to look forward is to look back for inspiration.

"A lot of people don't know that we have a large-scale assessment model, which was successful in California and other places, that provides the kinds of data that people need to make decisions but is not divorced from the rich context of students' actual work," Peg Syverson of the Learning Record told me. "One of my biggest heartbreaks out of the No Child Left Behind Act is that it pretty much demolished the very successful implementation of the Learning Record."

The Learning Record was originally developed in London and grew out of the need to identify the progress of students for whom standard assessments weren't working.

In London inner-city schools, where there was an influx of children from all over the world, the teachers had few resources. These were teachers who recognized that students were learning, but that this wasn't being captured by the standardized tests because the students were still learning English. So the teachers became determined to find a way to capture and document the learning they were actually witnessing. They worked together with Myra Barrs and Hillary Hester, and a couple of other people who were university education researchers, and they were also very interested in Lev Vygotsky, who was the person who provided the framework for the dimensions of learning that are used in the Learning Record. They were mostly concerned with reading and writing, and with the teachers they began to put together what you would need to know to understand how kids were taking on their literacy learning. They developed this robust system called the Primary Language Record. It was eight pages long, and they could document teachers' observations. They did an interview with the parents that had to be done in the parents' home language, asking the parent, "What does your child like to do?" Then they would do an interview with the student, so you'd get a little sense at the very beginning of what they're coming out of. The teachers became enchanted. The parents became enchanted because the teachers were trying find out what the kids enjoyed doing. They would find out that this was a kid that loved science but doesn't like reading. Then the teacher would start thinking of creative solutions, like, "How about science fiction?" They began looking for ways to honor the students' literacy development in their home languages.

They became convinced that they could use what is really an empirical model—what you would use if you wanted to study change in any adaptive system. First, you take a snapshot of the system at the beginning, and then you observe over time and you gather samples of work, and then you do an analysis. "This is where most of the portfolio systems fall apart—there's no analysis. An analysis has to be principled. It has to be built on some theoretical framework. You want to know if water is drinkable? Is it supporting frog life, or whatever? Vygotsky gave us a framework that allows us to talk about students' learning in a sort of multivalent way. They were able to talk to parents about what the students were learning. "He's getting more confident in reading books that are unfamiliar to him." "He's gaining skills in decoding words he hasn't seen before." The parents began to develop immense respect for the expertise of teachers.

"This became a really robust model in the U.K. Teachers got so excited because it's asking them to think creatively about their work and to think differently about the kids that they used to think were problems. They started to get curious about those kids. What would help them learn? What are they showing me?"

At this time, Myra Barrs was the head of the California Literacy Project, and she invited the Primary Language Record team to California. Together, they began working on a design for K–12 and began using it in pilot projects in schools. At this point, Peg came on board as a research associate to help refine the assessment tools.

"We were not using rubrics; we were using developmental scales that contained descriptors of what you would typically see from students moving through different stages of literacy learning. This was based on thousands and thousands of hours of observation of actual kids. For example, we could say on the very first scale that when a kid scribbles on a piece of paper and points to it and babbles something to you, that's readiness for literacy learning, because they're beginning to make an association between language and marks on paper. That helped the teachers enormously, because they could see what stage the child was moving into and how they could provide the resources for that stage.

"We knew we had something then. We needed to get this accepted as an alternative to standardized testing, especially for inner city schools. You're showing students on a trajectory of learning, not as failing at something." Their efforts with the Department of Education in California brought them to the state's chief psychometrician. According to Peg, after seeing a demonstration of the Learning Record, he responded, "Oh, you're talking about *real* assessment. We only have symbolic assessment now."

The state of California allowed it as an alternative to standardized testing, the only thing they have approved as an alternative to date. "We were all over California and in New York and in Ohio, and teachers were ecstatic. The parents were ecstatic. They couldn't believe the careful look the teachers were taking. And these learning records are public, so the parents could look at them and see what was being observed of their children's work. Then they could see the analysis. For the children, it was absolutely revolutionary to be looked at in that way, because the teacher was busy looking for what they were showing they knew how to do. "We had a complete success and it got completely wrecked by No Child Left Behind."

FairTest called the Learning Record "a powerful assessment process . . . a process through which students take charge of their own learning and document their learning. It is also a means to more strongly integrate parental involvement into the school."[23] After NCLB pressured school systems into sticking to one standard for assessment, the Learning Record foundered. These days, Peg is a professor at the University of Texas, where she has developed a version of the Learning Record at the college level, with notable success.

"Graduate students of mine are using it all over the country. At the college level mostly, because the public education system is such a hermetically sealed environment and so politically fraught. I do consulting for college-level faculty who want to take it on."

Meanwhile, she still keeps the torch burning for the K–12 version. "The Learning Record is completely open and completely available. I make it available on the website for anyone who wants to download it. I get emails from music teachers in Peru."

Assessment as Learning

The Learning Record showed that it is possible to assess how well a large number of students were learning with a commonly agreed-upon set of standards without resorting to standardized tests.

Sam Chaltain is the editor of *Faces of Learning: 50 Powerful Stories of Defining Moments in Education* and author of *Our School: Searching for Community in the Era of Choice*, among other books. For Sam, assessment and standardization are not the problem; the problem is what we choose to standardize. The United States has chosen to standardize testing and accountability, and the results have been underwhelming. Finland has chosen to standardize the way they prepare teachers rather than tests, and the Finnish education system is lauded around the world. "That says to me that standardization itself is not a dirty word," Sam said to me. "It's just what we've done with it."

"When it comes to assessment, the traditional model of assessment is assessment for learning. What people like to talk about now is that the twenty-first-century model is assessment of learning. But if assessment is merely the way we are able to determine how much learning has occurred, then the ultimate goal is assessment as learning, where assessment occurs in real time and is the process by which people reflect on their own thinking and diagnose how they've changed. There are schools that do this. There's a remarkable school in New Hampshire that, for them, the thing that matters the most is that people who graduate from their school have seventeen specific habits of mind and work—everything from collaboration and leadership to curiosity and wonder. They've developed these really thoughtful behavioral rubrics that break down each of those habits by subskills.

"If we're serious about curiosity and wonder, then we have to think, 'What are the sub-habits that lead to that?'" This school recognizes that the path to curiosity and wonder is through openness to new ideas, comfort with complexity, ability to ask questions. For each of those sub-habits, there are different descriptions, so this is what a person looks like when they're a novice, when they're a beginner, when they reach expert stage. This is not something that only teachers look at. Those rubrics are used by students and parents all the time. That's what I mean by assessment as learning. Young people at that school are constantly reflecting on where they're at on the continuum. As a result, I've never met young people who are better able to articulate their strengths and weaknesses and what they want to do with their lives and why.

Sam suggests that before embarking on any course of assessment, a school community first needs to identify the characteristics of an ideal graduate: What should those graduates know? How should they be able to use what they know? What will this knowledge do for them? Once the school has identified this, they can then decide how to assess for this, both in terms of student performance and how effectively the school community (teachers, administrators, and parents) is creating an environment that allows students to flourish.

"It's not like we need to come up with the same set of skills for the ideal graduate at every school, because the importance is in giving communities the space to reflect on these questions and answer them themselves, and then have those questions drive all of their strategic thinking and planning. Otherwise, what you get is schools that, by default, focus exclusively on what the federal government sets out in terms of accountability."

Monty Neill agrees. "Portfolios, projects, and extended tasks are the way to go. That doesn't mean you can't use short answers and multiple-choice tests as components of that. We want kids to be able to think, reason, write, speak, and show that they can apply their knowledge in complex ways. We know that well-conceived projects and tasks can do that. . . . To improve learning and provide meaningful accountability, schools and districts cannot rely solely on standardized tests. Because of their inherent limits, the instruments generate information that is inadequate in both breadth and depth. States, districts, and schools must find ways to strengthen classroom assessments and to use the information that comes from these richer measures to inform the public."

A Snapshot of the Future

Earlier in this chapter, I introduced you to Joe Bower, who took the bold step of eliminating grades from his classroom. Some schools are doing this at a much broader level. Surrey, British Columbia, is one of several school districts around the world involved in a pilot program that does away with letter and number grades, replacing them with a more holistic form of assessment.

Using an online portfolio program called Fresh Grade, teachers in these schools take photos of each student's work to form a continuous glimpse into each child's progress that parents and students can share. Teachers work with students to define individual goals and markers of progress, and success is defined through those goals and markers.

"The movement is, in part, a response to calls from employers for the school system to emphasize skills such as creativity and communication, not just knowledge of traditional subjects," said journalist Erin Millar.[24] "The move away from grades matches a growing belief among employers that traditional assessment is not the best way to help students develop the skills they need to succeed in today's world. In national and global surveys, employers don't complain about applicants lacking specific knowledge or technical skills, which are easy to test and express in a letter grade; they want employees who can analyze critically, collaborate, communicate, solve problems, and think creatively."

In British Columbia, where the program has been in use for a while, the results are very encouraging. While some parents are confused about how to navigate through a world without grades, many more love the immediacy of the program because they're getting nearly daily progress reports. One advantage is the opportunity for early intervention; when their children are struggling, they can get them help much sooner, as opposed to the traditional grading system, where they might not discover that their child was having trouble until the end of an assessment period. Teachers are excited about the program too, even though it means more work for them.

"Teachers are spending a ton of time sitting down with students one-on-one, setting goals together," Erin told me. "They're saying things like, 'You need to have the skills to assess your work. You need to have the skills to assess other people's work.'"

Interestingly, but perhaps not surprisingly, the biggest push-back is coming from those for whom the traditional form of grading worked. "I heard from teachers that the students who struggled the most with it were the high-achieving students in the old system, because under this new paradigm, you can't get an A without progress. For a student who was accustomed to doing well in the old system because they were very good at playing the game and could identify what the teacher wanted, the rules have completely changed. The middle kids and the lower kids responded to it wonderfully, because all of a sudden they were able to set their own goals and see progress."

This new program is not without its challenges. Universities, for example, are still trying to figure out how to compare student transcripts based on this new assessment system to those based on traditional grades. But the effort to do so is under way, especially at smaller universities that have the scale to consider portfolios without numbers. And even bigger schools are attempting to adjust. "I would say there's a willingness," Erin said, "but a lot of questions need to be answered first."

At least they are the right questions to ask and, like all the best ones, there is no single answer. That's how life usually is, and that's what real assessment in education should reflect.

Assessment is an integral part of teaching and learning. Properly conceived, both formal and informal assessments should support students learning and achievement in at least three ways:

- **Motivation:** Effective assessment spurs students to do well. It provides constructive feedback to help them understand how they're doing and to encourage them to improve where they can.
- **Achievement:** Effective assessment provides information on what students have actually done and achieved. It also provides relevant comparisons with how others have done against simi-

lar criteria so that students and others can make their own judgments of their progress and potential.

- **Standards:** Effective assessment sets clear and relevant standards that can raise students' aspirations and contribute to the guidance and practical support they may need in reaching them.

Assessment should not be seen as the end of education, in either sense. It is an essential part of the whole process and should interweave naturally with the daily processes of teaching, learning, and curriculum development. It should be an integral but supportive part of the ordinary school culture. Getting that balance right is one of the roles of school leadership.

CHAPTER EIGHT

Principles for Principals

A T THE CENTER of any great learning experience are two essential figures—a learner and an educator. For a school to excel, a third figure is critical: an inspired school leader who brings vision, skill, and a keen understanding of the kinds of environments where learners can and want to learn. I know many great schools that practice most, if not all, of the principles we discussed so far. What they all have in common is the leadership of a visionary and passionate principal. This type of leadership is what sustains Boston Arts Academy.

Identifying the need for a local arts-driven high school, the six colleges in the Boston area devoted to educating professionals in the arts (Berklee College of Music, Boston Architectural College, the Boston Conservatory, Emerson College, Massachusetts College of Art and Design, and the School of the Museum of Fine Arts) collaborated to create Boston Arts Academy in 1998. The academy is a pilot school within Boston public schools, which means that they operate under the purview of the school district but have certain areas of autonomy, such as budget, calendar, and staffing.

As an inner-city public school, Boston Arts Academy deals with the academic challenges facing every school with a large proportion of economically disadvantaged students. For this school, the poverty level is very high: 65 percent of the students qualify for free and reduced-cost lunch. In addition, a third of the school's incoming students arrive reading below grade level, often far below grade level. Yet 94 percent of their graduates go to college, a dramatically higher percentage than the national norm. Interestingly, most Boston Arts Academy graduates do not go on to an arts college, largely because of leadership that opens up a larger world to the students. "Among our graduates, the top majors they choose are design and engineering," headmaster Anne Clark told me. "Those are things they never would have understood if they weren't being taught in an interdisciplinary way, where they could see they had this strength.

"We're operating from a different sense of what education should and could be, and a different sense of success. It's not narrowly defined through standardized assessments, but also through the types of things the arts teach, like persistence and collaboration and creativity and vision and voice. We have found that many of our students who were not successful before coming to Boston Arts Academy find their way to engaging with school through the arts, because school isn't just another thing that they hate and are bad at."

Still, Boston Arts Academy is a public school and, like all other public schools in Massachusetts, they are required to administer standardized tests. For the staff and the administration, that means doing some teaching to the test.

"We would be doing our students a disservice if we didn't prepare them for the tests," Anne said. "We're *always* preparing them for the tests. By the time they finish their state-required tests, we have to switch gears and prepare them for the SAT, which is a very different kind of test."

The school offsets this requirement with an environment that keeps students inspired even in the face of high-stakes testing. "Students are generally here from eight to four. If it's during a performance period or a portfolio period, they could be here much later. They spend half their day in the arts, and half in academics. They do a full academic program, though we teach through the arts and through interdisciplinary modes as much as possible. We teach math, humanities, world languages, and science. Then they all have an art major: music (instrument or vocal), dance, theater, visual arts. They mostly have to focus on one, but there are times during the day when the underclassmen especially get to explore other majors."

While every student at the school is an individual, what unites them is their passion for the arts. And this is what influences their approach to every element of their education. Anne Clark was one of the founding teachers at the school before taking a leadership role, and she has seen the value of this passion more times than she can say.

"The kids are happy to be here, and that makes a big difference for all of us. Most of our academic faculty has an arts background, and they teach in both arts and academics. When I was a teacher, one of the things I did was teach reading to the lowest readers. These were seventeen-year-old young men reading on a third-grade level. If they get to spend two to three hours a day on the thing that lets them show their strengths, it's a lot easier to work with them one-on-one on the thing that makes them feel most disempowered. A parent said to me recently, 'This is the only school that started with what my daughter could do, not what she couldn't do.' The school is about showcasing the student's gifts and strengths. It changes the conversation."

The Boston Arts Academy model substantiates what I've seen in all my work with schools around the world: building the curriculum around students' interests leads to them performing at higher levels in all areas. There's something else too. Because it is an arts-based program, and because artists are accustomed to receiving criticism and responding to that criticism quickly, the school is also creating students far better prepared for what will be asked of them once they leave school.

"Creativity and interdisciplinary thinking are what the world demands. I think that's why our graduates are so successful. That's what we've heard from colleges. Our kids are willing to take risks, imagine, work hard, work collaboratively. They take critique, which is a really important part of an arts-based education. Formal revision, review, and feedback is inherent to the arts. I worry about my biological children growing up in a world of 'Is it right? Well, I'll find out when the test grader tells me.' Our students are being invited to imagine their own answers, defend them through critique, and revise—but not just because there's some standard to meet. That's the kind of thinking that we need. When your whole education is based on learning a specific way, filling in bubbles, and then waiting for your number, you don't learn the same way.

"There's a member of our board who is a high-ranking executive. He said that he's here because when he's hiring, he always wants to look for the violinist. He's looking for someone with an arts background because he knows that person is creative and imaginative. That person has been trained to meet problems with fresh eyes. That's what an arts-based education provides."

Far more students want to attend Boston Arts Academy than there are slots. The school admits about 120 new students a year and gets more than 500 applications. The school looks at each application carefully, but there is one thing it ignores completely when making its selections.

"We're unique among art schools in the country because we're academic-blind," Anne said. "We don't look at previous grades, test scores, or anything else. We believe that an arts-based education should be accessible to all. One would never say, 'You can't study history because your math scores stink.' Why would we say you can't study art because your math scores stink? Functionally, that's what happens around the country. They'll include academic records in admissions, or they say they won't, but they'll say something like you have to have Algebra 1, and that becomes a functional barrier.

"We choose through auditions. But if we only took kids who knew how to do a formal audition, we wouldn't get a population that's reflective of the city of Boston, which is our mission. We're looking for students who are responsive and invested, but not necessarily formally skilled. I like to say we're looking for the kid who cannot *not* dance. Most of our students have not had formal training, because the resources aren't there in the Boston public schools. We have a lot of musicians who can't read music; a lot of visual artists who haven't had many art classes, because those have been cut from the lower grades. A lot of dancers who danced in the community but never had any formal ballet training. We're looking for the kid who would flourish with the opportunity for formal training, but hasn't necessarily had that before."

What Anne is describing is the heart of a principal's role: appreciating the individuality of the student body, seeking potential at every turn, and constantly striving to move the school forward in the face of constant change.

Roles for Principals

It's hard to overestimate the impact of leadership on the vitality and purpose of a community. A change of president, a new CEO, a different head of a department, or a new principal can transform the expectations of everyone they lead.

There's a difference between leadership and management. Leadership is about vision; management is about implementation. Both are essential. Great leaders may be great managers, and vice versa. The difference is in the role they take in any given context. High performance is driven by motivation and aspiration, and great leaders know how to conjure up those in the human spirit. They can bring hope to the hopeless, resolve to the forlorn, and direction to the lost.

Of course, vision is not enough. People need support, resources, and the skills to do the job. The role of management is to make sure that there are systems and resources available for the vision to be realized. But resources on their own are not enough. Let's step away from schools for a moment for another illustration.

I recently shared a platform at a corporate convention with Sir Alex Ferguson, one of the most successful and admired soccer coaches in the history of the game. During his twenty six and a half years managing Manchester United, a team that had had very little success before his arrival, he won thirteen Premier League championships and five FA Cups while being named Manager of the Year four times and Manager of the Decade in the nineties. He developed some of the best-known and most successful soccer players of all time, including David Beckham, Cristiano Ronaldo, and Wayne Rooney, and he went out on a high note, winning the Premier League championship in his final season.[1]

Manchester United is the most valuable sports franchise in the world (worth $2.33 billion according to *Forbes*, or 26 percent more than the New York Yankees),[2] so one might attribute the club's extraordinary run of success to wealth and resources rather than Alex Ferguson's brilliance at getting the most from his players—until you consider what happened immediately after Ferguson retired. With largely the same roster of players, and certainly with access to the same resources Ferguson had, new manager David Moyes not only didn't win the Premier League championship (as Ferguson had done the year before), but the team failed to qualify for the Champions League for the first time in two decades. Moyes was fired in April 2014, less than a year into his six-year contract.[3]

What does this have to do with school leadership? Quite a bit. The Premier League is filled with hugely talented players. One could argue—and certainly those of us from the U.K. regularly do—that the Premier League has the highest concentration of talent of any league in the world. What separates the consistently successful teams like Manchester United from the rest is the teaching and motivation that comes from their leaders who bring the best out in their players. How else does one explain the enormous drop-off in performance from Ferguson's last year to Moyes' only year with the club, when most other conditions remained the same?

There is no single style of leadership, because there is no one type of personality that makes a leader. Some leaders are collaborative; others are commanding. Some aim for consensus before they act, and some act on conviction. What unites them is an ability to inspire those they lead with the sense that they are doing the right thing, and that they are capable of doing it too. Different situations call for different styles of leadership. In the heat of battle, a military leader may have neither the time nor the inclination to consult with others. But the leaders who are most revered in any field are those who genuinely care for those they lead and whose compassion is evident not only in what they say but also in what they do.[4]

In schools, great principals know that their job is not primarily to improve test results; it is to build community among the students, teachers, parents, and staff, who need to share a common set of purposes. They know too that the established conventions of schooling are secondary to these purposes. Even so, challenging those conventions can be sensitive work. It's more likely to succeed if everyone involved believes in the changes enough to give them a chance. Richard Gerver showed his understanding of this in how he nurtured the changes at Grange that we discussed in chapter 2.

Richard knew he had to introduce this idea slowly or risk losing the support of those resistant to sweeping change. "First we had the Grangeton project, which was the idea of replicating the town." He introduced Grangeton initially as an after-school activity, separate from the standard timetable and curriculum. "We did that because it felt more gentle; it allowed time for it to evolve and develop. If I'd walked in on day one and presented this structure to the parents, I think there would have been open rebellion. I don't think the teachers were ready to go at it on day one, either. But most important, I don't think the students were ready, particularly the older ones. I wanted everyone to immerse themselves in a way that didn't feel high-stakes or totally alien.

"We needed to avoid predefining a massive transformation and then imposing it on the school community. You have to build the context and capacity within your community to take on ideas that don't feel threatening. Running Grangeton initially as an extracurricular program allowed everyone to dip their toes in and observe what was happening until they felt confident enough to dive in themselves."

Richard's decision to introduce Grangeton slowly allowed its progress to accelerate dramatically. When he started the after-school program, he saw it as the beginning of a five-year evolution for the school, one that would gradually find greater buy-in from parents, students, and teachers. The freshness of his approach made everyone more receptive. "Most school systems are used to having programs imposed on them either by their management teams or by governments. Everybody jumped in so fast here because they reveled in the freedom and the fact that this wasn't being done to them. As a result, the entire Grangeton program was up and running within six months."

Changing Cultures

I talked earlier about complex adaptive systems. Just as education systems are examples, so too are individual schools. Schools can and do adapt to change. The task for principals is to help them to do this consciously.

A good deal of management theory has focused on how to make organizations more efficient, and that is essentially what the standards movement is about too. The assumption is that organizations are much like mechanisms and can be run more effectively by tightening procedures, minimizing waste, and focusing on yield. If you look at the typical management charts of many organizations, you'll see that they are like technical drawings or wiring diagrams. Here is an example.

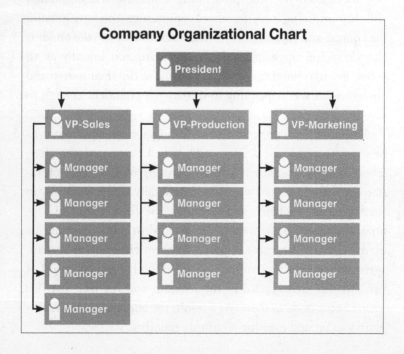

These sorts of images and the rhetoric of cost-efficiency and outputs that often goes with them reinforce the idea that organizations are like mechanisms. The trouble is, they are not. This metaphor may work well in some areas of manufacturing, but it doesn't in many other sorts of organizations, including schools. While focusing on efficiencies and cutting costs can be good goals in themselves, human organizations are not like mechanisms; they are more like organisms, each with their own culture.

In the social sense, culture means a community's way of life: its values, forms of behavior, and codes of coexistence. In the organic sense, culture implies growth and evolution. At their best, schools are living communities of individuals who come together in a shared venture of learning and development. How well they do this is all about the culture of the school.

Writing about the culture of organizations in *Out of Our Minds*, I made a distinction between *habits* and *habitats*. Transforming schools means looking at both, and how they affect each other.

HABITS

In the interest of getting things done, all institutions develop routines and procedures. That's understandable. Communities need to agree on ways of doing things so that things get done at all. The problem is that, over time, these procedures can become fixed and the community can lose touch with the purposes they were meant to serve. The institution becomes the procedures. As Winston Churchill once said, "We shape our buildings, and afterward our buildings shape us."[5]

Many of the conventional rituals of schooling are not fixed in law. Many schools are organized as they are because they always have been, not because they must be. Many of the examples we've looked at have involved breaking old habits that get in the way of learning. In his important study, *Creating Innovators*, Tony Wagner argues too that it is the ambient culture of the school and the attitudes and expectations it creates in teachers and students alike that is the critical factor in generating—or inhibiting—original thinking and the habits and mind-sets of innovators.[6] One of the best recent accounts of the transformative influence of school culture is *Comprehensive Achievements: All Our Geese Are Swans* that tells a twenty-year story of the transformation of Hampstead Comprehensive School, which became a highly successful state school in North London. The book documents the evolution of the culture of the school under the inspirational leadership of Tamsyn Imison and her bringing together an accomplished group of teachers to offer a "broad-based, holistic, and creative education, enabling children to love learning and develop as all-round people, in addition to passing examinations."[7] The book includes the voices of students, teachers, governors, and parents who together tell "how it is possible for a well-led school with well-chosen staff to hold firm to their professional and moral beliefs, and in doing so resonate with their pupils, parents, and the wider school community." Like many of the schools we've featured, the key to this transformation was to challenge accepted habits in school culture and to develop ways of being together that were customized to the needs and interests of the school's particular community.

HABITATS

The physical environment of a school affects not only how it feels but also how it actually works. You get a feel for a school as soon as you walk through the door. Whether they are in old buildings or new, some schools feel impersonal and institutional. Others feel vibrant and alive: the walls are covered with student and staff work, there are displays, installations, performances, and a buzz of activity. The tones and features of the physical environment are more than cosmetic. They affect the mood, motivation, and vitality of the whole school community. In *The Third Teacher*, Bruce Mau and a team of international architects and designers look closely at the intimate and powerful relationships between how students learn and the spaces in which they do it.[8] They show how the physical environment embodies the philosophy of the school and they offer a series of practical design ideas and strategies to transform school spaces.

Different activities need different sorts of spaces and atmospheres. The spaces given to different activities are often an indication of the importance attached to them. So too is the configuration of the school. When facilities are set apart from each other, this often reflects the separation of subjects in the curriculum. If classrooms are always laid out with rows of separate desks facing the front, they send a clear message to students and teachers alike about the sort of learning that's meant to go on in them. The physical space of High Tech High was designed to promote the interaction between disciplines, which is a central part of its philosophy. The transformation of much of Grange into a working town was embodied in the physical reorganization of the school itself. There are many other models for redesigning the school environment to embody different and more innovative concepts of curriculum and learning.

Cultivating the Ground

For several years I worked with the state of Oklahoma on a comprehensive strategy of creativity and innovation. In the developmental phase, I had a series of meetings with the governor and various members of his administration. I remember one of them saying how important it was to Oklahoma's future for the state to develop a culture of innovation. "But I'm just not sure," he said, "where all these great ideas are going to come from." I told him they would come from all over the state. People everywhere have ideas they would like to develop, but they need permission to try them out and see if they work. If they fear failure or humiliation or disapproval, they will usually hold back. If they're encouraged to try their hand, they usually will.

Culture is about permission. It has to do with what's acceptable and what is not, and who says so. Sometimes changes in permission happen slowly, and it's only when we look back over time that we can see the true scale of them. When I was in my twenties in the U.K., almost everybody smoked cigarettes. I did, and so did everyone I knew. Restaurants, pubs, and people's homes were constantly enveloped in a gray haze of smoke, which clung to everything and created what we felt was a proper atmosphere for hanging out. If you'd said that ten years from then it would be unacceptable to smoke indoors, you would have been ridiculed. But it did and it still is.

As I write, state after state in the United States is passing laws to allow same-sex marriage. At the height of the permissive sixties, that would have been unthinkable. Now it's perfectly acceptable, as it should be. The lines of permission have been gradually redrawn. Change is often the result of many complex forces interacting with each other. For all the reasons we've discussed, schools are changing too. How quickly they change will depend, in large part, on the vision of the people who run them, especially the principals, on how they set expectations, and where they draw the lines of permission.

One of the most impressive people I know in education worked for many years as a principal in Oklahoma's public schools. Her work there and later in her career shows how effective the vision and leadership of a great principal can be in changing the culture and achievement of schools.

Jean Hendrickson was principal of three different elementary schools over the course of fifteen years. Socially and economically one of her schools was at the top in Oklahoma City. "It was at the edge of a country club, and it had every advantage that a public school could have," Jean told me. "What the school district couldn't provide, the parents and community could provide. Yet even at that school, of course, there were children who needed more attention, and there were things that we needed to do differently. We needed to make sure every child was seen as an individual.

"I had been there for six years, and we had done some systematic reorganizing of the way teachers communicate and had brought the arts into the school. I was then asked to take a school that was fourth-generation poverty, that had a high Hispanic population, and that had had a very horrible year when they brought a principal in who thought it was his job to tear the inside out and the teachers thought it was their job to protect themselves. I was asked if we could do some of the things in that school that I had promoted at my previous one. It took me about five minutes to say yes.

"By the time I got there, there were two distinct communities. There was the immigrant community—very low income—and there was a fourth-generation pioneer, rugged, white community as well. When I went to that school for the first time in my life, I saw there was graffiti everywhere. It was a completely devastating environment. I was angry to know that there were kids in my town going to school in a place like that."

She asked a pointed question at that school: "Do you believe the kids here deserve the same kind of full educational opportunity as my other kids received?" No one said no. "So we set about doing some things there that I felt you'd do anywhere you had kids in schools. It was about building out the kind of school that you would want your own child to attend. We needed to have arts involvement. We needed to have community inside the school. We needed to have a beautiful place where people felt that they were respected. Basically, you need it all, and all at the same time. The first thing I did to help the school pull out of its doldrums was to double arts and music time, and I used Title I money to do it.

"Oklahoma decided to canvas the country to look for better models of education. They were looking for a few conditions: it needed to be a whole-school model, not just one grade or subject area; it needed to have an arts component; and it needed to have some research to show what it was doing was effective. One of those models was the A+ initiative in North Carolina. I was one of the team members who went to North Carolina to explore the model.

"A+ started in North Carolina when school accountability was just beginning to resonate across the United States. It began as a project of the Keenan Institute for the Arts, where those folks asked the question, "What would happen in schools if you took the arts seriously? If you taught through and about the arts, would there be any impact? And if so, what might the impact be?" That created a pilot program with twenty-five schools from across the state, and they watched the schools grapple with that question for about four years. What they discovered was that there were eight commitments that schools make when they say they are part of the A+ network.

"They commit to the arts every day for every child; to a curriculum that is connected, shared, and planned across time; to hands-on, real-world learning, not just on worksheets; to multiple learning pathways; to enriched assessment; to deliberate collaboration—not just between teachers, but between the home and the school, between the children and their teachers; they commit to changing infrastructure; and they commit to creating a positive climate, so you have students who are joyful, teachers who are happy to be there, and parents and a community who feel they are part of the learning."

In 2001, Jean was embedded in one of the school teams that was undergoing their summer institute training. She was part of the school team during the day and joined the planners and facilitators in the evening as they discussed how the day had gone. As a principal, she realized that this was the kind of model that she'd been looking for throughout her professional career. In 2003, she was invited to become the executive director for A+ Schools.

The experience and research of A+ Schools has shown that what makes or breaks achievement and effectiveness in schools is not the type of school or its location. It is the presence of three main drivers, which can transform any school setting: They are principal leadership, a faculty willing to engage in the change, and quality professional development.

A+ Schools have higher-than-average test scores. So that's OK. But more than that, they have fewer discipline problems and referrals. They also have what they call a "joy factor" based on measures of student engagement. The teacher opinion surveys show higher teacher satisfaction and higher teacher capacity—a sense that they are more empowered and capable as professionals.

"I think the first takeaway," Jean says, "is to get really clear on what you want for your children. If what you seek is something more than a high standardized test score. If what you're seeking is joyful engagement, completion of tasks, high achievement, well-rounded opportunities for learning. If what you seek is to have culture and community visible and unique and valued in your school, then look for a framework that can systematically hold and work with those things."

I assume that we do want these things for all students. Or did I miss a meeting?

Beyond the Gates

Great schools are continuously creative in how they connect to the wider communities of which they are part. They are not isolated ghettos; they are hubs of learning for the whole community. For example, we are used to thinking of education in separate stages: elementary school, high school, community college, college, and adult and lifelong learning. But learning can often happen best across age groups and between as well as within institutions. Although elementary school, high school, and college are usually separate stages in education, some students are now working together to dissolve the barriers that often separate them. Take Clark University, in Worcester, Massachusetts.

David Angel, the president of Clark, has been working with faculty and students to build bridges between the campus and the city, and to the lives that the students may live after college. During a recent conversation, he said to me, "We asked ourselves the question, 'If we want to be intentional at Clark at graduating students who are both strong on the traditional liberal arts criteria and can carry their education out into the world and be impactful, how do you cultivate the resilience of a young person when they hit a road bump?' How do they develop three-way creative solutions to problems? If you want to build those skills intentionally, you're much more effective if you do it in an authentic context. If a student is put on a project team and has a real problem to overcome, you see far more development."

LEEP (Liberal Education and Effective Practice)[9] is a program that combines interdisciplinary studies with out-of-class, real-world challenges of the kind that students are going to face once their college days are through. Clark alumnae and a range of other professionals host students on project themes. This goes far beyond the traditional internship, where students get only a taste of a career path. The objective is to put students on project teams where there's a real problem to solve or outcome to accomplish.

One Clark student group, All Kinds of Girls, works with teenage kids from the neighboring community around issues of identity and bullying. The group addressed this task from the ground up by creating a program for more than fifty teenage girls on campus every Saturday. "This isn't about getting a grade," David said. "This is about helping a particular thirteen-year-old girl. It reaches into their hearts and their heads. Almost inevitably, you see this flourishing of capability when you see someone become passionate about what they do and when the work they're doing is authentic."

They also get involved in Clark initiatives like University Park Campus School. Clark helped found University Park as a way to address the difficult conditions for high school students in the impoverished area that surrounds the university. Three-quarters of the students qualify for free lunch, and students tend to come into the school several years behind academically.[10] Yet, through personalized attention to each of its two hundred–plus students, which begins at a camp kids attend prior to seventh grade,[11] nearly all University Park graduates go on to college, with nearly all of them being first-generation college students. Clark students play an active role at University Park as part of the college's overall effort to incorporate them into real-world scenarios where they can serve a vital function at the undergraduate level.

The reimagining of the ideal Clark graduate led David to a dramatic new approach to the curriculum. Traditionally, colleges think in terms of freshman year, sophomore year, and so on. Clark decided instead to establish three developmental phases around which to organize the curriculum at the university: transition (establishing yourself as part of the academic university community), growth and exploration ("breaking frame" and discovering your deepest passions and interests), and synthesis and demonstration (pulling together what you've learned in your major and nonmajor courses and putting that to work in a practical way). Students are encouraged to go through these phases on their own timeline.

What David Angel is doing at Clark is a particularly refined version of what every head of a school should be aiming to do: honing and reshaping the school as necessary to fit the evolving needs of students and society. David sees our time as a watershed moment for such an approach to school leadership.

"In my view, education is at a transition point where an increasing focus on learning outcomes is becoming the basis for assessing the educational experiences available to students. That can be a very powerful tool for engaging in greater reflection on the future of education in this country. We're asking the questions, 'What kinds of outcomes and what kinds of educational practices matter in this regard?'"

Breaking Ranks and Breaking Through

The National Association of Secondary School Principals (NASSP) has been asking these particular questions for more than three decades now. In 1996, the NASSP released its report, *Breaking Ranks: Changing an American Institution*. Based on decades of testing and observation, the report identified a series of recommendations designed to help school leaders do a better, more personalized job of serving their students and the school community.[12] Every year since 2007, the NASSP, working with the MetLife Foundation, has named a handful of schools in the country Breakthrough Schools, based on a combination of leadership; personalization; and curriculum, instruction, and assessment.[13]

Recently, the organization created the Breaking Ranks Framework, built along lines similar to the criteria for awarding Breakthrough School status. It is not intended to standardize behavior among schools all across the country. Instead, it provides a model that school leaders can follow to personalize a program specific to their schools' needs. NASSP addresses three core areas that they feel every school leader needs to address:

- **Collaborative leadership:** creating a shared vision, developing a defined and sustainable improvement plan, identifying meaningful roles among staff
- **Personalizing your school environment:** banishing the culture of anonymity that allows so many students to slip through school virtually unnoticed, developing personal plans for students
- **Curriculum, instruction, and assessment to improve student performance:** prioritizing depth of knowledge over breadth of knowledge, offering alternatives to tracking and grouping, providing students with real-life connections to the material they are learning[14]

They also provide a process for evolving the culture of a school to allow for sustainable change. This process runs in six stages, from gathering data and identifying priorities to communicating the plan, monitoring the plan, and adjusting where necessary. In addition, they've identified ten skills that "encompass the bulk of what school leadership entails." These include setting instructional direction, developing leadership in others, and building a meaningful sense of teamwork.[15]

What NASSP offers through Breaking Ranks is a template that can be applied throughout K–12 education. While it is not the only approach to the school leader's role, it has served a considerable number of schools over the nearly twenty years since NASSP first issued the report.

The Roots of Achievement

In chapter 2, I described the four general principles of organic farming—health, ecology, fairness, and care—and recast them for education. In organic farming, the focus is not only on output, it is on the vitality of the soil and the quality of the environment on which natural, sustainable growth depends. In education, natural, sustainable learning depends on the culture of the school and the quality of the learning environment. Sustaining a vibrant culture of learning is the essential role of the principal.

We looked earlier at a management chart based on mechanistic principles. Such charts give some sense of the structure of an organization; they give hardly any sense of how it actually works. Some years ago, I worked with a design company in New York City on issues of change and innovation. We discussed the power of organic metaphors. Some weeks later, the company had an off-site meeting and redrew its organizational chart on organic principles. Here it is:

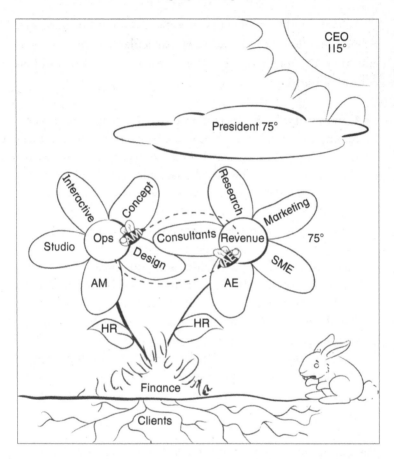

They explained that the roots of the organization are in its client base, which is where its income is created. The growth of the company depends on the cross-pollination of its two main stems of activity, operations and revenue, and their various elements. When that dynamic works well, the company flourishes. When it doesn't, it doesn't. The role of the president is partly to shield the company from the overheated expectations of the board and to maintain a climate in which people can work comfortably and do their best. (I don't know what the rabbit is for.)

Schools are like companies in some ways, but not in others. Schools that flourish have their own particular dynamics. In general, they all promote these essential features of an empowering culture of learning:

- **Community:** Its members all feel part of a compassionate community that supports each other's needs and aspirations. There is a strong sense of shared identity and purpose that extends beyond the gates to embrace the aspirations of all the families it serves and all the organizations with which it collaborates.
- **Individuality:** Its members feel respected as individuals, each with his or her own talents, interests, and needs. They are encouraged as individuals to develop a deeper understanding of themselves, of their own values and aspirations, and of their fears and anxieties. They all feel part of the larger community but know they will not be lost in the crowd.
- **Possibility:** The school provides hope and opportunity for all who are part of it. It recognizes the great range of talents in its members and provides multiple pathways to fulfill their aspirations. It provides opportunities for what everyone needs to know in common, as well as for everyone to excel on their own terms.

The culture of the school is expressed through the curriculum, teaching, and assessment practices. In previous chapters, I've identified key characteristics associated with them. As I see it, they all relate to the overall culture of the school in this way:

Conditions for Growth

Culture	Curriculum	Pedagogy	Assessment
Community	Diversity	Inspiration	Motivation
Individuality	Depth	Confidence	Achievement
Possibility	Dynamism	Creativity	Standards

Organizations thrive by adapting to their environments. This process depends on the flow of fresh ideas and the willingness to try new approaches. The role of a creative leader is not to have all the ideas; it is to encourage a culture where everyone has them. From this perspective, the main role of a school's principal is not *command and control*, it is *climate control*.

The culture of schools is also deeply affected by the more general climate in which they work. Creating the best opportunities for schools is the essential role of policymakers in education, and we will be coming to that shortly. But first, let's consider the most important partners with schools: the families and parents of the students who go to them.

CHAPTER NINE

Bring It All Back Home

CHILDREN AND YOUNG PEOPLE typically spend more time out of school than in it. Parents and families have a major influence on their achievement in school. When schools, parents, and families work together in the right ways, there are all kinds of benefits for everyone involved, and they apply across all social and economic groups. That said, one of the great complexities now for schools and students alike is the profound changes in the nature of the family. So, who do we mean by parents?

There's a biological answer, usually, but the social answer is often more complicated. In the United States, only a minority of children now live with both biological parents in what was a conventional nuclear family.[1] Many live with only one parent, because of divorce or separation, or because the parents were not a fixed couple in the first place. Some siblings have the same mother but different fathers, or the other way around, who live separately from them. Some live in blended families with more than two parents. Some are raised by siblings or other relatives. Some raise themselves.

A small but increasing number of children are being raised by same-sex parents through surrogacy or adoption. And many parents, whoever they are, are now working very long hours, often at several jobs if they can get them, to make ends meet. As a result, large numbers of young people are left to look after themselves anyway.

So the picture is complicated. For our purposes, the students' parents are whoever is most responsible for their welfare outside of school. In some cases, this will be one or both of their biological or adoptive parents, and in some cases not. One of the common challenges for schools and students is in knowing who exactly the parents are.

Being a parent can be very much harder than you imagined before you were one. Trust me. There can be wonderful fulfillment in seeing your children grow and feeling your relationships with them deepen. But many parents struggle more and more now with the practical and financial challenges of raising a family and with balancing the emotional demands of the many different roles that being a parent involves.

Children are changing too. They are maturing physically more quickly than ever before. They are under intense pressure from their peers, from the wider cultural environment, from the relentless demands of the digital world and social media, and from the incessant noise of advertising that badgers them for their attention, sense of identity, and money.

If you are a parent, what is the right sort of support? This is a complicated question, but let me offer two general pieces of advice based on research and experience. In doing this, it's as well to acknowledge that there are no universally agreed-upon rules on how best to raise and educate your children. Much depends on cultural background and personal experience. There are longer books than this one on this subject alone, and shelves of reports and learned papers. Some "tiger moms" believe that firm direction, control, and discipline is the right way;[2] others believe that a more facilitating and guiding role is best.[3]

Where you stand on the spectrum will depend on many factors. Inevitably, any advice I give here is similarly flavored by my own background and disposition. I offer it in the sure knowledge that much of what other people have to say in this area is flavored by theirs.

SEE THE INDIVIDUAL

I have often made a bet with people who have two children or more. I've never lost this bet, and I never will. My bet is that those children are completely different from each other. I know this because all children are unique, just as you are. They may be alike in some ways. They may be similar to some of their relatives. I am, and I'm sure you are. But in most respects, individuals are most like themselves, with their own temperaments, interests, talents, and dispositions. You can help your children by treating them as individuals and by not assuming that they should follow the same paths or be judged against the same criteria in school.

One of the reasons that so many students struggle in school is that they are not treated as the individuals they are. Their particular strengths are not recognized or provided for. Attentive parents know their children better than most do—including their children's teachers. As a parent, you have an essential role in helping the schools evolve a more rounded understanding of your children's unique qualities and capabilities.

Our children are always sending signals about who they are becoming. It is critical for us as parents and teachers to be vigilant and to pay attention. In the Element books, we gave many examples of people who were drawn early in their lives to different sorts of activities. Sometimes their real talents were hiding in plain sight, even though their families and schools alike ignored them at the time. They include children who played endlessly with LEGOs, and then went on to become accomplished architects, obsessive doodlers who became celebrated cartoonists, "hyperactive" toddlers who became professional dancers or gymnasts, quiet readers who became studious academics.

LIFE IS NOT LINEAR

One of the perils of standardized education is the idea that one size fits all and that life is linear. The truth is that there are many routes to fulfillment. The lives of most people have not followed a standard course. People commonly move in unexpected directions, discover new interests, or take unplanned opportunities. It's important at school not to limit your children's futures by assuming that the sort of education that you had will inevitably be right for them. You may assume that some subjects will necessarily be more useful than others for finding a career. As the world continues to change, that may simply not be true. The best you can do is to help your children develop in their different ways the general competencies we discussed in chapter 6 and to identify the personal talents and interests that engage them most. They will create and live their own lives, as you have done. Care as you must and try as you might, you cannot do that for them.

WHAT'S YOUR CHOICE?

I said in the introduction to this book that if you're involved in education in any way you have three options: you can make changes within the system, you can press for changes to the system, and you can take initiatives outside the system. Parents have these choices too. When they work with schools, and work to change them, they can get two sorts of benefits.

Parents' engagement in their children's education has a direct relationship to *motivation and achievement*, regardless of socio-economic standing or cultural background. According to the report *A New Wave of Evidence*, when parents "talk to their children about school, expect them to do well, help them plan for college, and make sure that out-of-school activities are constructive, their children do better in school."[4]

By connecting with families, schools can understand more deeply the interests and characters of the students they teach. When schools, families, and community groups work together to support learning, children are more likely to go to school more regularly, stay in school longer, like school more, get better grades, have higher graduation rates, and enroll in postsecondary education.[5]

Many of the challenges that schools commonly face—including drug abuse, bullying, violence, and discipline problems—may turn up in classrooms, but they don't originate there. They spill over from the world outside, in which students spend most of their time and energy. Developing closer ties with families and the community is one of the best ways to understand and tackle these issues.

In 2010 the University of Chicago published a report of a seven-year study that evaluated school improvement in low-income elementary schools in urban Chicago.[6] "The study found that elementary schools with strong family engagement were ten times more likely to improve in math and four times more likely to improve in reading than schools weak on this measure."

There are other benefits to collaboration for parents and schools. Collaboration between schools and families is a powerful source of *school improvement*. As we've shown, there are numerous opportunities for schools to enrich their teaching and curriculum through creative partnerships with the communities they are part of. When they build positive partnerships with families and listen to their ideas and concerns about their children's education, schools tend to create better and more successful learning environments.

According to the University of Chicago report, "parent-community ties" are one of the "five essential supports" for success in reform that include strong school leadership, the quality of the faculty and staff, a student-centered learning climate, and strong curriculum alignment. The report credited parent and community organizations with leading the charge for improved school facilities and staffing, positively influencing curriculum decisions, and providing more and better extracurricular school activities. At the same time, when families and communities organize to hold poorly performing schools accountable, school districts are more likely to make positive changes in policy, practice, and resources.[7]

Parental Guidance

One of the things I've found confounding over the years is how reluctant some school systems are to use the expertise of parents and other community members to offer enhancements to their programs. As we saw with Steve Rees and Minddrive earlier, such participation can lead to profound achievements, so it seems counterintuitive that most districts don't make greater use of—or even shun—these resources.

My collaborator, Lou Aronica, has been similarly puzzled when dealing with his children's schools. At the beginning of every year, Lou tells his kids' teachers that he'd be happy to help out in any way he can with writing projects. Lou is not only a best-selling author of fiction and nonfiction, he's also an award-winning editor, plus he minored in education in college and has been certified to teach English in the state of New York. So it wasn't as though he was volunteering to perform amateur microsurgery on a whim. Yet, year after year, teachers and administrators declined to take him up on his offer, other than to have him come to a couple of career days. Lou's neighbors reported similar experiences when they tried to offer help in their areas of expertise.

Finally, this year, his youngest daughter's elementary school began a series of enhancement programs called "clusters" and they invited Lou to run a short-story workshop with a small group of fourth and fifth graders. The students in Lou's group responded enthusiastically. Despite arguing that theirs was the only cluster in the entire school that required participants to do homework, the majority of the members of the group completed a short story over the course of the five-session program, and their work improved dramatically from the first session to the last. When Lou had to miss the second session, a teacher at the school subbed in for him and marveled at the students' level of engagement.

This didn't surprise Lou. This group of students had chosen to be in his cluster, so they were likely to be engaged. However, because they were all extremely interested in writing, they responded to his background more than they might if the same session had been run by a teacher. This is the value in bringing the community into the classroom and why it is important for parents to offer themselves up to their children's schools. There is no substitute for a great, trained, dedicated teacher. If a parent or another member of the community can supplement what the school is offering, everyone wins.

Hovering Overhead

One caveat. While the evidence supporting the value of parent involvement in schools is very strong, there are some lines that are better left uncrossed. According to Patrick F. Bassett, the president of the National Association of Independent Schools, over-parenting occurs when parents adopt the "helicopter" mode:

"hovering over their child incessantly and swooping down to the rescue when the first hardship occurs."[8]

Bassett is talking about those parents whose concern for the welfare of their children extends to the point where they justified micromanaging the child's success, often to the detriment of the child's growth. He points out that the most dangerous of these are the helicopter parents who lobby teachers for better grades or make excuses for a student's misdeeds, even going as far as threatening legal action if their child is punished.

"The lessons students learn from such over-parenting is life-long dependency: 'I'm not capable of fighting my own battles or accepting the consequences for my bad behavior, so thank God my parents will rescue me.' This may be why colleges are reporting problematic parents trying to register classes for their children, why workplace employers are reporting parents trying to negotiate their children's first job contracts, and why an increasing number of parents are seeing their college-graduate, adult children moving back home 'to save money.' "[9]

Chris Meno, a psychologist at Indiana University, agrees. When she sees students engaged in this sort of codependent relationship at a time in their lives when they should be fully emerging as individuals, she goes out of her way to "talk them down." Meno acknowledges that helicopter parenting often comes from a good place—genuine concern for their children, a sense of "friendship" with their kids that earlier generations didn't enjoy, the desire to protect them from the dangers of the world—but that these kinds of parents are potentially doing a good deal of harm and offering very little benefit.

"When children aren't given the space to struggle through things on their own, they don't learn to problem-solve very well. They don't learn to be confident in their own abilities, and it can affect their self-esteem. The other problem with never having to struggle is that you never experience failure and can develop an overwhelming fear of failure and of disappointing others. Both the low self-confidence and the fear of failure can lead to depression or anxiety."

While Meno is specifically speaking about college-age students, the same point applies to parenting throughout a child's school years. Staying connected to what your child is learning and how he or she is being taught is a great thing. Doing the work for your child or insisting that he or she is a top-achieving, perfectly behaved student when the evidence suggests otherwise is not. Letting your voice be heard at PTA meetings and school board sessions is a plus. Throwing your weight around to get special entitlements for your child is not.

Home to School

What are the best ways for schools and parents to work together? Many of the examples we've given feature parents and other adults working in partnership with schools on joint projects. Some of these were initiated within schools and some came from outside of them. All of them help to reframe the conventional relationships between schools and families.

In *Out of Our Minds*, I describe the innovative work and unique ethos of Blue School, an elementary and middle school in Manhattan. Founded by the Blue Man Group, the aim of this school is "to reimagine education for a changing world." Underpinning the school's approach are two questions: "What matters in an education that is worthy of the lives our children will live, and worthy of the world we want them to live in?" Blue School's answer is to nurture "communities of creative, joyful, compassionate learners who use courageous and innovative thinking to build a harmonious and sustainable world." The school's work is based on "an inquiry-based approach to education that fosters creativity, promotes academic excellence, nurtures human relationships and inspires a growing passion for learning."

The school aims to help children flourish by "providing opportunities for deep human connections to permeate all aspects of their lives. Our educational approach supports children in practicing mutual respect, cooperation, leadership, mentoring, listening, personal integrity, valuing differences, and conflict resolution. We help foster the social skills children need to thrive in the relationships they form throughout their lives."[10]

The head of the school is Alison Gaines Pell. "What if," she asks, "a school speaks up rather than down to the intellects of children? What if a school's curriculum is built from children's questions and wonderings about the world, built on our human and natural desire to create and do? What if we develop educational practices that foster—instead of hamper—creativity and innovation? What if, freed from the what-has-always-beens that hold some schools back, and from the standardized testing that has paralyzed our nation's discourse and practice, a school launches the inventors, artists, and change makers who will act boldly and courageously in the face of a changing world? What if we align learning in school with the kinds of lives our children are likely to lead? The kind of lives we hope for them?"

At the core of Blue School is a belief in the partnership between family and school in raising and educating children. Throughout the year, parents are closely involved in the work and development of the school—and not just as parents of the students but as learners themselves. Parents, students, teachers, and staff come together to learn, make connections, and play together as an essential part of school life. Family events each year include "discussion groups, community gatherings and meet ups, and more formal events as well . . . to support the mission and vision of the school as well as to make connections between and among our vibrant community of adults."

During the year, parents are invited to join roundtables, and other events, which aim to

- support the educational mission and objectives of Blue School
- strengthen the connection between home and school
- assist parents in being active participants in the school community
- build a strong community among families
- facilitate effective communication between all members of the Blue School community
- foster a deeper understanding of the educational framework of Blue School

These close working relationships between the school and its community of partners and parents are not public relations or promotional exercises; they are at the heart of the school's philosophy and understanding of itself. They are an essential part of Blue School's success in reimagining education and the world they and their families want their children to inhabit and sustain. They are not alone. National PTA (parent-teacher association) is America's largest and oldest organization involved in advocating for children with regard to schooling. It involves millions of families, educators, and community members. They've released a set of National Standards for Family-School Partnerships that serves as a template for the kind of engagement that allows students to prosper. The six standards are:

1. *Welcoming all families into the school community.* Families are active participants in the life of the school, and feel welcomed,

valued, and connected to each other, to school staff, and to what students are learning and doing in class.

2. *Communicating effectively.* Families and school staff engage in regular, two-way, meaningful communication about student learning.

3. *Supporting student success.* Families and school staff continuously collaborate to support students' learning and healthy development both at home and at school, and have regular opportunities to strengthen their knowledge and skills to do so effectively.

4. *Speaking up for every child.* Families are empowered to be advocates for their own and other children, to ensure that students are treated fairly and have access to learning opportunities that will support their success.

5. *Sharing power.* Families and school staff are equal partners in decisions that affect children and families and together inform, influence, and create policies, practices, and programs.

6. *Collaborating with community.* Families and school staff collaborate with community members to connect students, families, and staff to expanded learning opportunities, community services, and civic participation.[11]

According to National PTA president Otha Thornton, "Family engagement is not limited to helping children with homework, attending meetings at school, and checking in with teachers." "It also encompasses advocating with local school boards and state and federal government to ensure schools have the resources they need to provide a world-class education to every student."[12]

The U.S. Department of Education has also weighed in on the subject of family engagement, releasing its (rather stodgily titled) report, "Partners in Education: A Dual Capacity-Building Framework for Family–School Partnerships."[13] The document stresses the importance of families and schools working together and lists a series of conditions, goals, and outcomes that it believes parents and educators should seek to achieve. The framework shows the process of moving from an ineffective partnership, in which both schools and families lack the ability to collaborate, through the "four C's" (capabilities, connections, cognition, and confidence), to an effective one that allows schools and households to work together to support student achievement.

For educators, the framework offers the opportunity to acknowledge the wisdom and interconnectedness of families, create a culture that welcomes parental involvement, and channel parent-school interactions toward improvement in student learning. For families, "regardless of their race/ethnicity, educational background, gender, disability, or socioeconomic status," the framework offers an environment under which parents can support, encourage, and advocate for their children while also serving as models for learning.[14]

Family involvement is vital, but it is only possible if schools make such involvement accessible. Schools often need to be active in getting parents on the team, recommending parent workshops, regular face-to-face meetings, and building trusting collaborative relationships among teachers, families, and community members.

Edutopia, a nonprofit launched by the George Lucas Educational Foundation, offers ten tips for educators to make their schools more inviting, which parents can use to guide their interactions with their children's schools:[15]

- Go Where Your Parents Are—Use social networking sites, like Facebook, Twitter, and Pinterest, to keep parents in the loop and encourage interaction.
- Welcome Everyone—Acknowledge that many families in your community are nonnative English speakers, and use technology to help communicate with them.

- Being There, Virtually—Use Web-based tools to offer "virtual windows into the classroom." Edutopia calls out classroom social networking site Edmodo and assignment management tool Blackboard Learn, among others.
- Smart Phones, Smart *Schools*—Edutopia advocates using these devices to engage families, suggesting the use of group texts and a number of apps that can facilitate this.
- Seize the Media Moment—Use current media (the release of a new education-related book or film, for example) as a platform for creating an open forum for discussing school activities and education reform.
- Make Reading a Family Affair—Use programs like Read Across America, First Book, and Experience Corps to promote reading as a family activity.
- Bring the Conversation Home—Flip the parent-teacher conference upside down by having teachers visit student homes.
- Student-*Led* Parent Conferences—Allow students to direct the parent-teacher meeting, presenting some of their work and exhibiting their strengths, challenges, and goals.
- Get Families Moving—Create school events that encourage exercise and play as a family activity.
- Build Parent Partnerships—Use a range of tools, such as starting a parent-based book club or creating assignments that include family interviews, to actively involve parents in schoolwork.

In the late nineties, an initiative was launched in Los Angeles County public schools to create a comprehensive approach to improving schools in the inner city. One of the key takeaways from this initiative was the vital importance of engaging parents. Getting that engagement is a particular challenge in inner-city schools, because many parents speak little or no English and they often work multiple jobs and couldn't be available for school functions or teacher meetings.

On top of that, non-English-speaking parents often felt marginalized by school systems, effectively being told that if they couldn't speak English, they couldn't participate in their children's education. Out of this study came Families in Schools, whose goal is to bring parents, students, and educators together behind a common purpose, in spite of all of the hurdles.[16]

Oscar Cruz is president of Families in Schools. "We understand the importance of parents being involved to support their kids and their education," he told me. "What was less understood was what the role was of the school to promote that. Parent engagement was seen as solely the responsibility of the parent. A parent comes asking for resources. But that parent speaks another language. The staff looks at that person and says, 'Look, you should be learning English. Go learn English first, and then we can help you.' That's an obstacle a parent is facing. A parent-engagement strategy for us would be professional development training for staff to make sure that every single parent that comes into that school feels welcome and feels valued.

"Once you really start looking at how education is treating parents, there are very strong entrenched interests. Would a union support parent feedback as part of teacher evaluations? Would a union support having parents have a greater voice in district negotiations of contracts? The bureaucracy is very powerful, and the politics of education are strong, and many times they supersede the interests of student achievement.

"We've always known that parents matter. The question is what are the conditions that need to change within schools to make them more welcoming and more supportive of parents, especially in predominantly low-income communities?"

Families in Schools addresses the issue on three fronts. One is the creation of culturally relevant materials that parents can use to learn how they can become more actively involved in their child's school. Another is assisting in the training of school staff to show how to effectively connect with parents. The third is in advocating for policy change at the district level to encourage investment in the first two initiatives. On occasion, Families in Schools will even conduct school staff training themselves in situations where funding wouldn't allow the schools to do such training otherwise.

Oscar understands that the only way to get more parent engagement is to help more parents to participate in their children's learning at home. To that end, they've launched two programs of note. One is the Million Word Challenge, in which the organization sponsors a contest in Los Angeles–area schools to encourage reading outside of the classroom. Parent participation is central to the event, as they help their kids create an activity log and sign off on their progress. The second program is Read With Me, a lending library in which they give twenty bags filled with books to a large number of classrooms for students to bring home and read with their families. Reading time has increased by twenty minutes a day, thanks to the accessibility of these books.

"More and more, there's an elevated discussion about parent engagement," Oscar said. "We can see it in the news, we can see it in policy on the state level. You can see parents taking control of schools and demanding changes. People are getting more information that is making them proactive. I think the other positive is that as more Latinos and minority leaders are having positions of power, they carry with them a decent understanding of what the problems are, and they are shaping the solutions.

"The way parent engagement is framed in the schools, there are very formal ways in which parents have a voice," Oscar said. "There might be a PTA, a school-side council, but the real notion of what a democratic organization is—where there's a flow of information for people to make decisions, there are partnerships, there is common understanding, there is common respect—this hasn't yet been achieved. For parents to be partners, they have to be well informed, and that's the responsibility of the school."

Oscar Cruz and the staff at Families in Schools have dedicated themselves to changing the dynamic between parents and inner-city schools for a reason that is relevant to everyone: regardless of where you live and what your socioeconomic status might be, when parents take an active interest in their child's education, that child has a far better chance of thriving.

Teach Your Children Well

The highest level of parental involvement in a child's education is homeschooling, a practice that has gained traction over the past several years. Where once it was considered the domain of eccentrics, it is now entering the mainstream. According to the U.S. Department of Education, approximately 3 percent of school-age children were homeschooled in the 2011–2012 school year.[17] There are many compelling reasons to consider homeschooling as an option. One is that it addresses a number of issues we've brought up elsewhere regarding personalization of education by avoiding a reliance on teaching to standardized tests and giving kids room to discover their truest passions and interests. Evidence seems to indicate that homeschooled students tend to outperform their peers on academic achievement tests and the SAT.

Quinn Cummings is the author of *The Year of Learning Dangerously*, a memoir of her experiences homeschooling her daughter Alice. In it, she writes:

Alice's father and I both knew our daughter better than anyone and we could no longer ignore the fact that she wasn't working very hard in school. As people say when they've run out of polite variations of "slacking off," she "wasn't reaching her full potential." At the same time, I was also concerned that her homework load would increase with each passing year, leaving her less free time to follow a sudden curiosity, delve deeper into a random subject, absorb herself with a pointless activity or create something for no better reason than the muse struck her. I was greedy. I wanted her to stretch her mind and her self-confidence, but I also wanted her to play with friends, read books, listen to music and glaze over with the pleasant boredom of a long afternoon with no place to be and nothing to do.[18]

What Quinn Cummings is getting at here is the greatest argument for homeschooling: that it allows you to push your child where your child needs pushing (Alice, for example, tended to pretend she couldn't do long division with remainders) while also letting you give the child enormous room for improvisation and discovery.

Logan LaPlante would support this perspective. Logan is a teenager who has been involved with homeschooling since fourth grade. He feels that getting his education this way allows him to extend himself in certain areas while still getting a broad education. "I'm definitely focusing on certain things," he told me, "but I'm not ignoring other things. I still do every single topic in school; I just do it differently. My curriculum is a mash-up. I do math traditionally—I do that online. But I also learn math through design when I'm at my internships. We do all the stuff that you need to learn in a certain grade."

Logan sees this approach as much more valuable than the experiences of his traditionally educated friends. "My friends are struggling a lot because they're just going from history, straight to

math, straight to science, or whatever, and they're not really div-
ing deep enough into their classes. They'd like to dive deeper and
integrate more subjects into one topic like I did in a government
class this fall where we learned about the government, we learned
about the history of it all the way back to the Civil War, and we
did art—we integrated several subjects into that one subject."

In 2013, Logan spoke at a TEDx event at the University of
Nevada. There he talked about how he "hacked" his education by
using a variety of resources at his disposal to pull together the
curriculum that he believes is best for him. "I take advantage of
opportunities in my community and through a network of my
friends and family," he said during the speech. "I take advantage
of opportunities to experience what I'm learning. And I'm not
afraid to look for shortcuts or hacks to get a better, faster result."[19]

While some parents homeschool their children entirely by
themselves, supplementing with online courses, specialty tutors,
and enrichment programs in their communities, Logan accesses a
wider group of teachers within his community. He does this with
a core group of other homeschooled kids. "Some of our teachers
are chemistry professors at University of Nevada–Reno. Some of
them are just regular school moms that take classes over the summer, like that government class. Some of them mastered in literature, so they're our writing teachers. We all get together for about
eight weeks, one or two classes a week."

Homeschooling doesn't come without its challenges. The National Education Association recently weighed in, saying that it
"believes that homeschooling programs based on parental choice
cannot provide the student with a comprehensive education experience."[20] Some are also concerned that homeschooling stunts so-
cialization. And of course there's the matter of cost, which can be
anywhere from a few thousand dollars a year to more than ten
thousand. Finally, there's the commitment to spending that many

hours with your children every day, which is a level of parental involvement few imagine when they have children. None of these are issues to be considered lightly, but for a growing number of parents, the pros outweigh the cons. Certainly it's hard to deny that homeschooling is the ultimate expression of family involvement in personalized learning. And whether it's at home or school, making education more personal, engaging, and fulfilling is what this is about.

CHAPTER TEN

Changing the Climate

HOWEVER MUCH SCHOOLS DO to transform themselves, their cultures are critically affected by the political climate that envelops them. The changes that are needed in schools will take root more readily if local and national policies actually support them. For that to happen, policymakers need to understand their particular roles in helping those changes to come about.

Who are the policymakers? They are whoever sets the terms and the practical conditions under which schools are required to work. They include school board members, superintendents, politicians, and union leaders. This is a complex web of different, often conflicting, interests. I have worked with policymakers at all levels of education around the world. Most of those I know are passionately committed to the success of the schools they affect and want to do the right thing for students. Many do the best they can in difficult circumstances. Some pursue well-intentioned policies that inadvertently frustrate the goals they are trying to achieve.

As we've seen, it's a complex environment and a difficult challenge for policy. But it's made worse when policies are focused on the wrong objectives, or strategies are misaligned with how schools really need to work. So, in general, what should be the roles of policymakers in transforming schools? And what should they actually do to help schools meet the four basic purposes of education: *economic*, *cultural*, *social*, and *personal*?

. . . . . .

Before I set out my answers, let's look at how a group of policy-makers and educators is working to change the culture of education in one of the poorest areas of the United States. They are going beyond the limitations of the standards culture to effect transformative changes in their local public schools.

The Roots of Achievement

In South Carolina, the numbers don't look great. According to the National Assessment of Educational Progress (NAEP), in 2013 the percentage of fourth and eighth graders (which is when the NAEP assessments are taken) who were at or above proficient in both reading and math was lower than the national average. About a quarter of students did not graduate high school in four years, and of those who did, 40 percent needed remedial help before entering college.[1] Those remedial programs cost the cash-strapped state around twenty-one million dollars a year. A public poll showed that three-quarters of parents with children in South Carolina public schools thought the system needed to make major changes. But that meant getting past entrenched beliefs within these same communities about how schools should actually look and work.

These were daunting conditions for transformation, but a group of dedicated educators took up the challenge. In October 2012, they submitted an innovation report to the state board of education. The report set out the issues and the challenges. It also asked who in the state could help to bring about the necessary changes. Some state leaders suggested New Carolina, a nonprofit organization that focuses on economic development. The group met with New Carolina, and together they launched Trans-formSC. As I'm writing this, the program is still gathering momentum, but its ambitions and approach promise to move the state's education system in significant new directions.

Moryah Jackson is the director of education initiatives at New Carolina. She told me that New Carolina prides itself "as an organization that connects the dots and is able to bring people together in a nonpartisan way." The first step was to go into communities to get the sense of what the public saw as the most important changes that are needed to improve education in the state. They had the innovation document, but it had to align with public feelings if they were to have the kind of buy-in they needed to make wholesale changes stick. "I was just overwhelmed with the responses," Moryah said. "Senators, house members, city officials, parents, teachers. We felt that we'd really struck a nerve and that people really cared about what was going on. That laid a very solid foundation for us.

"We want to show people that change can occur. Short term, we are working to get everybody on the same page. We've had our school administrators agree on the characteristics of a twenty-first-century graduate and our state Chamber of Commerce just adopted those same characteristics. That was important, because so often educators and business leaders talk in different languages."

It became clear through these outreach sessions and meetings with school superintendents that there was a real desire in many parts of the state to focus more on the kinds of practical, collaborative programs we've discussed in this book. These South Carolina schools are prioritizing technology, shifting to project-based learning models, developing undervalued skills like problem solving and communication, and giving teachers significantly more freedom, while still holding them accountable for outcomes. Throughout the state, there was also a very strong feeling that new forms of assessment were needed. Moryah said, "We know the importance of having formative and summative assessment. We need to have real-time data. Teachers shouldn't have to wait until the end of the year and then not receive test results until the next year. They need to have the noncognitive assessments. If we're talking about project-based learning, how do you assess leadership? How do you assess communications skills?

"Long-term, we want at least 90 percent of our students to graduate career- or college-ready. It doesn't necessarily mean that test scores are going to go up. We're really trying to be smart about this. We want our classrooms to reflect the real world more. The world is changing. We need to be sure that our students are prepared to compete in the knowledge economy."

The New Carolina initiative is based on empowering principals and teachers to improve the overall culture of achievement in their own schools. "They have a lot of flexibility, and there are a lot of innovations they can try on their own, but they really need someone to say, 'Hey, it's OK; we have your back. We're going to advocate for you in the legislature.' It's a really fine line for us in South Carolina in terms of our structure. Each school district has a local school board, and the school board hires a superintendent. At the state level, the state superintendent does not have a lot of power. If a local community is dissatisfied with a superintendent, you're gone. So we're telling people that what these superintendents and teachers are doing is right, so we can back them up."

As the program rolls out, one of the biggest challenges is dealing with entrenched thinking about schools and education, even among parents and legislators who think that change is critical. "For the first time in decades, everybody agrees that we need to change, but it's difficult to change culture. Everybody knows what schools usually look like, so we have some very strong ties to our schools. When we start talking about completely redesigning a building so it doesn't even look like a school anymore, we run into some issues in the community."

Many have marveled at the progressive design of River Bluffs High School in Lexington, South Carolina, its Expeditionary Learning curriculum, and its lack of textbooks or lockers. Others have complained that it looks like a Starbucks and not nearly enough like a school. What TransformSC is seeing here is something that reformers have faced elsewhere around the world—the disconnect that happens when a new vision dramatically contradicts a long-held vision.

"One powerful way to change is to change how we're talking about public education. We're trying to emphasize the bright side, and maybe the naysayers will say, 'You know what, maybe this isn't so bad' or, 'Maybe we can do this.' We're very intentional in how we talk about what we're doing. Instead of saying, 'Oh, that school is failing because it's high poverty,' we'll find the high-poverty schools that are succeeding." As the program moves beyond its launch phase, it is beginning to gain momentum. In the fall of 2013, there were thirty-seven schools taking part in the initiative, covering a wide demographic range.

Policies for Growth

With TransformSC and many other examples we've given, the policy from the top is focused on encouraging innovation from the ground up. It's about creating the conditions in which schools can transform themselves. So what exactly are those conditions?

As I said earlier, the real role of effective leaders in education is not *command and control*; it is *climate control*. Just as teachers and principals should create the conditions for growth for their own students and communities, the role of policymakers is to create similar conditions for the networks of schools and communities they are appointed to serve. I've suggested that education should be based on the principles of *health*, *ecology*, *fairness*, and *care*. To practice these principles, policymakers need to facilitate particular conditions. These are implicit in the many examples we've given throughout the book. Let me make them explicit here.

FOSTERING HEALTH

Enthusiastic learners

The basic prerequisite for effective education is to cultivate students' enthusiasm for learning. That means understanding how students learn, providing a diverse curriculum, and supporting methods of teaching and assessment that motivate rather than inhibit learning. If students are not engaged at school, everything else that goes on in the name of education is pretty much beside the point. The costs of students turning off or dropping out are far higher than those of investing in schools that excite students to learn in the first place.

Expert teachers

I made a distinction at the beginning between learning and education. The role of teachers is to facilitate learning, and that is an expert professional task. This is why all high-performing school systems put such a premium on the recruitment, retention, and continuous professional development of high-quality teachers. There is no system of education in the world that is reliably better than its teachers.

Uplifting vision

People will achieve miracles if they are motivated by a driving vision and sense of purpose. That vision has to connect with them personally. I can't imagine that many children wake up in the morning wondering what they can do to raise their state's reading standards. But countless children do want to read and write and calculate for their own purposes and to sing and dance and explore and experiment. Countless parents and teachers want to support them. They need policies and visions that speak to their own interests and circumstances and not to be reduced to data points in some abstract political competition.

Nurturing the Ecology

INSPIRING LEADERS

Great systems need great leaders. Just as students can be inspired to new heights by inspirational teachers, and schools can be inspired by a visionary principal, networks of schools need to believe in the leadership that affects them. They need to know that policymakers really understand the day-to-day challenges of teaching and learning, and they need to believe that they have the best interests of schools in mind in the policies they are pursuing. Policymakers cannot raise achievement in schools without the confidence and commitment of those who actually do the work.

ALIGNMENT AND COHERENCE

Healthy systems work holistically; each element sustains the others. Education should be the same. In a complex system like this, with many subsystems and dynamics, the constant risk is that the preoccupations of different interest groups become misaligned. In quality systems, the vision for education is closely aligned with practice across all phases and levels of the system. It is living people who are moving through the system, and the coherence of their experiences is a primary, not incidental, consideration.

WELL-FOCUSED RESOURCES

High-performing systems of education are well resourced. The resources are not only financial. The quality of education is not inevitably related to the amount of money spent on it—we have seen some excellent examples in this book of schools delivering very high-quality education in spite of limited funding. Overall, however, the United States spends more money per capita on education than any other country in the world, but it would not claim to have the best system. Everything depends on where the resources are focused. High-performing systems invest especially in professional training, in appropriate technology, and in common support services that would be beyond the reach of individual schools.

Promoting Fairness

PARTNERSHIP AND COLLABORATION

The standards movement is rooted in competition between students, teachers, schools, districts, and now between countries. There is a place for competition in education, as there is in the rest of life. But a system that sets people against each other fundamentally misunderstands the dynamics that drive achievement. Education thrives on partnership and collaboration—within schools, between schools, and with other groups and organizations.

STRATEGIC INNOVATION

Moving from the status quo to a new paradigm takes imagination and vision; it also needs care and judgment. "Care" is about safeguarding what is known to work while being prepared to explore new approaches in a responsible way. One of the most powerful strategies for systemic change is to test the benefits of doing things differently. Innovation is strategic when it has significance beyond its immediate context—when it inspires others to innovate in similar ways in their own situations.

ADVOCACY AND PERMISSION

One of the roles of policymakers is to create conditions in which local innovation is actively encouraged and supported. Change is often difficult, not least when it involves challenging practices that have long been taken for granted. I said earlier that culture is a set of permissions about what is and what is not acceptable behavior. Policymakers can facilitate change at all levels by advocating for it and by giving schools permission to break old habits in the interests of breaking new ground.

Providing Care

HIGH STANDARDS

It's essential to have high standards in schools in all areas of learning. That has never been in doubt. High standards can inspire achievement and enable people to accomplish more than they imagined they could. This is as true of music and dance as it is of math and engineering. To be effective, reaching the standards should be a spur to achievement rather than an end in itself. It's essential to have an agreement on what those standards should be and a collaborative process of mutual respect to reach that agreement.

INTELLIGENT ACCOUNTABILITY

High standards are not only about what students do. They are essential in teaching, administration, and leadership. Accountability should not be a one-way street. Certainly, educators should be accountable for their effectiveness. So too should the policymakers who affect their work. Accountability implies responsibility and control. If people are to be accountable, it should be for factors they can control. An intelligent system of accountability should take proper account of factors in students' lives that schools may mitigate but cannot control, and it should operate across all areas and levels of the system.

CONTINUOUS PROFESSIONAL DEVELOPMENT

Teaching is a highly demanding profession. As the world changes and the demands increase, it's essential that teachers have regular opportunities to hone their professional expertise. School development is really a process of professional development. Continuing professional development of teachers is not a luxury. It is an essential investment in the success of students, their schools, and their communities.

Changing Course

If the standards movement were working as intended, there would be no reason to change course. But it is not. Policymakers around the world know that. Some of the most interesting changes are happening in states that formerly championed it. NCLB was largely based on policies that originated in the state of Texas. Parts of that state are now leading the way to more personalized strategies that take proper account of the different talents of students and the needs of different parts of the state itself.

This is exactly what veteran Texas state representative Jimmie Don Aycock had in mind when he noted to me that "The economic and social issues across Texas are vastly different—from someone up in the panhandle in the wind farms, to someone in the petroleum refineries, to all points in between. Giving the local districts the means to craft different educational strategies for their part of the state is very important."

Jimmie is the author of House Bill 5, which passed unanimously in 2013 in both the Texas House and Texas Senate and made significant changes in graduation requirements and the number of state tests Texas students need to take. It also offers new paths to graduation that recognize that different students coming out of high school have many different goals for their futures.

"All my service in the legislature has been education-related. In fact, I tell people it was the only thing that was important enough to bring me out of retirement. Close to 40 or 50 percent of our students were simply either being pushed aside with very little offering of job readiness or adequate educational background to find a job. That's just unacceptable. Hopefully, this bill will include reasonable educational offerings for kids that are not bound for college. Some of them are not bound for college for academic reasons, some are not bound for financial reasons, and some just don't want to go—they've got something they want to do that doesn't require a four-year degree.

"I think most people agree that most kids will require some form of advanced skill training, whether they get those skills in high school or after high school. The bill gives the flexibility to let students start toward getting an employable skill and/or an employable skill set that gets them a job. Just because kids aren't headed toward a college degree, they aren't failures. What we're finding is that once kids see that some goal is achievable, they and their parents are reengaging and seeing a goal to education that they simply weren't seeing before. I think we may actually see not only improved vocational and career decisions, but we may see improved college-going decisions that say, 'Oh, I can really do that if what I take is important.' These are conversations that were just not taking place. If it does nothing but engage the students and the parents, I think it will be worthwhile.

"We're reducing the number of high-stakes tests from fifteen to five. Still, we might be looking at one in four students next year who are not ready to graduate on time. If we had done fifteen, I think that number might have exceeded 40 percent and even approached 50 percent. Many of them will have completed their course work and gotten a grade in the course that was successful. If you have a lot of high-stakes end-of-course exams, you're going to face a situation where kids have done well in school, have done everything they think they need to do, and still don't get through that end-of-course exam. The question is, do they get the grades too easily? Is the test flawed? Or do they not take tests well? It's probably some of all of the above.

"The bill is somewhat nuanced in that in order for it to work properly, we have to deal with all three pieces: testing, curriculum, and accountability. There was a conscious decision to roll all three together. If we dealt with any one piece without dealing with the other two, I think it would have had some potentially really bad consequences. When you balance all three together, I think it's a functional compendium of legislation that says, 'This is for students, this is for the needs of the state, and here's a better way for holding districts accountable.' It's a very workable bill, and most educators are pleased with it. Parents and students seem pleased with it. Some of the reform folks seem pleased with it, and some don't.

"The folks who have expressed the most concern about the bill had heavily bought into No Child Left Behind and felt that if you test students more, raise high standards, and keep the pressure on, we will excel and move forward in our educational results for children. I've got to admit that there was a time that I felt that way. The thing we missed in that thinking was that that's a nice mechanical view of education. It's like a factory-production view. What that fails to take into account is that human beings are not all alike. You can do the same thing and get very different results sometimes. So I backed away from that thinking and I realized that No Child Left Behind is left largely on that kind of thinking and I just don't believe that anymore."

The transition from standardization to personalization, from conformity to creativity, is not only happening in the United States. It's happening in many parts of the world, with equally dramatic results.

Doing It Differently

Policymaking is a collective process, and a complicated one too. But the real agents of change know that an impassioned individual can transform the process and change the world. Sometimes that sort of leadership comes from answering a call.

LIGHTNING STRIKES IN ARGENTINA

When the Argentinian economy crashed in 2001, Silvina Gvirtz realized that her life in academia needed to take a dramatic turn. She had been awarded her PhD and had been focused on educational research, but with so many newly impoverished children in her country, she knew she needed to step out from behind her desk. Accessing grants from many large companies, she created an ambitious project to improve the quality of education at underfunded schools. Working with poor districts around the country, she spearheaded an initiative to involve communities in making their schools better. The results were inspiring, with the dropout rate going from 30 percent to 1 percent and the repetition rate (the rate at which students needed to repeat a grade) going from 20 percent to 0.5 percent.

"We worked with local partners," she told me. "We territorialized to make the local policies stronger. We worked with the local teachers and the principals. It was important that the principals knew the goals we wanted to achieve with them, and that they could give their input to the teachers. We never used negative reinforcement. We would get into the classroom with the teachers and work with them on concrete problems. We worked a lot like doctors do, where they sit together to solve a case. The teachers felt there was someone there for them, to help them."

As effective as the program was and continues to be, Silvina realized that she had a problem with scale. If she truly wanted to help as many students as she could, she was going to have to go into politics, even though that wasn't her natural inclination. She became minister of education of the province of Buenos Aires, serving in that role for nearly eight years. Most recently, she started Conectar Igualdad, a program dedicated to linking Argentinian students with technology. As I write this, Conectar Igualdad has distributed more than three and a half million netbooks to students in her country. The netbooks are filled with open-source applications to facilitate learning, but the goal with the program has always been to light a spark.

"For me, you have three kinds of kids," she said. "You have

passive consumers of technology. They consume the most well-known programs, but they don't understand the technology. Then you have intelligent consumers, which are the kids that distinguish the right from wrong on the Web. They know more about technology, but they don't produce. Then there are the kids who are also producers. Open source allows them to do that. If you want a kid who's creative, you have to teach them how to program. When you give a kid a computer who never had one, you reduce the digital gap. This can be an incredible device for other disciplines and for making them more creative."

Once satisfied to work exclusively at the theoretical level, Silvina Gvirtz now assumes a position of leadership in a number of domains. She's executive director of Conectar Igualdad, a professor at the University of San Martin, a researcher at the National Council for Scientific and Technical Research in Argentina, a visiting professor at the State University of New York in Albany, and she's the series editor for two education book programs. Circumstances demanded that she become a leader, and she answered the call.

CREATIVE CHINA

Jiang Xueqin saw a problem in China. The numbers were great—as I mentioned earlier, Shanghai ranked at the top of the latest PISA league tables—but it came as a result of relentless drilling and nearly exclusive focus on test-taking performance, a process that he feels "rewards utilitarian, unethical, short-sighted behavior that destroys a student's intrinsic curiosity, creativity, and love of learning. In general, any education system that highlights achievement and goals above process and attitude is, in my opinion, bad for students."[2] This system is known as the *gaokao* system (the *gaokao* is China's college entrance exam). Much as Western education was modeled on a system appropriate for the Industrial

Revolution, the *gaokao* system was designed for a time when China needed as many engineers and middle managers as it could generate. The system was about generating big numbers and then sending a huge quantity of students to the United States for graduate school. But China is changing. The middle class is expanding, and it is less reliant on manufacturing—and it needs to produce a different kind of student. "If China is to progress, it needs people with different skill sets. It needs entrepreneurs, designers, managers—the sort of people China doesn't have," he said.[3]

So in 2008, Jiang Xueqin started working on a new kind of school, in the city of Shenzhen. The students didn't take the *gaokao*. They spent more time writing. They helped run a coffee shop and a newspaper. They learned to be entrepreneurs, and how to empathize. They participated in social service.

Jiang Xueqin has since moved on to Tsinghua International School, where he is deputy principal and has continued to promote this next-generation approach to educating Chinese students. He also recently published a book, *Creative China*, where he talks about his experiences teaching creativity and offers a platform for broadening his approach.

ASKING FOR CHANGE IN THE MIDDLE EAST

Dr. Amin Amin sees human capacity building as the biggest challenge in the Arab region. "The need for twenty-first-century human capital is creating new pressure on the existing education systems to be effective and fully capable of catering to the specific needs of each student," he said.[4] This led him to found ASK for Human Capacity Building (the acronym stands for "attitude, skills, and knowledge").[5] One of the primary goals of ASK is to provide education services that will raise a new generation of critical thinkers in the region. These services operate on five platforms:

professional development for educators, teacher licensing, customized content development, monitoring and assessment, and consultancies with both NGOs and schools.

Dr. Amin's work has already had a widespread effect, touching nearly four thousand schools since 2011. For this, he was named Global Endeavor Advocate and Mentor of the Year by the mentoring organization, the Mowgli Foundation.[6]

TRANSFORMING SCOTLAND

Currently, one of the most interesting national education initiatives is in Scotland. It illustrates many of the principles and conditions we've been considering. At the center of the initiative is the Curriculum for Excellence, a general framework for whole-school transformation. Like the curriculum in Finland,[7] but unlike many reform initiatives in the U.K. and the United States, the Curriculum for Excellence was developed through a long process of consultation with educators, parents, students, and business and community leaders throughout Scotland. It presents a bold vision for the future of education in the country and a broad framework for bringing it about. This is not a prescriptive framework, imposed from above. Like A+, it allows schools considerable room for interpretation to meet the particular needs of their own students and communities. Underlying this process is a thoughtful analysis of the challenges of implementation and a cogent theory of change.

This strategy has been developed in association with the International Futures Forum (IFF), a worldwide group of educators, policymakers, and researchers. As I have done, the IFF identifies three forms of understanding in effecting change, which they call their three horizons: Horizon 1 is the existing system, Horizon 2 is the process of transition, and Horizon 3 is the new state of affairs, which the process of change is intended to bring about. These same principles lie at the heart of the transformation that is taking place across the Atlantic from Scotland, in the Canadian city of Ottawa.

LISTENING TO OTTAWA

Like me, Peter Gamwell is originally from Liverpool, the U.K. He is now the superintendent of instruction for the Ottawa-Carleton District School Board (OCDSB), an organization that has proven to be a standard-bearer for school boards throughout the world because of its dedication to inclusion and creativity.

According to Peter, the breakthrough moment for OCDSB came during a 2004 meeting about leadership with a range of staff within the district. Peter and the others involved had been running the program for about a half hour when a hand went up in the back of the room. The man asked what he was doing at the meeting, and he was told that he was there to share his ideas on leadership. The man seemed surprised by this response and said he'd been working in the district as a custodian for twenty years and had never had any indication that his ideas on leadership had any value. That was when Peter realized he needed to conduct a districtwide initiative to embrace creative contributions from everyone involved, including staff, parents, and, of course, students.

"Everyone has a creative capacity," he told me. "Everyone has inner brilliance. We need to recognize and value that and find ways of tapping into it. If you can do that, you'll maximize your opportunity to develop a culture of engagement, belonging, and creative capacity."

One way in which Peter fosters a climate of creativity is by canvassing everyone involved to "find out what people have to offer, listen to the stories they tell, find out their unique capacities, and grow them from there." Another is to help everyone involved in the system understand that they really do have innate capacities to be creative.

"If you go to a kindergarten class and you look at the kids, they're bouncing with creativity. If you go into an intermediate class and ask, 'Who's creative?' they do the most incredible thing. They point to one or two of the kids in the class. It's so sad. That's what we were finding with our adults as well. Our goal was to get people to stop pointing away from themselves and to point into themselves, to recognize that every single one of them had creative capacities."

The organization followed this with a districtwide call for creative initiatives. At first, the responses were measured and limited. Once Peter and his team made it clear that they genuinely wanted these contributions, they received hundreds of them. The ideas ranged from new classroom programs, to efforts to reach out to autistic children by introducing them to entrepreneurialism, to cost-cutting contributions from the maintenance staff.

Many of the initiatives have been targeted on personalizing the education the students receive by making a wider range of course offerings available to them and broadening their horizons.

"This is not about saying that mathematics and language aren't important. Of course they are. They're absolutely vital. It's about making sure that we don't let kids go through school not knowing what their strengths are. That happens with many kids. This is about achieving a balance so we don't have one kid leaving the school saying, 'I don't know what I'm good at.' When you have teachers in classrooms who are excited about sharing their passions and their abilities, it's going to have a very positive impact on the learning environment."

I asked Peter what he would recommend for policymakers in other districts who wanted to foster the air of creativity and potential that exists at OCDSB. His first response was "prepare for a bumpy ride." Effecting these changes at OCDSB was neither immediate nor smooth. But then he sent the following list:

- Take the temperature of your learning organization. Find out how people are feeling about the learning culture. Ask serious and thought-provoking questions. What are people's views on learning, leadership, and creativity? Where does imagination fit in the organization on the individual, group, and organizational levels? What do people believe about leadership and the characteristics and behaviors of ideal leaders? Does the organizational culture foster informal leadership and personal creativity? What is the organization doing to help or hinder individual, group, and organizational creativity? How could we improve? Be prepared for honest answers. Tell people that you are sincere in wanting their real opinions.
- Use the information to take a strength-based approach to culture change. Start this immediately. Create a collaboratively designed vision or leadership narrative that captures the ideas that emerge from what you have learned. This collaborative model needs to be inclusive of employees from across employee groups. The hierarchies need to be flattened, and people need to see that this is the case.
- Put in place practices and structures that demonstrate to people that you are listening to their ideas and responding from an appreciative and strength-based perspective.
- The conversation needs to be long term and continuous. You need to develop structures through which people's voices can be heard. A culture of listening and storytelling is crucial. People will respond in different ways to this, so you need to provide multiple opportunities for input. Once people feel a genuine sense of belonging, then the learning culture ignites.
- Break down the barriers of your organization and bring in peo-

ple from the outside. They will provide a totally different perspective. There are amazing transformational stories all around as businesses, municipalities, arts and science organizations, and a host of others try to figure out how to respond to and operate in this new creative age. Seek them out. Invite them in. Visit them. Engage them in dialogue. Through this collision of ideas, this sparking of curiosity, you start to spark a different kind of dynamism.

Wherever these sorts of approaches are properly practiced—from Argentina to Ottawa, from Texas to Dubai—the results are similar. So, if the principles and conditions are so clear, why are they not being adopted everywhere?

What's the Problem?

There are many obstacles to the sorts of transformation we have been discussing. Some have to do with the inherent conservatism of institutions, including schools themselves, some with conflicting views about the sorts of changes that are needed, some with culture and ideology, and some with political self-interest.

RISK AVERSION

In *Weapons of Mass Instruction*, John Taylor Gatto speaks about a matrix of constraints on innovation in schools. A former New York City Teacher of the Year, he retired in disillusion with the impact of the factory-oriented, standards culture on teachers and students alike. After a lifetime in education, he said, he had come to think of schools "with their long-term, cell-block-style forced confinement of both students and teachers as virtual factories of childishness." He could not see why they had to be that way.

"My own experience revealed to me what many other teachers must learn along the way too, yet keep to themselves for fear of reprisal: if we wanted we could easily and inexpensively jettison the old, stupid structures and help kids take an education rather than merely receive schooling. We could encourage the best qualities of youthfulness—curiosity, adventure, resilience, the capacity for surprising insight—simply by being more flexible about time, texts, and tests, by introducing kids to truly competent adults, and by giving each student the autonomy he or she needs in order to take a risk every now and then. But we don't do that."[8]

This resistance to change old habits can operate at all levels of the system, from classroom to state assemblies. There are other factors too.

CULTURE AND IDEOLOGY

Education policy is inevitably enmeshed in other cultural interests, and local and national cultures deeply affect how education is conducted. In parts of Asia, for example, there is a strong culture in school of compliance and of deference to authority, which is rooted in more general traditions in Asian thought and culture.

In the United States and the U.K., right-wing politicians in particular often favor the breakup and commercialization of public education. Their general commitment to market economies leads naturally to the view that education can be improved by applying that thinking to schools and parental choice. The political enthusiasm for these initiatives has as much to do with the general values of capitalism in these cultures as it has to any real understanding of their efficacy in education itself.

PROFITS AND INFLUENCE

There is a push by some politicians to open public education to market forces—through charter schools, preschools, and independent schools operated by for-profit corporations. None of these has been shown as a category to be better than well-supported public schools.[9]

POLITICS AND AMBITION

Not all policymakers in education actually care about education. Some are career politicians or administrators who are using education as a platform for professional advancement. Their own ambitions in education may be tied up with other political interests and motives. One of the reasons they put such a premium on test results is that they are preoccupied with short-term gains they can use in the next election cycle. In many democracies, these happen every four years or so. With the increasing clamor of the news cycle, campaigning starts eighteen months or more before. So politicians have a couple of years in office to get results they can use on the stump. They go for measurable results in politically sensitive areas like literacy, numeracy, and job readiness. The PISA rankings are tailor-made for political posturing.

COMMAND AND CONTROL

Politicians are often drawn naturally to command-and-control approaches. For all the rhetoric of promoting individual fulfillment and the public good, there is a well-documented history in education of social control, conformity, and mass compliance. In some respects, mass education is, and always was, a process of social engineering. Sometimes the political intentions have been benign and sometimes not. I said at the beginning that education is an "essentially contested concept." It is, and sometimes we disagree not only about means but also about the ends of education. No amount of debate on strategy will result in consensus if the purposes we have in mind are opposed.

Organizing Change

We noted the need for inspiring leadership to create a climate of innovation and possibility in education. I've been privileged to work with many inspiring leaders in education. One of the most inspiring is Tim Brighouse. A distinguished thought leader in the U.K., he has also been a transformative chief executive in two major school districts—Oxfordshire and Birmingham—and led important programs of strategic innovation in London and throughout the country. He knows from long experience that there is not a simple line from vision to change. It is a constant process of action, improvisation, evaluation, and reorientation in light of experience and circumstances. He sometimes uses this chart to summarize the essential elements: vision, skills, incentives, resources, and an action plan:[10]

Effecting change needs all of these elements. People need a vision of the future they are being asked to move toward. They need to feel that they are capable of change and have the skills that are needed for it. They need to believe that there are good reasons for changing and that the place they aim to be will be better than where they are now, and that it will be worth the effort of making the transition. They need to have the personal and material resources to make the transition. And they need a convincing plan of action to get them there; or at the very least, one that will get them on their way, even if it changes as they go.

One of the biggest obstacles to change is the lack of alignment between the various elements that are needed to bring it about. If one or more is missing, the process can stumble and usually does. It happens like this:[11]

	Skills	Incentives	Resources	Action Plan	=	Confusion
Vision		Incentives	Resources	Action Plan	=	Anxiety
Vision	Skills		Resources	Action Plan	=	Resistance
Vision	Skills	Incentives		Action Plan	=	Frustration
Vision	Skills	Incentives	Resources		=	Diffusion

If all of these elements are in place, there's a reasonable chance of helping people move from where they are now to where they want to be. The role of leaders is to help ensure that they are moving in the right direction. And in the end, that too is the role of policy and of policymakers in education.

Your Move

Many of the principles and conditions we've discussed throughout this book are as old as education itself. They lie at the heart of well-rounded, successful schools everywhere, and they always have. My own work with schools and governments over the last forty years has always been based on these principles, and, in one way or another, the many examples of transformation that we've looked at in this book clearly illustrate them. The challenge now is to apply them everywhere. As we have emphasized repeatedly, there are many wonderful schools, with great and hopeful people working in them. But too many of them are laboring against the dominant culture of education rather than being helped by it.

Benjamin Franklin, the American statesman and polymath, knew that a balanced, liberal education for all was essential for the proper flourishing of the American dream. It is essential to the fulfillment of the dreams of people everywhere. As the world becomes more complicated and perilous, the need to transform education and create schools for people has never been more urgent.

Franklin once said that there are three sorts of people in the world: those who are immovable, those who are movable, and those who move. We know what he meant. Some people don't see the need for change and don't want to. They squat like boulders in a stream while the flow of events rushes around them. My advice is to leave them alone. Tide and time are on the side of transformation, and the currents of change may leave them behind.

There are those who are movable. They see the need for change. They may not know what to do, but they're open to being convinced and to act if they are. Work with them and go where their energy is. Form partnerships and make dreams and plans.

And there are those who move: the change agents who can see the shape of a different future and are determined to bring it about through their own actions and by working with others. They know that they don't always need permission. As Gandhi said, if you want to change the world, you must be the change you want to see. Because when enough people move, that is a movement. And if the movement has enough energy, that is a revolution. And in education, that's exactly what we need.

Afterword

WHEN I LEFT HIGH SCHOOL in the U.K. in 1968, I went to college and, by an unaccountable stroke of fortune, found myself at Bretton Hall, the renowned college of the liberal and performing arts in West Riding of Yorkshire. Bretton was a jewel in the crown of an outstanding education district led by the inestimable Sir Alec Clegg, a pioneer of transformation in public education. It was a triple treat. Bretton was led by a young scientist of penetrating intelligence, Dr. Alyn Davies. He was also a subtle educational leader who honed the wits and sensibilities of staff and students alike with charm, erudition, and political savoir faire.

The college was populated with an array of idiosyncratic and passionate faculty who in their different ways intrigued and exasperated us into producing our best. And then there were the students. We were an eclectic crowd in ages, talents, and inclination, and we found ourselves intensively immersed for several years in each other's company, around a grand mansion house, set in hundreds of acres of the most magnificent countryside in the U.K. And it was free, courtesy of the enlightened government policies of the day. I know.

I left with a degree in education and a qualification to teach English and drama in elementary and secondary schools. Along the way, I got to learn from some of the best teachers I've ever met, work alongside some of the most talented students I've known, and teach in some of the most interesting and creative schools I've ever been in. I also became intrigued by the perturbations of public education and the need to make it personal.

Personalizing education might sound revolutionary, but this revolution is not new. Its roots are deep in the history of education. In the seventeenth century John Locke advocated the simultaneous education of the body, character, and mind—in other words, the whole person. Many different individuals and types of institutions have carried the torch of personalized forms of education that follow the natural grain of children's development, and the importance of these forms of education for more equitable and civilized societies.

Advocates and practitioners of personalized and holistic education come from many cultures and perspectives. They include Jean-Jacques Rousseau, Johann Heinrich Pestalozzi, John Dewey, Michael Duane, Kurt Hahn, Jiddu Krishnamurti, Dorothy Heathcote, Jean Piaget, Maria Montessori, Lev Vygotsky, Sir Alec Clegg, Noam Chomsky, and many more. These various approaches don't add up to a single school of thought or practice. What they have in common is a passion for forming education around how children learn and of what they need to learn to form themselves.

Maria Montessori was a physician and educator. She began her career in education in San Lorenzo, Italy, in the early twentieth century, working with poor and disadvantaged children. Montessori stressed personalized education. "The teacher shall observe whether the child interests himself," she said, "how he is interested in it and for how long, even noticing the expression of his face. The teacher must take great care, she said, not to offend the principles of liberty. For, if she provokes the child to make an unnatural effort, she will no longer know what is the spontaneous activity of the child."[1] There are now more than twenty thousand Montessori schools throughout the world that follow Montessori's approach to learning.[2]

Rudolf Steiner was as an Austrian philosopher and social reformer who developed a humanist approach to pedagogy now called the Steiner Waldorf Schools Fellowship. The Steiner approach is built around the individual needs of the *whole* of each child—academic, physical, emotional, and spiritual. The first Steiner school opened in 1919. Today there are nearly three thousand of them in sixty countries using Steiner's philosophies and methods.[3]

Interestingly, Steiner also developed a particular system of organic agriculture based on the principles of ecology and sustainability. His system of biodynamic agriculture follows the natural cycles of the seasons and makes no use of chemical fertilizers or pesticides. It is now in wide use in many parts of the world as a specific practice within the general field of organic farming.

A. S. Neill founded the Summerhill School in 1921, creating the model for all democratic schools that followed. The school's philosophy is "to allow freedom for the individual, each child being able to take responsibility for their own life, and following their own interests to develop into the person that they personally feel that they are meant to be. This leads to an inner self-confidence and real acceptance of themselves as individuals."[4]

The list goes on.

These various approaches to personalized learning are often grouped together under the general banner of "progressive education," which some critics seem to imagine is the polar opposite of "traditional education." This is a damaging misconception that tends toward many false dichotomies. The history of education policy has been an oscillation between these supposed poles. The standards movement is the latest swing. Effective education is al-

ways a balance between rigor and freedom, tradition and innovation, the individual and the group, theory and practice, the inner
world and the outer world.

As the pendulum moves back, as it invariably does, the task,
as it has always been, is to help schools and students find equilib-
rium. There is no permanent utopia for education, just a constant
striving to create the best conditions for real people in real communities in a constantly changing world. That's what living in a
complex, dynamic system means. The need is urgent. The experience of education is always personal but the issues are increasingly global.

Revolutions are defined not only by the ideas that drive them
but by the scale of their impact. Whether or not ideas provoke
revolutions depends on circumstances—on whether they resonate with enough people at the right time to move them to action. The ideas behind the revolution that I'm encouraging have
been around for a long time. But the appetite for them is growing
now and the changes are gathering pace.

Many of the principles and practices that I'm advocating have
been practiced successfully, though in limited ways, throughout
the history of education—in public schools, in whole districts, in
experimental and laboratory schools, in deprived urban areas, in
bucolic private schools, and now in at least one entire country. So
what is new? First, there is the rapidly changing context in which
we are living that makes it urgent that these approaches are properly understood and applied on a mass scale. Second, we now
have technologies that make it possible to personalize education
in wholly new ways. Third, there is a groundswell of feeling in
many parts of the world that a tectonic shift in how we think
about and practice education is essential.

The schools that we have looked at in this book are all trying
to offer the kind of rigorous, personalized, and engaged educa-

tion that everyone needs but that so many have too long been denied. They are part of a long revolution. This time it has to be for everyone, not for a select few. The stakes have never been higher, and the outcomes could hardly matter more.

Notes

INTRODUCTION: **One Minute to Midnight**

1. I've written in more detail in other books and publications about some of the concepts and practices that underpin my overall arguments in this one. They include *Learning Through Drama* (1977), *The Arts in Schools: Principals, Practice and Provision* (1982), *All Our Futures: Creativity, Culture and Education* (1999), *Out of Our Minds: Learning to Be Creative* (2001 and 2011), *The Element: How Finding Your Passion Changes Everything* (2009), and *Finding Your Element: How to Discover Your Talents and Passions and Transform Your Life* (2013).

2. Especially since my TED talks have become popular, I've debated my ideas with all sorts of people around the world and seen them written about too, sometimes by people who say they agree with me and sometimes by people who do not. Sometimes people say they agree with me but probably wouldn't if they understood what I was really saying. And there are those who misrepresent what I think and then criticize me for thinking that. I'm always happy to account for what I do think, but not for what I do not. If we're to make progress in education, it's important to know what we're agreeing or disagreeing about. I'll try to be as clear as possible about my position so that you can decide one way or the other. See http://edition.cnn.com/2002/ALLPOLITICS/01/19/bush.democrats .radio/index.html.

CHAPTER ONE: **Back to Basics**

1. Having helped Smokey Road to make progress that might have seemed unimaginable nine years earlier—progress that came because she chose to find the wiggle room within the mandates—Laurie has moved on to her next challenge. We actually conducted our interview while she was driving to Kalispell, Montana, where she has become superintendent of the Evergreen School District. I haven't had a chance to reconnect with

her since she's been there, but my guess is that she isn't letting either tradition or external dictates define what's best for her students.

2. "Bush Calls Education 'Civil Civil Rights Issue of Our Time.'" CNN .com, January 19, 2014. Retrieved from http://edition.cnn.com/2002/ ALLPOLITICS/01/19/bush.democrats.radio/index.

3. In 2012, the President of China, Xi Jinping, said, "Our people have an ardent love for life. They wish to have better education, more stable jobs, more income, greater social security, better medical and health care, improved housing conditions, and a better environment." "Transcript: Xi Jinping's Speech at the Unveiling of the New Chinese Leadership (video)." *South China Morning Post*, November 15, 2012. See http://www.scmp.com/news/18th-party-congress/article/1083153/ transcript-xi-jinpings-speech-unveiling-new-chinese.

4. "Only when there's progress in the quality of education," Rousseff argues, "can we form young people that are . . . able to lead the country to the full benefits of technology and knowledge." Edouardo J. Gomez. "Dilma's Education Dilemma." *Americas Quarterly*, Fall 2011.

5. Organisation for Economic Co-operation and Development (OECD). "PISA Key Findings." Retrieved from http://www.oecd.org/pisa/key findings.

6. See, for example, http://internationalednews.com/2013/12/04/pisa-2012 -headlines-from-around-the-world/or http://www.artofteachingscience .org/pisa-headlines-from-the-uk-world-league-standings.

7. U.S. Department of Education. "The Threat of Educational Stagnation and Complacency." Remarks of U.S. Secretary of Education Arne Duncan at the release of the 2012 PISA, December 3, 2013. See http://www .ed.gov/news/speeches/threat-educational-stagnation-and-complacency.

8. "Race to the Top marks a historic moment in American education. This initiative offers bold incentives to states willing to spur systemic reform to improve teaching and learning in America's schools. Race to the Top has ushered in significant change in our education system, particularly in raising standards and aligning policies and structures to the goal of college and career readiness. Race to the Top has helped drive states nationwide to pursue higher standards, improve teacher effectiveness, use data effectively in the classroom, and adopt new strategies to help struggling schools." The White House. "Race to the Top." Retrieved from http:// www.whitehouse.gov/issues/education/k-12/race-to-the-top.

9. "Background and Analysis: The Federal Education Budget." *New America Foundation Federal Education Budget Project*, April 30, 2014. Retrieved from http://febp.newamerica.net/background-analysis/education-federal -budget.

10. Sean Cavanagh. "Global Education Market Tops $4 Trillion, Analysis Shows." Education Week.com, *Marketplace K-12*. February 7, 2013. Retrieved from http://blogs.edweek.org/edweek/marketplacek12/2013/02/size_of_global_e-learning_market_4_trillion_analysis_how.html.
11. Elizabeth Harrington. "Education Spending Up 64% Under No Child Left Behind But Test Scores Improve Little." CNSNews.com, September 26, 2011. Retrieved from http://www.cnsnews.com/news/article/education-spending-64-under-no-child-left-behind-test-scores-improve-little.
12. U.S. Department of Education. "A Nation at Risk: The Imperative for Educational Reform." April 1983. See http://datacenter.spps.org/uploads/sotw_a_nation_at_risk_1983.pdf.
13. World Bank Education Statistics. Retrieved from http://datatopics.worldbank.org/education/EdstatsHome.aspx.
14. "Given a common structure, but distinct environments and a still separate and unequal experience for many students, what is the purpose of high school in the twenty-first century?" asks Johns Hopkins research scientist Robert Balfanz. "The weight of evidence," he says, "suggests a growing consensus among both the students who attend the schools and the school districts and states that organize them that regardless of the characteristics of a school or its students, the primary purpose of high school today is to prepare students for college."
15. For a useful analysis of this trend, see Diane Ravitch. *Reign of Error: The Hoax of the Privatization Movement and the Danger to America's Public Schools.* New York: Knopf, 2013.
16. National Center for Education Statistics. "PISA 2012 Results." Retrieved from http://nces.ed.gov/surveys/pisa/pisa2012/index.asp.
17. OECD. "PIAAC Survey of Adult Skills 2012—USA." Retrieved from http://www.oecd.org/site/piaac/surveyofadultskills.htm.
18. Paul R. Lehman. "Another Perspective: Reforming Education—The Big Picture." *Music Educators Journal*, Vol. 98, No. 4 (June 2012), pp. 29–30.
19. "2006 National Geographic Roper Survey of Geographic Literacy." *National Geographic.* Retrieved from http://www.nationalgeographic.com/roper2006/findings.html.
20. See, for example, this from 2008: http://www.theguardian.com/education/2008/nov/19/bad-at-geography, and this from 2013: http://www.britishairways.com/en-gb/bamediacentre/newsarticles?articleID=20140115072329&articleType=LatestNews#.VG226zB1-uY.
21. In the U.K., graduate unemployment increased from 5.6 percent in 2000 to 12 percent in 2011. There were increases over the same period

throughout most of mainland Europe with one or two exceptions, notably Finland where the rate dropped from 14.8 percent to 7.4 percent. In October 2011, the unemployment rate for twenty- to twenty-nine-year-olds in the United States who had graduated from college in 2011 was 12.6 percent. The rate was 13.5 percent for those who recently had earned bachelor's degrees and 8.6 percent for those who recently had earned advanced degrees. Despite modest improvement since the most recent peak in October 2009, the unemployment rates of recent college graduates remained above the rates prior to the 2007–2009 recession. http://www.bls.gov/opub/ted/2013/ted_20130405.htm. In the United States in 2014, 8.5 percent of young people between ages twenty-one and twenty-four, 3.3 percent over twenty-five, 16.8 percent new grads were "underemployed." http://www.slate.com/blogs/moneybox/2014/05/08/unemployment_and_the_class_of_2014_how_bad_is_the_job_market_for_new_college.html. See also http://www.epi.org/publication/class-of-2014/ and http://www.bls.gov/emp/ep_chart_001.htm.

22. European Commission. "Youth Unemployment Trends." Eurostat Unemployment Statistics, December 2013. Retrieved from http://epp.eurostat.ec.europa.eu/statistics_explained/index.php/Unemployment_statistics#Youth_unemployment_trends.

23. During the period 1990–2012 unemployment rates for college graduates in the United States peaked in 2010 at the height of the recession and had averaged around 2.9 percent for all college graduates and averaged 4.3 percent for recent college graduates. Jaison R. Abel, Richard Deitz, and Yaquin Su. "Are Recent College Graduates Finding Good Jobs?" Federal Reserve Bank of New York report, *Current Issues in Economics and Finance*, Vol. 20, No. 1 (2014), pp. 1–8.

24. In 2008, more than 35 percent of college graduates were underemployed; by June of last year, the Federal Reserve Bank of New York reported that a whopping 44 percent of graduates were underemployed. And it's not just because of the recession. The number has been rising since 2001. More education doesn't exactly help; in fact going to graduate school can make things worse. In 2008, 22 percent of people with PhDs or professional degrees were underemployed. That number rises all the way to 59 percent for people with master's degrees.

25. "Sustainable and Liveable Cities: Toward Ecological Civilization." *China National Human Development Report 2013*. February 2, 2014. Retrieved from http://www.cn.undp.org/content/dam/china/docs/Publications/UNDP-CH_2013%20NHDR_EN.pdf.

26. OECD. *Education at a Glance 2013: OECD Indicators*. OECD Publishing, 2013. DOI: 10.1787/eag-2013-en.

27. Unlike other forms of debt, student debt cannot be relieved through bankruptcy. This fact was welcome news to the debt collection industry. Since the recession of 2008, debt collectors have been having lean times. Many corporate debtors defaulted and went into bankruptcy proceedings, thwarting debt collectors of their commissions. Student debt is different. It must be paid. I read an interview with the head of a collection agency, who said delightedly that the future of his industry now looked bright again. In what struck me as a chilling epithet, he indicated that the prospects for recovering student debt were "mouthwatering"—a grim example of a system decomposing.

28. Donghoon Lee. "Household Debt and Credit: Student Debt." Federal Reserve Bank of New York media advisory, February 18, 2013.

29. For more on this, see, for example, Tony Wagner. *The Global Achievement Gap: Why Even Our Best Schools Don't Teach the New Survival Skills Our Children Need—and What We Can Do About It*. New York: Basic Books, 2014.

30. Yong Zhao. "Test Scores vs. Entrepreneurship: PISA, TIMSS, and Confidence." Zhaolearning.com, June 6, 2012. Retrieved from http://zhaolearning.com/2012/06/06/test-scores-vs-entrepreneurship-pisa-timss-and-confidence/.

31. "The Enterprise of the Future." IBM 2008 Global CEO Study. Retrieved from https://www-935.ibm.com/services/uk/gbs/pdf/ibm_ceo_study_2008.pdf.

32. http://zhaolearning.com/2012/06/06/test-scores-vs-entrepreneurship-pisa-timss-and-confidence/.

33. Yong Zhao. "'Not Interested in Being #1': Shanghai May Ditch PISA." Zhaolearning.com, May 25, 2014. Retrieved from http://zhaolearning.com/2014/05/25/not-interested-in-being-#1-shanghai-may-ditch-pisa/.

34. U.S. Census Bureau. "Current Population Survey 2013." *Annual Social and Economic Supplement 2012*. Retrieved from http://www.census.gov/hhes/www/cpstables/032013/pov/pov28_001.htm.

35. In D.C., Oregon, Alaska, Georgia, and Nevada, and in many inner-city districts, for example, graduation rates are well below 70 percent.

36. Henry M. Levin and Cecilia E. Rouse. "The True Cost of High School Dropouts." *The New York Times*, January 25, 2012. Retreived from http://www.nytimes.com/2012/01/26/opinion/the-true-cost-of-high-school-dropouts.html?_r=3&.

37. Daniel A. Domenech. "Executive Perspective: Real Learning on the Vocational Track." AASA, May 2013. Retrieved from http://www.aasa.org/content.aspx?id=28036.

38. Mariana Haynes. "On the Path to Equity: Improving the Effectiveness of Beginning Teachers." Alliance for Excellent Education report, July 2014.
39. Richard M. Ingersoll. "Is There Really a Teacher Shortage?" University of Washington research report R-03-4, September 2003.
40. Carla Amurao. "Fact Sheet: How Bad Is the School-to-Prison Pipeline?" PBS.com, *Tavis Smiley Reports*. Retrieved from http://www.pbs.org/wnet/tavissmiley/tsr/education-under-arrest/school-to-prison-pipeline-fact-sheet/.
41. "School-to-Prison Pipeline." ACLU. Retrieved from www.aclu.org/school-prison-pipeline.
42. http://www.cea-ace.ca/sites/cea-ace.ca/files/cea-2012-wdydist-report-1.pdf.
43. "South Korea: System and School Organization." NCEE. Retrieved from http://www.ncee.org/programs-affiliates/center-on-international-education-benchmarking/top-performing-countries/south-korea-overview/south-korea-system-and-school-organization/.
44. Reeta Chakrabarti. "South Korea's Schools: Long Days, High Results." BBC.com, December, 2, 2013. Retrieved from http://www.bbc.com/news/education-25187993.
45. "Mental Health: Background of SUPRE." World Health Organization website. Retrieved from http://www.who.int/mental_health/prevention/suicide/background/en/.

CHAPTER TWO: **Changing Metaphors**

1. Edward Peters. "Demographics." Encyclopedia Britannica Online. Retreived June 17, 2014, from http://www.britannica.com/EBchecked/topic/195896/history-of-Europe/58335/Demographics.
2. Thomas Jefferson. *The Works of Thomas Jefferson*, ed. Paul Leicester Ford. New York: G. P. Putnam, 1904.
3. Secondary education in France, for example, has a two-stage structure. Stage one, *le collège*, caters to students age eleven through fifteen; stage two, *le lycée*, provides a three-year course preparing fifteen to eighteen-year-olds for the baccalaureate. Italy divides secondary education into two stages: The first stage, *la scuola secondaria di primo grado*, lasts three years and covers all subjects. The second stage, *la scuola secondaria di secondo grado*, lasts five years. The curriculum in the first two years of this second stage is mandatory; for the last three years, paths can be freely chosen. Secondary education in the United States refers to the last four years of statutory formal education (grades nine through twelve) either at high school or split between a final year of "junior high school" and three in high school.

4. We discuss this process in detail in *Finding Your Element*.

5. Richard won the school Head Teacher of the Year Award at the British National Teaching Awards in 2005, and in 2006 his work was celebrated at the UNESCO World Arts Education Conference in Lisbon, Portugal. These days, he travels around the globe working with a wide variety of organizations in the public and private sectors on education, leadership, change, and human capacity.

6. http://www.silentspring.org/legacy-rachel-carson.

7. For an account of how industrial and rural lifestyles have affected human health, see, for example, T. Campbell, T. Colin, and Thomas M. Campbell, *The China Study: The Most Comprehensive Study of Nutrition Ever Conducted and the Startling Implications for Diet, Weight Loss, and Long-term Health*. Dallas, TX: BenBella, 2005.

8. "Principles of Organic Agriculture." IFOAM. Retrieved from http://www.ifoam.org/en/organic-landmarks/principles-organic-agriculture.

9. See Partnership for 21st Century Skills website, http://www.p21.org.

10. James Truslow Adams. *The Epic of America*. Safety Harbor, FL: Simon Publications, 2001.

11. "Los Angeles, California Mayoral Election, 2013." Ballotpedia. See http://ballotpedia.org/LosAngeles,_California_mayoral_election,_2013.

CHAPTER THREE: **Changing Schools**

1. See North Star website, http://northstarteens.org/overview/.

2. "The Story of Liberated Learners." Retrieved from http://www.liberatedlearnersinc.org/the-story-of-liberated-learners/.

3. U.S. Department of Education. "A Nation at Risk: The Imperative for Educational Reform." April 1983. See http://datacenter.spps.org/uploads/sotw_a_nation_at_risk_1983.pdf.

4. Ibid.

5. For more on the Finnish education system, see P. Sahlberg. *Finnish Lessons 2.0: What Can the World Learn from Educational Change in Finland?* New York: Teachers College Press, 2014.

6. "What Are Complex Adaptive Systems?" Trojanmice.com. Retrieved from http://www.trojanmice.com/articles/complexadaptivesystems.htm.

7. For a general discussion around the dynamics of emergence, see Steven Johnson. Emergence: The Connected Lies of Ants, Brains, Cities and Software. New York: Scribner, 2002.

8. For a fascinating account of the possibilities of new technologies in transforming learning, see Dave Price. "Open: How We'll Work, Live and Learn in the Future," 2013.

9. Dave Price. *Open: How We'll Work, Live and Learn in the Future City*: Crux Publishing, 2013.

10. Marc Prensky. *Digital Game Based Learning*. New York: McGraw Hill, 2001. Also www.janemcgonigal.com and McGonigal, ed. *Reality Is Broken: Why Games Make Us Better and How They Can Change the World*. Penguin, 2011.

11. Peter Brook. *The Empty Space: A Book About the Theatre: Deadly, Holy, Rough, Immediate*. New York: Touchstone, 1996.

CHAPTER FOUR: **Natural Born Learners**

1. Sugata Mitra. "The Child-Driven Education." TED talks transcript. See http://www.ted.com/talks/sugata_mitra_the_child_driven_education /transcript?language=en.

2. Ibid.

3. Chidanand Rajghatta. "NRI Education Pioneer, Dr. Sugata Mitra, Wins $1 Million TED Prize." *The Times of India*, February 27, 2013. Retrieved from http://timesofindia.indiatimes.com/nri/us-canada-news /NRI-education-pioneer-Dr-Sugata-Mitra-wins-1-million-TED-Prize/ articleshow/18705008.cms.

4. "The School in the Cloud Story." School in the Cloud. Retrieved from https://www.theschoolinthecloud.org/library/resources/the-school-in-the-cloud-story.

5. To be fair, not everyone buys into Sugata Mitra's research, especially those who feel that he might be advocating too strongly for a lessening of traditional teaching techniques and systems. In *The Journal of Education*, Brent Silby wrote, "Mitra believes the intellectual traditionalist model of education from the past will not equip our students with what they need to face modern world problems. But I disagree. I worry that the top-down approach to learning provides students with knowledge that has insecure foundations and therefore cannot be easily built upon. While Mitra holds that ideas of the past cannot be used to solve current problems I think we ignore the past at our peril. The intellectual traditionalist model of education provides students with solid foundations upon which to build knowledge. This is crucial if we are to address novel problems. Without the solid base, any attempt at acquiring new knowledge risks failure. Twenty-first century problems need to be addressed with the benefit of the expertise and knowledge of history—precisely that knowledge which enabled us to build this 21st century world."

6. If you want to know more about free schools, go to newschoolsnet work.org.

7. Jeffrey Moussaieff Masson. *The Pig Who Sang to the Moon: The Emotional World of Farm Animals*. New York: Ballantine, 2003.

8. "Are Crows the Ultimate Problem Solvers?" *Inside the Animal Mind*, BBC. 2014. Available at https://www.youtube.com/watch?v=AVaITA7eBZE.

9. See http://www.koko.org/history1.

10. See, for example, *Out of Our Minds: Learning to Be Creative*, chapter 4, *The Academic Illusion*.

11. "The Components of MI." MIOasis.com. Retrieved from http://multipleintelligencesoasis.org/about/the-components-of-mi/.

12. Karl Popper. *Conjectures and Refutations: The Growth of Scientific Knowledge*. New York: Routledge Classics, 2003.

13. For a fascinating and helpful discussion of this and of other dynamics of learning and intelligence, see Daniel T. Willingham. *Why Don't Students like School?: A Cognitive Scientist Answers Questions about How the Mind Works and What It Means for the Classroom*. San Francisco: Jossey-Bass, 2009.

14. Carl Honoré. *In Praise of Slowness: How a Worldwide Movement Is Challenging the Cult of Speed*. San Francisco: HarperSanFrancisco, 2004.

15. Joe Harrison. "One Size Doesn't Fit All! Slow Education at Holy Trinity Primary School, Darwen." Retrieved from http://sloweducation.co.uk/2013/06/13/one-size-doesnt-fit-all-slow-education-at-holy-trinity-primary-school-darwen/.

16. Monty Neill. "A Child Is Not a Test Score: Assessment as a Civil Rights Issue." *Root and Branch* (Fall 2009), pp. 29–35.

17. Peter Gray. "The Decline of Play." TEDx Talks: Navesink. See https://www.youtube.com/watch?v=Bg-GEzM7iTk.

18. Peter Gray. *Free to Learn: Why Unleashing the Instinct to Play Will Make Our Children Happier, More Self-reliant, and Better Students for Life*. New York: Basic, 2013.

CHAPTER FIVE: **The Art of Teaching**

1. Melissa McNamara. "Teacher Inspires Kids to Love Learning." CBS Interactive, January 31, 2007. Retrieved from http://www.cbsnews.com/news/teacher-inspires-kids-to-love-learning/.

2. Ibid.

3. Rafe Esquith. *Teach Like Your Hair's on Fire: The Methods and Madness Inside Room 56*. New York: Viking, 2007.

4. John Hattie. *Visible Learning: A Synthesis of Over 800 Meta-analyses Relating to Achievement*. London: Routledge, 2009.

5. Alistair Smith is an education consultant who has worked with teachers

throughout the world. In his book, *High Performers: The Secrets of Successful Schools*, he says, "Students with the best teachers in the best schools learn at least three times more each year than students with the worst teachers in the worst schools. Therefore investing in the quality of teaching and teachers is a must." Alistair Smith. *High Performers: The Secrets of Successful Schools*. Carmarthen, Wales: Crown House Pub, 2011.

6. "Gove, the Enemy of Promise." Times Higher Education, June 13, 2013. Retrieved from http://www.timeshighereducation.co.uk/features/gove -the-enemy-of-promise/2004641.article.

7. He's not alone in thinking like this. There's a view that universities are filling potential teachers up with needless theory and social critiques. In the United States, many charter schools have waivers that allow them to avoid state and federal mandates, which means that they can bring in teachers who might know a tremendous amount about what they're teaching, but have not had to learn the other necessary skills of teaching.

8. Jessica Shepherd. "NUT Passes Unanimous Vote of No Confidence in Michael Gove." TheGuardian.com, April 2, 2013. Retrieved from http:// www.theguardian.com/education/2013/apr/02/nut-no-confidence -michael-gove.

9. "Minister Heckled by Head Teachers." BBC.com, May 18, 2013. Retrieved from http://www.bbc.com/news/education-22558756.

10. In Singapore, there is only one teacher training institution—the National Institute of Education—and it is extremely selective, choosing from among the top third of high school graduates. The program takes prospective teachers through a rigorous program with an intensive focus on the craft of teaching as well as subject mastery. In South Korea, the effort to provide students with only the most qualified teachers extends to the point that even part-time lecturers are required to have teaching certifications.

11. Thomas L. Friedman. "Foreign Affairs: My Favorite Teacher." *The New York Times*, January 8, 2001.

12. Hilary Austen. *Artistry Unleashed: A Guide to Pursuing Great Performance in Work and Life*. Toronto: University of Toronto, 2010.

13. *Wright's Law*, dir. Zack Conkle. 2012.

14. Ibid.

15. Rita Pierson. "Every Kid Needs a Champion." Ted.com, May 2013.

16. Joshua Davis. "How a Radical New Teaching Method Could Unleash a Generation of Geniuses." Wired.com, October 13, 2013. See http:// www.wired.com/2013/10/free-thinkers/.

17. Taken from http://www.buildinglearningpower.co.uk. Visit the site for more on the principles, techniques, and impact of BLP.

18. Eric Mazur. Keynote Session, SSAT National Conference. Retrieved from http://youtube/lDK25TlaxVE.
19. Cynthia J. Brame. "Flipping the Classroom." Vanderbilt University Center for Teaching report. Retrieved from http://cft.vanderbilt.edu/guides-sub-pages/flipping-the-classroom/.
20. "Up Close and Personal in a Khan Academy Classroom." Khan Academy blog, September 6, 2013. Retrieved from http://www.khanacademy.org/about/blog/post/60457933923/up-close-and-personal-in-a-khan-academy-classroom.
21. Former U.K. Secretary of State for Education Michael Gove once pronounced that children have to learn the necessary skills before they can start to be creative. In English, he says, "creativity depends on mastering certain skills and acquiring a body of knowledge before being able to give expression to what's in you. . . . You cannot be creative unless you understand how sentences are constructed, what words mean, and how to use grammar." In mathematics, he went on, "unless children are introduced to that stock of knowledge, unless they know how to use numbers with confidence, unless multiplication, long division, become automatic processes, they won't be able to use mathematics creatively . . . to make the discoveries which are going to make our lives better in the future." Even if you're musically gifted, he says, "you need first of all to learn your scales. You need to secure a foundation on which your creativity can flourish." This all sounds like common sense. But like a lot of common sense it's wrong or, at best, a half-truth.
22. I made these points in a piece for *The Guardian* newspaper (May 17, 2013) in response to then U.K. Education Secretary Michael Gove. http://www.theguardian.com/commentisfree/2013/may/17/to-encourage-creativity-mr-gove-understand.

CHAPTER SIX: **What's Worth Knowing?**
1. See http://www.hightechhigh.org/.
2. Jeff Robin. "Project Based Learning." Video, October 15, 2013. Retrieved from http://dp.hightechhigh.org/~jrobin/ProjectBasedLearning/PBL_is.html.
3. See, for example, http://www.coreknowledge.org/ed-hirsch-jr. "About the Standards." Common Core State Standards Initiative. Retrieved from http://www.corestandards.org/about-the-standards/. The site goes on to say that Common Core is research and evidence based; clear, understandable, and consistent; aligned with college and career expectations; based on rigorous content and application of knowledge through higher-order thinking skills; built upon the strengths and les-

sons of current state standards; and informed by other top-performing countries in order to prepare all students for success in our global economy and society.

4. Reflecting on his own experiences in school, Charles Darwin (1809–1882) said: "Nothing could have been worse for my mind than this school, as it was strictly classical; nothing else being taught except a little ancient geography and history. The school as a means of education was to me a complete blank. During my whole life I have been singularly incapable of mastering any language. . . . The sole pleasure I ever received from such [classical] studies was from some of the odes from Horace which I admired greatly." Charles Darwin. *The Autobiography of Charles Darwin*. Retrieved from http://www.public-domain-content.com/books/Darwin/P2.shtml.

5. I go into these developments in a little more detail in *Out of Our Minds*.

6. In chapter 1, I said there are many variations in how different national systems operate and that different countries are looking at curriculum in different ways. That's true. It's also true that there is a dominant shape to the curriculum in many countries. In Shanghai, for example, major curriculum reform began in the eighties with a shift in focus toward conceptual and experiential learning. The curriculum is divided into three components: compulsory classes, elective classes, and after-school programs, and a regular refrain is "to every question there should be more than a single answer." This is a major shift from the period before this, when the curriculum was focused on a handful of subjects and teachers spent much of their time making their students better test takers. It's also true that there is a dominant shape to the curriculum in many countries.

7. The term was coined in the 1960s by the British educator, Andrew Wilkinson. See, for example, Terry Phillips and Andrew Wilkinson. *Oracy Matters: The Development of Talking and Listening* (Education, English, Language, and Education series), ed. Margaret Maclure. Bristol, PA: Open University Press, 1988.

8. See, for example, William Damon. "Peer Education: The Untapped Potential." *Journal of Applied Developmental Psychology*, Vol. 5, Issue 4, October–December 1984, pp. 331–43.

9. For more on this, see the great work of the Citizenship Foundation. http://www.citizenshipfoundation.org.uk/index.php.

10. Elliot Washor and Charles Mojkowski. "High Schools as Communities in Communities." *The New Educator* 2 (2006), pp. 247–57.

11. Elliot Washor and Charles Mojkowski. *Leaving to Learn: How Out-of-*

School Learning Increases Student Engagement and Reduces Dropout Rates. Portsmouth, NH: Heinemann, 2013. I was delighted to write the foreword for this book.

12. Washor and Mojkowski. *Leaving to Learn*.

13. "Big Picture Learning—A School for the 21st Century." Innovation Unit, November 18, 2013. Retrieved from http://www.innovationunit.org/blog/201311/big-picture-learning-school-21st-century.

14. See http://www.mmhs.co.uk/we-are-different.

15. See http://www.yaacovhecht.com/bio/.

16. Yaacov Hecht. "What Is Democratic Education?" Schools of Trust YouTube Channel. Retrieved from http://youtube/BlECircdLGs.

17. Yaacov Hecht. "Democratic Education: A Beginning of a Story." *Innovation Culture*, 2010.

18. See http://www.educationrevolution.org/store/jerrymintz/.

19. I haven't tried to set out in detail how that can and does work in practice, but have done so elsewhere. See, for example, K. Robinson. "All Our Futures: Creativity, Culture and Education." 1999.

CHAPTER SEVEN: **Testing, Testing**

1. Ronda Matthews. "What Testing Looks Like." Retrieved from https://www.youtube.com/watch?v=KMAjv4s5y3M&feature=youtube.

2. "Washington State's Loss of No Child Left Behind Waiver Leaves Districts Scrambling." Associated Press, May 11, 2014. Retrieved from http://www.oregonlive.com/pacific-northwest-news/index.ssf/2014/05/washington_states_loss_of_no_c.html.

3. For information on Kohn's work and proposals, see http://www.alfiekohn.org/bio.htm.

4. Yong Zhao. "Five Questions to Ask About the Common Core." Zhao learning.com, January 2, 2013. Retrieved from http://zhaolearning.com/2013/01/02/five-questions-to-ask-about-the-common-core/.

5. "National Resolution on High-Stakes Testing." FairTest. Retrieved from http://fairtest.org/national-resolution-high-stakes-testing.

6. Catey Hill. "Will New SAT Raise Test-Prep Prices?" MarketWatch .com, March 9, 2014. Retrieved from http://www.marketwatch.com/story/test-prep-industry-expects-banner-year-from-new-sat-2014-03-06.

7. Zach Schonfeld. "Princeton Review Founder Blasts the SAT: 'These Tests Measure Nothing of Value.'" Newsweek.com, April 16, 2014. Retrieved from http://www.newsweek.com/princeton-review-founder-blasts-sat-these-tests-measure-nothing-value-246360.

8. "Unions Opposed to Testdriven Education." M2 PressWIRE, July 31, 2012.

9. "Colleges and Universities That Do Not Use SAT/ACT Scores for Admitting Substantial Numbers of Students into Bachelor Degree Programs." FairTest. May 13, 2014. Retrieved from http://fairtest.org/university/optional#5. They include Bard College, Brandeis University, Colorado State College, Grambling State University, Providence College, the University of Texas, and many others.

10. "Testing & Educational Support in the U.S." IBISWorld Market Research Report, October 2014. Retrieved from http://www.ibisworld.com/industry/default.aspx?indid=1549.

11. "2013 Domestic Grosses." Box Office Mojo Yearly Box Office Results. Retrieved from http://boxofficemojo.com/yearly/chart/?yr=2013.

12. Monte Burke. "How the National Football League Can Reach $25 Billion in Annual Revenues." Forbes.com, August 17, 2013. Retrieved from http://www.forbes.com/sites/monteburke/2013/08/17/how-the-national-football-league-can-reach-25-billion-in-annual-revenues/.

13. Alyssa Figueroa. "8 Things You Should Know About Corporations Like Pearson That Make Huge Profits from Standardized Tests." *Alternet*, August 6, 2013. Retrieved from http://www.alternet.org/education/corporations-profit-standardized-tests.

14. Ibid.

15. Jim Armitage. "Watch Your Language: The Tories' U-turn on Testers." NewsBank, February 19, 2014.

16. Leonie Haimson. "The Pineapple and the Hare: Pearson's Absurd, Nonsensical ELA Exam, Recycled Endlessly Throughout Country." *NYC Public School Parents* (blog), April 19, 2012. Retrieved from http://nycpublicschoolparents.blogspot.com/2012/04/pineapple-and-hare-pearsons-absurd.html.

17. OECD. "PISA 2012 Results." Retrieved from http://www.oecd.org/pisa/keyfindings/pisa-2012-results.htm.

18. "Singapore: Instructional Systems." Center on International Education Benchmarking. Retrieved from http://www.ncee.org/programs-affiliates/center-on-international-education-benchmarking/top-performing-countries/singapore-overview/singapore-instructional-systems/.

19. Anu Partanen. "What Americans Keep Ignoring About Finland's School Success." TheAtlantic.com, December 29, 2011. Retrieved from http://www.theatlantic.com/national/archive/2011/12/what-americans-keep-ignoring-about-finlands-school-success/250564/#.Tv4jn7hW2CU.twitter.

20. Tien Phong. "Vietnam Stops Using Grades in Elementary Schools." PangeaToday.com, July 18, 2014. See http://www.pangeatoday.com/vietnam-stops-using-grades-in-elementary-schools/.

21. "OECD and Pisa Tests Are Damaging Education Worldwide—

Academics." TheGuardian.com, May 6, 2014. Retrieved from http://www
.theguardian.com/education/2014/may/06/oecd-pisa-tests-damaging
-education-academics.

22. Joe Bower and P. L. Thomas. *De-testing and De-grading Schools: Au-thentic Alternatives to Accountability and Standardization.* New York: Peter Lang, 2013.

23. "The Learning Record." FairTest, August 28, 2007. Retrieved from http://fairtest.org/learning-record.

24. Erin Millar. "Why Some Schools Are Giving Letter Grades a Fail." TheGlobeandMail.com, April 4, 2014. See http://www.theglobeand-mail.com/news/national/education/schools-that-give-letter-grades-a-fail/article17807841/.

CHAPTER EIGHT: **Principles for Principals**

1. See http://en.wikipedia.org/wiki/Alex_Ferguson.

2. Kurt Badenhausen. "Manchester United Tops the World's 50 Most Valu-able Sports Teams." Forbes.com, July 16, 2012. Retrieved from http://
www.forbes.com/sites/kurtbadenhausen/2012/07/16/manchester-united
-tops-the-worlds-50-most-valuable-sports-teams/.

3. Jamie Jackson. "David Moyes Sacked by Manchester United and Re-placed by Ryan Giggs." TheGuardian.com, April 22, 2014. Retrieved from http://www.theguardian.com/football/2014/apr/22/david-moyes
-sacked-manchester-united.

4. For a great discussion of this point, see Simon Sinek. *Leaders Eat Last: Why Some Teams Pull Together and Others Don't.* New York: Portfolio/Penguin, 2014.

5. T. Wagner. *Creating Innovators: The Making of Young People Who Will Change the World.* Scribner, 2012.

6. "House of Commons Rebuilding." *Hansard*, October 28, 1943, No-vember 10, 2014. http://hansard.millbanksystems.com/commons/1943/
oct/28/house-of-commons-rebuilding.

7. Tamsyn Imison, Liz Williams, and Ruth Heilbronn. *Comprehensive Achievements: All Our Geese Are Swans.* London: Trentham, 2013.

8. For details, see http://www.thethirdteacher.com.

9. "LEEP (Liberal Education and Effective Practice)." Clark University. Retrieved from http://www.clarku.edu/leep/.

10. "The School with a Promise." Clark University. Retrieved from https://
www.clarku.edu/departments/education/upcs/.

11. "University Park Campus School." *Dispelling the Myth.* Education Trust. http://action.org/content_item/university-park.

12. Since that initial report, NASSP has released six additional reports on

education reform and has launched an ongoing series of Breaking Ranks leadership programs.

13. "School Improvement." NASSP. Retrieved from http://www.nassp.org/School-Improvement.

14. "MetLife Foundation–NASSP Breakthrough Schools." MetLife Foundation—NASSP Breakthrough Schools. May 29, 2014. http://www.nassp.org/AwardsandRecognition/MetLifeFoundationNASSP-BreakthroughSchools.aspx.

15. *An Executive Summary of Breaking Ranks: Changing an American Institution.* Reston, VA: National Association of Secondary School Principals, 1996.

CHAPTER NINE: **Bring It All Back Home**

1. According to a 2014 report from the Pew Foundation, in 1960 73 percent of U.S. children lived with two heterosexual parents in their first marriage; in 1980 the figure was 61 percent, and in 2014 it was 46 percent.

2. For the standard manifesto on this approach to parenting, Amy Chua. *Battle Hymn of the Tiger Mother.* New York: Penguin Press, 2011.

3. For the counter-manifesto, see Tanith Carey. *Taming the Tiger Parent: How to Put Your Child's Well-being First in a Competitive World.* London: Constable and Robinson, 2014.

4. Anne T. Henderson, Karen L. Mapp, and Amy Averett. *A New Wave of Evidence: The Impact of School, Family, and Community Connections on Student Achievement.* Austin, TX: National Center for Family and Community Connections with Schools, 2002.

5. Ibid.

6. "Organizing Schools for Improvement: Lessons from Chicago." University of Chicago Urban Education Institute, January 30, 2010. Retrieved from http://uei.uchicago.edu/news/article/organizing-schools-improvement-lessons-chicago.

7. Ibid.

8. Patrick F. Bassett. "When Parents and Schools Align." *Independent School,* Winter 2009. Retrieved from http://www.nais.org/Magazines-Newsletters/ISMagazine/Pages/When-Parents-and-Schools-Align.aspx.

9. Ibid.

10. For more on the school, see http://www.blueschool.org.

11. "National Standards for Family-School Partnerships." National PTA. Retrieved from http://www.pta.org/programs/content.cfm?ItemNumber=3126&navItemNumber=3983.

12. Otha Thornton. "Families: An Essential Ingredient for Student Success

and Excellent Schools." HuffingtonPost.com, April 29, 2014. Retrieved from http://www.huffingtonpost.com/otha-thornton/families-an-essential -ing_b_5232446.html.

13. U.S. Dept. of Education. "Partners in Education: A Dual Capacity-Building Framework for Family–School Partnerships." Retrieved from http://www2.ed.gov/documents/family-community/partners-education .pdf.

14. "The knowledge distilled in the Dual Capacity-Building Framework is the result of decades of work by teachers, parents, researchers, administrators, policy makers, and community members. The Framework reveals that, in order for family-school partnerships to succeed, the adults responsible for children's education must learn and grow, just as they support learning and growth among students." U.S. Dept. of Education, "Partners in Education."

15. *Home-to-School Connections Resource Guide.* Edutopia. Retreived from http://www.edutopia.org/home-to-school-connections-resource-guide.

16. See http://www.familiesinschools.org/about-us/mission-history/.

17. "Fast Facts." National Center for Education Statistics. Retrieved from http://nces.ed.gov/fastfacts/display.asp?id=91.

18. Quinn Cummings. *The Year of Learning Dangerously: Adventures in Homeschooling.* New York: Penguin Group, 2012.

19. Logan LaPlante. "Hackschooling Makes Me Happy." TEDx Talks: University of Nevada. Retrieved from https://www.youtube.com/watch ?v=h11u3vtcpaY&feature=kp.

20. Lisa Miller. "Homeschooling, City-Style." NYMag.com, October 14, 2012. Retrieved from http://nymag.com/guides/everything/urban-home schooling-2012-10/.

CHAPTER TEN: **Changing the Climate**

1. "South Carolina Loses Ground on "Nation's Report Card." *FITSNews South Carolina Loses Ground on Nations Report Card Comments.* November 7, 2013. http://www.fitsnews.com/2013/11/07/south-carolina-loses -ground-on-nations-report-card/.

2. C. M. Rubin. "The Global Search for Education: Creative China." HuffingtonPost.com, August 10, 2014. Retrieved from http://www.huffing tonpost.com/c-m-rubin/the-global-search-for-edu_b_5665681.html.

3. Ian Johnson. "Solving China's Schools: An Interview with Jiang Xueqin. *New York Review of Books* blog, April 8, 2014. Retrieved from http:// www.nybooks.com/blogs/nyrblog/2014/apr/08/china-school-reform -jiang-xueqin/.

4. C. M. Rubin. "The Global Search for Education: The Middle East."

HuffingtonPost.com, August 5, 2014. Retrieved from http://www.huff ingtonpost.com/c-m-rubin/the-global-search-for-edu_b_5651935.html.

5. See ASK's mission statement at http://www.ask-arabia.com/?page_id =644.

6. Rubin. "The Global Search for Education: The Middle East."

7. Describing their reform programs, Krista Kiuru, Finnish minister of education and science, said, "We must take strong action to develop Finnish education.. . . . We will bring in not only experts in research and education and political decision-makers but also student representatives and parents . . . we must find means to improve and sustain motivation in learning and studying and make schools a good environment to be in."

8. John Taylor Gatto. *Weapons of Mass Instruction: A Schoolteacher's Journey Through the Dark World of Compulsory Schooling.* Gabriola Island, BC: New Society, 2009.

9. See, for example, Diane Ravitch. *Reign of Error: The Hoax of the Privatization Movement and the Danger to America's Public Schools.* New York: Vintage, 2014.

10. Adapted by T. Brighouse from T. Knoster (1991). Presentation at TASH Conference, Washington, D.C. (Adapted by Knoster from Enterprise Group Ltd.)

11. Ibid.

Afterword

1. Maria Montessori and Anne E. George. *The Montessori Method.* New York: Schocken, 1964.

2. "How Many Montessori Schools Are There?" North American Montessori Teacher's Assoc. Retrieved from http://www.montessori-namta .org/FAQ/Montessori-Education/How-many-Montessori-schools-are -there.

3. "What Is Steiner Education?" Steiner Waldorf Schools Fellowship. Retrieved from http://www.steinerwaldorf.org/steiner-education/what-is-steiner-education/.

4. See http://www.summerhillschool.co.uk/about.php.

Index

ALLEN LANE
an imprint of
PENGUIN BOOKS

Recently Published

Peter Hennessy and James Jinks, *The Silent Deep: The Royal Navy Submarine Service Since 1945*

Sean McMeekin, *The Ottoman Endgame: War, Revolution and the Making of the Modern Middle East, 1908–1923*

Charles Moore, *Margaret Thatcher: The Authorized Biography, Volume Two: Everything She Wants*

Dominic Sandbrook, *The Great British Dream Factory: The Strange History of Our National Imagination*

Larissa MacFarquhar, *Strangers Drowning: Voyages to the Brink of Moral Extremity*

Niall Ferguson, *Kissinger: 1923-1968: The Idealist*

Carlo Rovelli, *Seven Brief Lessons on Physics*

Tim Blanning, *Frederick the Great: King of Prussia*

Ian Kershaw, *To Hell and Back: Europe, 1914–1949*

Pedro Domingos, *The Master Algorithm: How the Quest for the Ultimate Learning Machine Will Remake Our World*

David Wootton, *The Invention of Science: A New History of the Scientific Revolution*

Christopher Tyerman, *How to Plan a Crusade: Reason and Religious War in the Middle Ages*

Andy Beckett, *Promised You A Miracle: UK 80–82*

Carl Watkins, *Stephen: The Reign of Anarchy*

Anne Curry, *Henry V: From Playboy Prince to Warrior King*

John Gillingham, *William II: The Red King*

Roger Knight, *William IV: A King at Sea*

Douglas Hurd, *Elizabeth II: The Steadfast*

Richard Nisbett, *Mindware: Tools for Smart Thinking*

Jochen Bleicken, *Augustus: The Biography*

Paul Mason, *PostCapitalism: A Guide to Our Future*

Frank Wilczek, *A Beautiful Question: Finding Nature's Deep Design*

Roberto Saviano, *Zero Zero Zero*

Owen Hatherley, *Landscapes of Communism: A History Through Buildings*

César Hidalgo, *Why Information Grows: The Evolution of Order, from Atoms to Economies*

Aziz Ansari and Eric Klinenberg, *Modern Romance: An Investigation*

Sudhir Hazareesingh, *How the French Think: An Affectionate Portrait of an Intellectual People*

Steven D. Levitt and Stephen J. Dubner, *When to Rob a Bank: A Rogue Economist's Guide to the World*

Leonard Mlodinow, *The Upright Thinkers: The Human Journey from Living in Trees to Understanding the Cosmos*

Hans Ulrich Obrist, *Lives of the Artists, Lives of the Architects*

Richard H. Thaler, *Misbehaving: The Making of Behavioural Economics*

Sheldon Solomon, Jeff Greenberg and Tom Pyszczynski, *Worm at the Core: On the Role of Death in Life*

Nathaniel Popper, *Digital Gold: The Untold Story of Bitcoin*

Dominic Lieven, *Towards the Flame: Empire, War and the End of Tsarist Russia*

Noel Malcolm, *Agents of Empire: Knights, Corsairs, Jesuits and Spies in the Sixteenth-Century Mediterranean World*

James Rebanks, *The Shepherd's Life: A Tale of the Lake District*

David Brooks, *The Road to Character*

Joseph Stiglitz, *The Great Divide*

Ken Robinson and Lou Aronica, *Creative Schools: Revolutionizing Education from the Ground Up*

Clotaire Rapaille and Andrés Roemer, *Move UP: Why Some Cultures Advances While Others Don't*

Jonathan Keates, *William III and Mary II: Partners in Revolution*

David Womersley, *James II: The Last Catholic King*

Richard Barber, *Henry II: A Prince Among Princes*

Jane Ridley, *Victoria: Queen, Matriarch, Empress*

John Gray, *The Soul of the Marionette: A Short Enquiry into Human Freedom*

Emily Wilson, *Seneca: A Life*

Michael Barber, *How to Run a Government: So That Citizens Benefit and Taxpayers Don't Go Crazy*

Dana Thomas, *Gods and Kings: The Rise and Fall of Alexander McQueen and John Galliano*

Steven Weinberg, *To Explain the World: The Discovery of Modern Science*

Jennifer Jacquet, *Is Shame Necessary?: New Uses for an Old Tool*

Eugene Rogan, *The Fall of the Ottomans: The Great War in the Middle East, 1914-1920*

Norman Doidge, *The Brain's Way of Healing: Stories of Remarkable Recoveries and Discoveries*

John Hooper, *The Italians*

Sven Beckert, *Empire of Cotton: A New History of Global Capitalism*

Mark Kishlansky, *Charles I: An Abbreviated Life*

Philip Ziegler, *George VI: The Dutiful King*

David Cannadine, *George V: The Unexpected King*

Stephen Alford, *Edward VI: The Last Boy King*

John Guy, *Henry VIII: The Quest for Fame*

Robert Tombs, *The English and their History: The First Thirteen Centuries*

Neil MacGregor, *Germany: The Memories of a Nation*

Uwe Tellkamp, *The Tower: A Novel*

Roberto Calasso, *Ardor*

Slavoj Žižek, *Trouble in Paradise: Communism After the End of History*

Francis Pryor, *Home: A Time Traveller's Tales from Britain's Prehistory*

R. F. Foster, *Vivid Faces: The Revolutionary Generation in Ireland, 1890-1923*

Andrew Roberts, *Napoleon the Great*

Shami Chakrabarti, *On Liberty*